Customer Relationship Management: A Strategic Approach

Customer Relationship Management: A Strategic Approach

Denise Lopez

Willford Press
www.willfordpress.com

Published by Willford Press,
118-35 Queens Blvd., Suite 400,
Forest Hills, NY 11375, USA

ISBN: 978-1-68285-981-0

Cataloging-in-Publication Data

Customer relationship management : a strategic approach / Denise Lopez.
p. cm.
Includes bibliographical references and index.
ISBN 978-1-68285-981-0
1. Customer relations--Management. 2. Relationship marketing.
3. Consumer affairs departments. 4. Strategic planning. I. Lopez, Denise.
HF5415.5 .C87 2021
658.812--dc23

For information on all Willford Press publications
visit our website at www.willfordpress.com

WILLFORD PRESS

Contents

Preface

Customer relationship management is concerned with managing a firm's association with current and prospective consumers. It seeks to improve business relationships with customers by using data analysis of customers' history with a company. It particularly focuses on customer retention in order to boost sales. The systems which compile data from varied communications channels form an integral part of customer relationship management. A few of these communication channels are telephone, email, marketing materials, live chat and social media. The main function of customer relationship management is to help companies understand their target audiences so that they can cater to their needs more efficiently. This textbook aims to shed light on some of the unexplored aspects of customer relationship management. While understanding the long-term perspectives of the topics, it makes an effort in highlighting their impact as a modern tool for the growth of the discipline. This book will provide comprehensive knowledge to the readers.

To facilitate a deeper understanding of the contents of this book a short introduction of every chapter is written below:

Chapter 1- The manner in which a business relates with the customers is known as customer relationship. One of the ways in which these relations can be managed is through customer relationship management. This is an introductory chapter which will introduce briefly all the significant aspects of customer relationship management and the different models through which customer management systems can be created.

Chapter 2- A framework which seeks to improve the relationship between a business and the customer is known as a customer relationship model. There are a number of models which detail the different actions and processes which can be used for effective customer relations. The topics elaborated in this chapter will help in gaining a better perspective about the different models such as IDIC model and Gartner's CRM model.

Chapter 3- Strategic customer relationship management deals with the development of a business culture which is focused on customers. One of the tools by which B2B companies develop profitable customer relationships is through customer portfolio. The chapter closely examines these key concepts of strategic CRM to provide an extensive understanding of the subject.

Chapter 4- The entirety of services which allow a business organization to take care of customers' needs is known as operational customer relationship management. Collaborative CRM is an approach to customer relationship management where the different departments such as sales, technical support and marketing share the information gained from the customers. All the diverse principles of operational and collaborative CRM have been carefully analyzed in this chapter.

Chapter 5- Analytical customer relationship management deals with the analysis of customer data which has been collected from various sources, and then presents it in a coherent manner to enable business managers to make informed decisions. The chapter closely examines the key concepts of analytical CRM such as data analysis and customer-related database to provide an extensive understanding of the subject.

Finally, I would like to thank the entire team involved in the inception of this book for their valuable time and contribution. This book would not have been possible without their efforts. I would also like to thank my friends and family for their constant support.

Denise Lopez

1

Customer Relationship Management: An Introduction

The manner in which a business relates with the customers is known as customer relationship. One of the ways in which these relations can be managed is through customer relationship management. This is an introductory chapter which will introduce briefly all the significant aspects of customer relationship management and the different models through which customer management systems can be created.

Customer Relations

The way a business relates to its customers, clientele and patrons is known as customer relations. Also called customer service, some companies hire people specifically to manage how the company interacts and communicates with people. The goal is to retain existing customers and to gain new ones by providing the best customer relations they can, and – hopefully, to find better customer services than those their competitors provide. There are several components that go into superb customer relations.

Marketing and Promotion

Strategically promoting services or resources that make a company stand out is a huge part of customer relations. When a company has a powerful marketing push behind its customer service, it reminds customers why people should choose their company in the first place. Often, the promotional events are differentiated to attract different target groups, made up of both existing customers, as well as new customers. Identifying the needs of customers and anticipating those needs before customers even realize it, enables a company to pull ahead in superlative customer service.

Consistency of Service

Customers want to know that they can rely on a business to be the same, wherever they go insofar as policies. If, for example, a hotel chain advertises complementary car side service, then patrons will expect that to be a policy at all hotels under the same chain. Some people may even choose to use that company, because they have come to rely on a particular aspect of it.

Making sure that a company is consistent not only in what they offer but in how it's offered, which inspires loyalty in existing patrons and repeat business in new patrons. This includes employee training. Cohesive customer service policies and features are important.

Responsiveness of Customer Relations

A prompt, positive response works to build trust in customer relations. There are almost always ways to help customers get what they need or want without sacrificing the bottom line. Most people want to feel that they are listened to and taken seriously. That is especially true when addressing a business' customers. It won't always be possible to give customers exactly what they are asking for, but if people that see you are trying, it can make all the difference.

Often, answers often cannot be rushed but customers should be kept in the loop as to how long it may be, and then the business must stick to that time frame. Part of customer relations is finding ways to make people feel that it's easy to do business with your company.

Technology and Responsiveness

The latest and most-supported technology is the newest and no less important aspect of customer relations. Make sure the website is updated and properly supported for the volume of traffic it gets. Phones should be answered promptly and with the same greeting. Ideally, emails should be answered on the same day they are sent, or if not, then by the end of the next business day.

Technology makes it easier for employees and customers to communicate quickly, and by ensuring that a company has all the systems in place to do, that then the relationship thrives.

It often seems insurmountable to make all of a company's clientele happy. That isn't the goal, however. The goal is to make each new customer in front of an employee feel happy. Take it one at a time, with concentrated attention, and that's what takes a company from just okay to a solid favorite.

Customer Relationship Management

Every business unit emphasizes on spurting a long term relationship with customers to nurture its stability in today's blooming market. Customer's expectations are now not only limited to get best products and services, they also need a face-to-face business in which they want to receive exactly what they demand and in a quick time.

Customer Relationship Management is an upright concept or strategy to solidify relations with customers and at the same time reducing cost and enhancing productivity and profitability in business. An ideal CRM system is a centralized collection all data sources under an organization and provides an atomistic real time vision of customer information. A CRM system is vast and significant, but it be can implemented for small business, as well as large enterprises also as the main goal is to assist the customers efficiently.

Usually an organization consists of various departments which predominantly have access to customer's information either directly or indirectly. A CRM system piles up this information centrally, examines it and then makes it addressable within all the departments.

Let's take an example of an international call center which uses a CRM tool called 'xyz' and is integrated with a phone and a computer system or laptop. Now this system automatically perceives which customer is calling. Before the executive attends the phone the CRM system brings forth the customer details on the computer or laptop screen and also indicates what the opportunity of deals is with that particular customer, what the customer had already purchased or ordered in past and what is the probability of buying in future. Not only this, it can also highlight what all products best suit this customer. For finance department it may show the information regarding the current balance and for accounting department it may pop out the information regarding the recent purchases by the customer. All these pieces of data are stored in the CRM database and are available as and when it is needed.

According to this example, CRM system provides a well-defined platform for all business units to interact with their clients and fulfill all their needs and demands very effectively and to build long-term relationship.

Wangling this kind of relationship with customers is not easy to manage and it depends on how the systematically and flexibly a CRM system is implemented or integrated. But once it's accomplished it serves the best way in dealing with customers. In turn customers feels gratitude of self-satisfaction and loyalty which results in better bonding with supplier and hence increasing the business.

A CRM system is not only used to deal with the existing customers but is also useful in acquiring new customers. The process first starts with identifying a customer and maintaining all the corresponding details into the CRM system which is also called an 'Opportunity of Business'. The Sales and Field representatives then try getting business out of these customers by sophistically following up with them and converting them into a winning deal.

Customer Relationship Management strategies have given a new outlook to all the suppliers and customers to keep the business going under an estimable relationship by fulfilling mutual needs of buying and selling.

Origin of CRM

CRM originated in early 1970s when the business units had a manifestation that it would be advisable to become 'customer emphatic' rather that 'product emphatic'. Birth of CRM was because of this heedful perceptiveness.

The famous writer and management consultant Peter Drucker wrote; 'The true business of every company is to make and keep customers'. Traditionally every transaction was on paper and dependent on goodwill which created hindrance in clutching customers. People used to work hard in entertaining customers by presenting new products with astonishing services; they were ready to work overtime for grasping more and more customers for increasing business. This too resulted in customer satisfaction and loyalty up to some extent, but at the end of the day there was no such bonding or relation between the two to carry on with future business smoothly.

Previously business was quite easy as it was mere a one-to-one dealing without any specific process. But with time, due to incoming complexities in communication, it found itself in troubled waters. Emerging of new strategies and technologies in global marketplace and a mammoth degree of competition in business, the approach needed to be changed to proactive rather than reactive. Origination of CRM turned out to be a piece of cake for all suppliers and customers due to its advantages. Customer relationship management came as a process that dealt with relationships with customers surpassing the whole business.

Originally customer relationship management was based on three major principles; shielding the current customers, fostering new customers and enhancing asset value of all the customers. With the advent of CRM which was integrated with high end software and technology, business perspectives were totally changed. A CRM system eventually emerged as consisting of company-full of information which is depicted sophistically to increase business profit and meliorate customer satisfaction and loyalty, on the same hand reduces business cost and investment.

The outgrowth in origin of CRM as a strategic approach is a result of some of the following important perspectives:

1. The belief that customers are the real assets and not just the people in the audience.
2. The maturation of one-to-one transaction advent.
3. Extensive use of software and technologies to maintain useful information and no manual labor.
4. The realization of the benefits of utilizing information proactively and not reactively.
5. The change of business view to relationship approach rather than transactional approach.
6. The approach of concentrating more on customer values rather than concentrating on how the product is delivered to the customer.
7. The approach of focusing on customer satisfaction and loyalty rather than focusing self-satisfaction and profit.
8. The acceptance of the fact that using high end technologies and software the cost can radically be decreased without compromising on quality and service of products.
9. The increasing tendency to retain existing customers and trying to get more and more business out of them.
10. The realization that the traditional trends of marketing and selling are increasingly fading out in the current economic scenario.

These additive approaches helped a lot in building up consequently the modern CRM. Today we have well defined and sophisticated CRM systems into being which are always in process of improvement.

Features of CRM

Customer Relationship Management is a strategy which is customized by an organization to manage and administrate its customers and vendors in an efficient manner for achieving excellence in business. It is primarily entangled with following features:

1. Customer's Needs: An organization can never assume what actually a customer needs. Hence it is extremely important to interview a customer about all the likes and dislikes so

that the actual needs can be ascertained and prioritized. Without modulating the actual needs it is arduous to serve the customer effectively and maintain a long-term deal.

2. Customers Response: Customer response is the reaction by the organization to the queries and activities of the customer. Dealing with these queries intelligently is very important as small misunderstandings could convey unalike perceptions. Success totally depends on the understanding and interpreting these queries and then working out to provide the best solution. During this situation if the supplier wins to satisfy the customer by properly answering to his queries, he succeeds in explicating a professional and emotional relationship with him.

3. Customer Satisfaction: Customer satisfaction is the measure of how the needs and responses are collaborated and delivered to excel customer expectation. In today's competitive business marketplace, customer satisfaction is an important performance exponent and basic differentiator of business strategies. Hence, the more is customer satisfaction; more is the business and the bonding with customer.

4. Customer Loyalty: Customer loyalty is the tendency of the customer to remain in business with a particular supplier and buy the products regularly. This is usually seen when a customer is very much satisfied by the supplier and re-visits the organization for business deals, or when he is tended towards re-buying a particular product or brand over times by that supplier. To continue the customer loyalty the most important aspect an organization should focus on is customer satisfaction. Hence, customer loyalty is an influencing aspect of CRM and is always crucial for business success.

5. Customer Retention: Customer retention is a strategic process to keep or retain the existing customers and not letting them to diverge or defect to other suppliers or organization for business. Usually a loyal customer is tended towards sticking to a particular brand or product as far as his basic needs continue to be properly fulfilled. He does not opt for taking a risk in going for a new product. More is the possibility to retain customers the more is the probability of net growth of business.

6. Customer Complaints: Always there exist a challenge for suppliers to deal with complaints raised by customers. Normally raising a complaint indicates the act of dissatisfaction of the customer. There can be several reasons for a customer to launch a complaint. A genuine reason can also exist due to which the customer is dissatisfied but sometimes complaints are launched due to some sort of misunderstanding in analyzing and interpreting the conditions of the deal provided by the supplier regarding any product or service. Handling these complaints to ultimate satisfaction of the customer is substantial for any organization and hence it is essential for them to have predefined set of process in CRM to deal with these complaints and efficiently resolve it in no time.

7. Customer Service: In an organization Customer Service is the process of delivering information and services regarding all the products and brands. Customer satisfaction depends on quality of service provided to him by the supplier. The organization has not only to elaborate and clarify the details of the services to be provided to the customer but also to abide with the conditions as well. If the quality and trend of service go beyond customer's expectation, the organization is supposed to have a good business with customers.

Let it be a newly brought up enterprise or a well-established organization the above aspects prove to be of prime importance in dealing with a genuine customer through a well-organized CRM system.

Customer Relationship Management

Customer Relationship management is the strongest and the most efficient approach in maintaining and creating relationships with customers. Customer relationship management is not only pure business but also ideate strong personal bonding within people. Development of this type of bonding drives the business to new levels of success.

Once this personal and emotional linkage is built, it is very easy for any organization to identify the actual needs of customer and help them to serve them in a better way. It is a belief that more the sophisticated strategies involved in implementing the customer relationship management, the more strong and fruitful is the business. Most of the organizations have dedicated world class tools for maintaining CRM systems into their workplace. Some of the efficient tools used in most of the renowned organization are BatchBook, Salesforce, Buzzstream, Sugar CRM etc.

Looking at some broader perspectives given as below we can easily determine why a CRM System is always important for an organization:

1. A CRM system consists of a historical view and analysis of all the acquired or to be acquired customers. This helps in reduced searching and correlating customers and to foresee customer needs effectively and increase business.

2. CRM contains each and every bit of details of a customer, hence it is very easy for track a customer accordingly and can be used to determine which customer can be profitable and which not.

3. In CRM system, customers are grouped according to different aspects according to the type of business they do or according to physical location and are allocated to different customer managers often called as account managers. This helps in focusing and concentrating on each and every customer separately.

4. A CRM system is not only used to deal with the existing customers but is also useful in acquiring new customers. The process first starts with identifying a customer and maintaining all the corresponding details into the CRM system which is also called an 'Opportunity of Business'. The Sales and Field representatives then try getting business out of these customers by sophistically following up with them and converting them into a winning deal. All this is very easily and efficiently done by an integrated CRM system.

5. The strongest aspect of Customer Relationship Management is that it is very cost-effective. The advantage of decently implemented CRM system is that there is very less need of paper and manual work which requires lesser staff to manage and lesser resources to deal with. The technologies used in implementing a CRM system are also very cheap and smooth as compared to the traditional way of business.

6. All the details in CRM system is kept centralized which is available anytime on fingertips. This reduces the process time and increases productivity.

7. Efficiently dealing with all the customers and providing them what they actually need increases the customer satisfaction. This increases the chance of getting more business which ultimately enhances turnover and profit.

8. If the customer is satisfied they will always be loyal to you and will remain in business forever resulting in increasing customer base and ultimately enhancing net growth of business.

In today's commercial world, practice of dealing with existing customers and thriving business by getting more customers into loop is predominant and is mere a dilemma. Installing a CRM system can definitely improve the situation and help in challenging the new ways of marketing and business in an efficient manner. Hence in the era of business every organization should be recommended to have a full-fledged CRM system to cope up with all the business needs.

Customer Relationship Management (CRM) and Marketing

CRM leverages and amplifies customer base of an organization through efficacious and efficient marketing. In fact CRM has brought up new dimensions in the field of marketing by significantly improving marketing functioning and execution. Intuitive CRM associated marketing strategies like direct marketing web marketing, e-mail marketing etc. have been matured during the recent past. These marketing strategies are more promising as compared to the traditional ways on marketing as they help delivering higher-up performance and walloping business. They also help meliorating response rates in marketing campaigns, cut cost on promotions due to low asset values and provide higher scrutiny on organizational investments.

The various aspects of CRM oriented marketing are discussed below:

1. Web Marketing: With the growing popularity of web, customers are tending towards web marketing or web shopping. This helps both customers and suppliers to transact in a real time environment irrespective of their locations. Some of the major advantages of Web Marketing are listed below:

- It is relatively very inexpensive as it reduces the cost for physically reaching to the target customers for interaction.
- Suppliers can reach to more number of customers in lesser amount of time.
- The online marketing campaigns can be easily tracked, traced, calculated and tested.
- The selection process of any product or brand is simplified due to proven online research and analysis techniques.
- Online marketing campaigns are more promotional as compared to manual campaigns.

2. Email Marketing: Email marketing has turned out to be more efficacious and inexpensive as compared to mail or phone based marketing strategies. Email marketing is direct marketing which is data driven and leads to more accurate customer response and effective fulfillment of customer needs. More attractive features include newsletters, sending of e-Coupons, e-Cards, provision of saving events into calendars etc.

3. Analyzing customers buying behavior online: A CRM system provides a platform to analyze the customers buying behavior online. This interactive strategy provides great accuracy with high speed which includes profiling services furnishing elaborated bits of information regarding customers purchasing habits or behavior. Individualized analysis of this behavior also helps to identify to which product or brand the customers are more tended. For example an online selling website www.xyz.com can analyze the customers buying behavior by installing an in-house service with the help of a full-fledged CRM that checks what all products are being purchased by a particular customer and under which specific group they fall. This is achieved by personalized analyzing the buying history of customers in the past which predicts the future business with those customers also. This accomplishes to build a long-term relationship with customers by properly canvassing customer needs and resulting in customer satisfaction. Analyzing this particular buying behavior of customers online also helps to fix or change of marketing techniques or strategies to mould the system according to the future perspectives.

4. Forecasting future marketing strategies: Down the line marketing strategies keeps on changing according to the emotional behavioral change of customers. CRM market forecasting techniques help to understand this change through regression and statistical analysis of customer behavior online. These are some complex but more accurate analysis techniques provided by CRM system which are proved to be one of best marketing strategies. This innovative approach is carried out with greater risks but is believed to outturn astonishing rewards.

5. Building business impact models: It is important for an organization to have check on marketing performance regularly so that the techniques never deteriorate and always match to yield greater results. These CRM oriented models help in delivering accurate measurement of marketing performance throughout the organization and to do better every time.

These synergistic marketing strategies make a part of CRM system to develop high-end marketing business. Hence it is very important for an organization to incorporate them by carefully anticipating change, testing their performance and assembling the best possible combination of these strategies to meet the needs of the customers and maximize its marketing growth.

Customer Relationship Management (CRM) and HR

Human Resources are those constituents of an organization that take care of the human facets and needs of all employees within that organization. Key functions of HR in an organization are:

- Employee recruitment and selection.
- Compensation calculation and reward program management.
- In-house training for all employees according to skill sets.
- Performance calculation and managing employee behavior.
- Portfolio management and area location management.
- Transformation and change management.
- Structuring hierarchy of employees.

- Employee relationship management.
- Hiring Campaign management.

Employees are the significant assets and the primary promoters of profitable business for an organization. Hence, apart from managing clients and customers for business purpose, it's a decisive responsibility of an organization to manage and fulfill all needs of its own employees. It would be improper to say that a CRM system is only used to manage clients and customer; most of the HR heads or managers are using CRM technologies for managing company's human capital. This approach is called as Employee Resource Management (ERM). An ERM is a business process that fills gaps between an organizations and its employee to create a strong emotional and professional bonding among them.

A well-integrated ERM provides a committed information base system for all Human resources. This is termed as Human Resource Information System (HRIS) in most of the renowned organizations which provides a better interface for HRs to deal with internal employees and screens all problems associated with relationship among organization and employee. Some of its features are listed below:

- Profile Management: A profile management technique is used to manage profiles of all the employees which contain the entire employee related information which is also exposed to the employees in HRIS tool. Employees are allowed to change or edit some of this general information whenever there is a need.
- Payment/Compensation: Details regarding employee payroll and employee branding can be easily managed under this. An employee can see all the payroll related features and the salary statements can be automatically mailed to every employee.
- Training: Notification to attend online and manual training can be easily distributed within the organization. These can be online tracked for internship which can be optional or mandatory.
- Leave Management: Employee have a dedicated portal for applying or notifying for leaves. They just have to apply for leave through this portal and the information is escalated to his/her manager. The manager has the option for approving or rejecting this application online. The applied leaves get deducted from the bundle of employee's annual leaves automatically for which he gets email notification regularly.
- Meetings and Certifications: Managers and employees have the facility to online schedules of meetings or to book available meeting rooms. A notification is sent automatically to all the attendees informing them to be present in the meeting on the specified timings and venue. All the employees also have the facility to complete or attain online certifications as and when needed.
- Generate online Letters and data: The human resource managers or executives have the zeal to furnish offer letters or response letters online to the newly joined employees. There is no need for the new employees to re-enter their respective information again and again whenever needed.

- Online Alerts: Online alters are generated whenever any employee have something due. For example, employees are used to get these alerts automatically when they need to complete any survey or review or when there is a need to renew any software license.
- Export/Import facility: Every employee does have the deftness to export or import any sort of data available on the portal to and from an excel sheets or comma separated files (CSV files).

An organization is always benefitted by Employee Relationship Management if it is implementing it with CRM strategies with clear rules and guidelines. For an organization an upright and healthy relationship with employees always acts as reciprocal commutation and leads to betterment of both.

Customer Modeling

Customer modeling is the process of predicting and forecasting behavioral aspects of customers' future perspectives. The process includes identification of marketing and campaigning targets and optimizing predictive analysis. Following are the broadly discussed aspects of customer modeling:

- Response modeling: Modeling enhances the organization's knowledge on each individual customer and identify if the customers under specific segment are good and effective for marketing campaigns and promotion. This process includes validation and testing of collected customer response data and information. After analyzing and computing this data, scores or ranks are assigned to customers that represent their willingness to respond to a specific program or promotion. The approach is to divide the customers into modules or sub groups and then assign probability of response to each sub group. Marketing professional and decision making personals then decide the exact number of customers to be included in that particular promotion or program.
- Predicting customer Behavior: All the organizations are interested in determining the future value of all their existing customers. Modeling techniques are used to predict life time value of customers and profit impacting customer behavior like probability of product purchase, frequency of product purchase, spending capabilities, loyalty, usage of support and services. These predictive models support various kinds of processes like marketing campaigns, forecasting of financial and developmental aspects, customer budget management and asset management.
- Return on investment (ROI) optimization: Modeling emphasizes on optimizing following marketing activities like pricing, channeling and response medium determination. Organization usually gets highest return on investment from their marketing promotions by modeling the price elasticity of customers so that a valid offer can be given to each customer. By this the profit margin of product increases with low cost to the organization.
- Measuring market impact: In today's scenario, organizations have to come up with efficient and attractive marketing programs to communicate with customers and convey their message because customers are exposed to the open market where marketing competition is inevitable. Due to this market stimulation on customers are properly accounted which brings confusions in customers and they become biased. Due to this biased behavior the predictions and analysis could defect from actual implementation. Modeling being

multidimensional in nature helps to measure and sustain this impact of marketing on customers' behavior in a controlled and efficient manner.

Modeling and profiling are mostly same but the basic difference between them is the factor of time involved in modeling processes; as the modeling is not a static process. Modeling is quite more sophisticatedly implemented and thus making it powerful technique to predict customer behavior. Modeling process is action oriented and is not at all static throughout the customer life cycle. Profiling on the other hand is static and no action is taken apart from just recording the actual information and doing analysis on that information. Modeling on other hand involves action to be taken over times. Modeling also increases the return on investment and enhances business perspectives by fetching out good profit. Being more powerful and effective technique, marketing professionals prefer customer modeling in place of customer profiling because they have to deal with actual customer data.

Customer Profiling

For a developing business it is very important to understand who are the best customers, how to find more customers like these and where to find. Customer profiling is the best strategy to accomplish this. It helps to find valuable new customers, enhance the profitability by retaining existing customers and also identify low valued customers so as to minimize the cost to reach them. Customer profiling is a behavioral relationship marketing technique which includes a variety of marketing strategies ranging from simple one's to most complex one's.

Customer profiling starts with identification of relevant information regarding all the satisfied existing customers and then try to target new prospects with matching profiles. The profiles of customers can be categorized differently according to some influential variables present in their profile.

For example, let's examine the following two customer profiles:

1. This profile shows, the customer is married and has two children. He lives in a high society area and continuously read Economic Times newspaper.

2. This profile shows, the customer visited the supplier's site regularly for 3 months, but has never visited in last 2 weeks.

The first profile clearly indicates that the customer characteristics are demographic. The demographic profiles always help the suppliers to attract the customers and generate good revenue in the amateur stages of projects; these projects are basically online projects. The first profile will be interesting for someone inside the organization who is in advertisement department or who is involved in deciding the content and matter of websites.

The second profile can be depicted as a behavioral profile. The basic questions arise regarding to this profile should be, will they buy again? Will they visit again? A behavioral profile indicates the prominence of the relationship with customer in near future hence these profiles are crucial for organizations that focus on retaining more customers to increase their business value. Although behavioral profiles are more prominent than demographic but a combination of both provides a powerful and strong database to decide the customer characteristics in efficient way.

The following steps depicts an ideal profiling technique:

- Gathering demographic related and influential information from existing customers.
- Encapsulate this information in profiling database to each customer record.
- Attach more relevant information like behavioral characteristics (recent purchases, sales historical view etc.) and some other related information to each of the profiles.
- Implement the variables and strategies that determine the best and worst customers.
- Applying these effective variables to non-customers' profiles to identify valuable prospects.

The above process is involved ideally for simple profiling which can become complex for complex strategies. After profiling is completed the customers are then segmented according to segmentation variables. Every customer has individual preferences, needs and behavior associated with products which are different from other customers. Substantially it becomes impossible for suppliers to manage customers separately on individual characteristics; hence they pool customers into separate segments according to the type and variables they have in common.

Invalid or wrong information passed while profiling process will result in suboptimal decisions and unworthy consequences and could fetch customer dissatisfaction and could even lead to customer defect. Hence all the information and data should be validated and corrected before profiling is done. Customer profiling is the basis of market research techniques and is proved to be the most useful strategy under any circumstances in customer acquisition approach.

Regression Scoring – Meaning its Process and Types of Scoring

Regression scoring is one of the difficult but more precise and faithful marketing technique as compared to profiling and modeling. For targeting new and esteemed customers all the organization substantially pursue regression scoring techniques.

Following is the process involved in regression scoring:

- Identify the prospect or probable customers from the population of all customers and draw random samples from them.
- Collect individual characteristics from the information and data available from these samples.
- Record which all prospects are converted into customers after performing the marketing campaign on individual prospects.
- Using this information and trend, produce a regression scoring model which is a series of important variables which are used to predict and which prospects can be easily converted into customers in accordance to their individual characteristics.
- After the estimated model is ready the researchers engage themselves in following process:
    - According to the model, create regression equations to implement information of future group of prospect customer.

- Plug the information and individual characteristics of prospects that are not in the sample to calculate scores.
- Rank the prospects according to the regression score according to highest and lowest values.
- Perform marketing campaigns at the prospects that have scores above the cutoff value. This cutoff score depend on most of the important marketing and financial factors.

Following are the general types of regression scoring which are implemented according to specific need by the organization:

- Linear Regression Scoring: This type of scoring is performed by implementing linear regression algorithm on the random sample of data. The process includes scoring techniques on variables that have linear dependencies. For example if scoring has to be done on 2 distinct data values and each these values is associated with 5 distinct characteristics, then 25 linear regression analysis are performed.
- Non-Linear Regression Scoring: This is an extension linear regression scoring process which includes performing scoring by implementing nonlinear regression algorithm on the random sample of data. This means that the algorithm does not perform analysis on direct linear relationships of sample value, and hence the more and specific nonlinear analysis techniques are performed according to the conditions expected.
- Weighted score tables: This type of scoring does not need any sampling of data before associating scores to prospects. Weighted and important variables are directly associated with sample of prospect to determine individual scores for them without creating historic regression model. This type of scoring is not as accurate as linear or nonlinear regression scoring but it takes less time to perform.

Regression scoring has many advantages over other marketing methods. The primary advantage is that it measures the usefulness of variables that helps in determining which prospect to target and when. Secondly it provides a sophisticated and scientific process to determine the cutoff values or scores for a particular marketing campaign. The outcome of regression scoring helps in enhancing marketing efficiency. The primary and the only disadvantage of regression scoring is that the whole process is very complex and costlier as compared to profiling which is easy to perform.

Even if regression scoring is considered as complex and costly process but it is hardly recommended for an organization to implement regression scoring as it usually targets high marketing efficacy and effectiveness. In acquiring new customers regression scoring is the most capable and important marketing process that yields great results, hence organization should usually compromise on complexity and cost.

Need of Relationship with Customers

Building relationship with customers in current market trends is the most important aspect that an organization should focus on. Distinction and eminence are now most sustainable and affirm for which developing good relationship with customers is must.

Some of the substantial outcomes of building a quality relationship is explained below by which need of relationship with customer are insight:

1. Better Customer perceptiveness: As the customer lengthens to deal with a supplier, the supplier tends to explicate a better insight of customer's needs and expectations. By this a high level of relationship can be developed between them. This will result in selling more products and retain the business with the customers which finally will lead to profitable business.

2. Lead to Customer Satisfaction: Customer satisfaction is the measure of how the needs and responses are collaborated and delivered to excel customer expectation. It can only be attained if the customer has an overall good relationship with the supplier. In today's competitive business marketplace, customer satisfaction is an important performance exponent and basic differentiator of business strategies. Hence, the more is customer satisfaction; more is the business and the bonding with customer.

3. Lead to Customer Loyalty: Customer loyalty is the tendency of the customer to remain in business with a particular supplier and buy the products regularly. This is usually seen when a customer is very much satisfied by the supplier and re-visits the organization for business deals, or when he is tended towards re-buying a particular product or brand over times by that supplier. To continue the customer loyalty the most important aspect an organization should focus on is customer satisfaction, hence it can be said that customer loyalty is also an outcome of good relationship.

4. Lead to Customer Retention: Customer retention is a strategic process to keep or retain the existing customers and not letting them to diverge or defect to other suppliers or organization for business and this only possible when there is a quality relationship between customer and supplier. Usually a loyal customer is tended towards sticking to a particular brand or product as far as his basic needs continue to be properly fulfilled. He does not opt for taking a risk in going for a new product. More is the possibility to retain customers the more is the probability of net growth of business.

5. Chances of getting referrals: It is always a cost-free advocacy by customers to provide referrals to supplier when they feel satisfied and encouraged and when they have a healthy relationship with customers. These referrals or customer's reference of other customers acts like a piece of cake for suppliers as there is no cost and struggle involved in this. This could be treated as the best outcome of quality relationship what a supplier can think of.

6. Growth in revenue: When suppliers have healthy relationship with customers the revenue of the organization always increases as customers tend to buy more and more. There is possibility that a satisfied customer seek to buy special category of related products apart from the regular ones from that particular supplier. For instance if a satisfied and loyal customer has a home insurance from an insurance company then there are positive chances that he could also insure his property and car also if he is fully satisfied with the services of that insurance company. This will definitely result in growth of business.

7. Cost to serve is low: Cost to serve existing satisfied customers is always very less for the supplier as they know and understand customers. Customers never come back with complaints and queries because they know the actual business flow and completely rely on the relationship with supplier.

By the above substantial outcomes it is prominent that creating and maintaining relationship with customer is always a key to success.

Model of Creation of Customer Relationship Management System

The interest in relationship marketing emerged only in the second half of the XX century. The first to mention relationship marketing was. Berry L.L. in 1953 (though he did not mention the content of the notion). Only in the 90s serious scientific works by Christopher, Morgan and Hunt, Christopher, Payne, Ballantyne, Gronroos appeared. One of the authors who presented the broadest definition of relationship marketing was Gummesson, who referring to the 30S model analysed possible relationship, into which an enterprise and their interested partners got involved.

Constant changes in the market, development of service market sphere as well as limitation of traditional marketing conception (it does not analyse how to sustain long-term relationship with customers and other participants of the market) were the premises for the formation of a new marketing paradigm. As the market relationship is changing, new forms of the change of competitiveness, customers' needs satisfaction and individual random interaction into long-term relationship with suppliers, customers, competitors and other participants of the market were searched for. The support of long-term relationship becomes a central axis of marketing, and the literature analysing relationship marketing points out that customers make the greatest influence upon marketing solutions. Marketing is not any longer perceived as business activity system including only the projection and creation of goods and services meeting customers' wishes, price-fixing and support as well as distribution in the markets. It is a more complicated process, which emphasises not only marketing mix elements, but also maintenance, support and strengthening of relationship with other market participants.

Referring to Gronroos, Morgan and Hunt, Sheth as well as Ballantyne, the essence of relationship marketing is based on the support of customers' (organisations or individual people) and supplier's (industrial organisations or service organisations) relationship based on trust, cooperation, power distribution, communication, commitment, dependence and other features as well as development of customers' loyalty.

Referring to the suggestion of Wilson, Žvirelienė on the model of relationship marketing research and its application on the level of applied researches, it is possible to state that it might be applied for CRM conception as well. The application of relationship marketing theory (model) in the narrower CRM conception is simply inevitable because customer relationship management cannot be only the illustration of the relationship, it is more important to perceive relationship management and development.

One of the main principles of relationship marketing is orientation to a customer, i.e. detection of customers' needs, appropriate reaction to them and their preservation because to attract new customers is more expensive. Relationship principles should be applied where expenditure of customers' in draft and preservation can be precisely identified. It can present valuable information about the expenditure of service use (buying) experienced by customers, changes of customers' number, and changes of each customer's service application.

One of the ways of customers' demand formation and cognition (business conceptions) is customer relationship managements (CRM). CRM notion as well as relationship marketing has a lot of definitions.

CRM is everything what it is related to satisfaction of customer's needs. It is necessary to start from the review of the following questions: What and how you are ready to present to your customers, what they expect from you and more than expect. Only afterwards it is necessary to choose necessary technologies, which can help you. Technologies are only an instrument, a technical solution, which will automate sales process.

Dick Lee state that CRM is perceived as "chain reaction", which is caused by new strategic initiatives of communication with a customer when high level of information technologies' development and constant customer's need to get better quality of service are achieved. Thompson, "CRM Guru", explains the definition of CRM: in big business, even if it consists of only several persons, there is no collective mind till all information is not saved by different media; and having saved it, it should be presented to "appropriate people" "at appropriate time". For this purpose personal computers, software, and the Internet are necessary.

In the aspect of information technologies CRM is understood as the complex of software and technologies, automating and performing business processes in the following areas: sales, marketing, service, and customer support. The software helps to coordinate the activity of departments interacting with customers (sales, marketing, service and support), as well as to coordinate different channels of communication with customers: individual communication, telephone, the Internet. The software also presents information about a customer for the mentioned departments in order to better meet his/her needs. At present in most organisations sales, marketing and customer support (customers' activity observation and sales organisation as well as relationship support after sales) function as independent departments. Common activity often is not coordinated. In this case CRM creates common platform of communicating with a customer.

Customer relationship management system is the system that integrates management of customer groups, establishment and management of marketing companies. Thus in summary it is possible to state that customer relationship management is:

- Multimedia that guarantees the integration of all technological resources used in a company and activity fields related to customers;
- First of all it is business strategy meant for development of customer relationship; and its results optimise profitability, income and meeting the needs of customers;
- Meant for maximum personalised satisfaction of customers' needs.

Companies that manage customer relationship acquire such customers who are useful in another indirect meaning of getting profit. The clients who help to popularize the company, its activity and offered products or provided services are very important. Well-organised and successful strategy of customer management guarantees that a client will be more indulgent if a misunderstanding takes place as well as he/she will be more indulgent if he/she was not fully satisfied with the quality of service or product. Due to such cooperation the situation, in which both parts win, occurs:

- A customer because he/she gets a qualitative service or product.
- An organisation because it gets profit and has a reliable client.
- An organisation can easier and more appropriately serve a customer when he/she is well-known, his/her needs and tastes are known.

Figure presents the scheme of relationship marketing, which shows what important place in CRM system customer understanding as well as appropriate information about him/her should take.

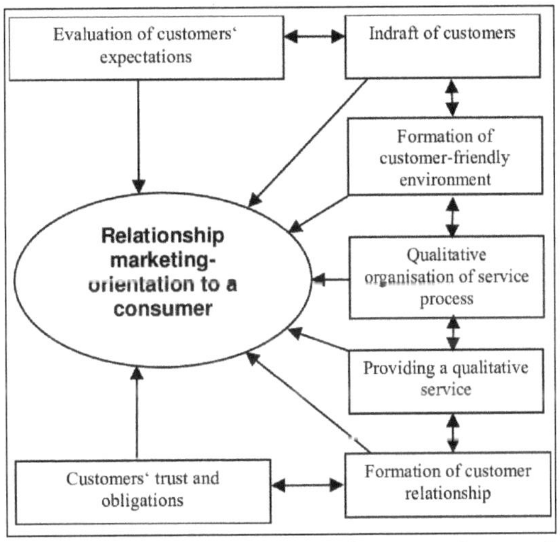

Figure: Coherence of relationship marketing and CRM elements

Customer relationship management (CRM) can help to select the most useful clients for an enterprise. Enterprises most frequently feel who their main customers are, but only some use systematised media of customers' stimulation, loyalty development. Collected data about consumers later become knowledge, and the latter determines profit for an enterprise. However the enterprise's activity can be based on such knowledge only when the data are processed and on their basis motivated decisions to attract or sustain customers are taken. Of course, it is necessary to possess special media, by means of which it is possible to perform the mentioned actions and which simplify the very decision-making.

At present most organisations recognise evident benefit of CRM and almost every enterprise either use certain CRM technologies, supporting their business, or evaluate specific benefit of CRM technology and plan its future realisation.

The achieved higher profit is the main benefit of CRM systems for proprietors, i.e.:

- Costs decrease: Increased total effectiveness, an automated process of sales, service and marketing companies; decreased costs of customers' management, automated routine work.

- Income increase: Greater quality of sales and services, management of customers' possibilities and problems (incidents, enquiries), better ratio of sales.
- Benefit of CRM systems for a customer: To get an offer in an appropriate form when it is necessary and what it is necessary, to be appropriately served, to feel important, to be informed in time, a possibility to choose a service channel (self-service, full service).
- Benefit of CRM systems for an employee: The system has to be a friend; it helps to fulfil more activity during the same time, and a higher salary is related to it; the feeling of self-control, a possibility to show oneself as leader and sound competition emerge.

CRM can be implemented within enterprises independent of enterprise's size or amount of goods or services selling; both within small, and big enterprises that value the quality of customer's service, his or her loyalty, less sensitivity for price changes and that recognise that to attract a new customer is much more expensive than to sustain the present one. CRM decisions are reasonably interesting for, namely: retail networks, telecommunication operators, banks, insurance companies, travel agencies, advertising and public relations agencies, and wholesale and logistics enterprises possessing a lot of customers.

Methodological Premises of CRM Model Formation

Creation of customer relationship management (CRM) system is a complicated process. Different authors present a lot of variants of creation (implementation) of CRM management system. Table presents 13 CRM models offered by different authors. The table shows components or process stages of CRM models.

Different authors distinguish similar CRM model formation elements or stages of its implementation process, which cannot be superposed because each author, according to his/her opinion, adds some important element.

CRM formation process consists of three important parts:

- Setting of CRM goal (objects) (e.g. To increase effectiveness);
- Choice of a team (or partners);
- Choice/creation of programs (relative schemes of activity), meant for customer relationship management.

Having chosen CRM program, the stage of relationship administration and management has to be considered, it involves the following decisions: creation of team structure, distribution of functions, communication, intercourse, process planning, and motivation of employees as well as supervision of process course. In the third stage of activity evaluation it is necessary to set goals, which are to be attained, i.e. what strategic, finance and marketing goals will be. Customers' loyalty and satisfaction are among basic marketing goals. The last stage of CRM development ends in actions of CRM support and improvement. A simple and clear CRM model is presented by Sin, Yim; it presents four elements groups: consumers (customers) characteristics, management of knowledge/data (information about customers), CRM structure (organisation structure, organisation obligations, sources, human resources, etc.) and CRM substantiation by IT technologies.

According to Jason, each customer is a unique personality, thus it is necessary to analyse his or her needs and features. It means that it is necessary to accumulate at least little information about a customer, to possess his or her contact information, work profile and main wishes. The author also assumes that certain reorganisation of an enterprise is necessary. If the level of customer service is not developed sufficiently, customer relationship cannot be managed effectively. For this purpose it is best to acquire the program of contact management, which permits to accumulate information about customers as well as to perform the analysis of accumulated information. Software is one of the means enabling the reorganisation of company's activity for the benefit of customers and enterprise.

Summarising all CRM creation models, their formats, it is possible to state that the diagnosis (analysis) of enterprise's customers is a primary stage when creating CRM system. Having analysed the most useful customers of an enterprise, it is advisable to prepare the appropriate program, which would contribute to the strengthening of current relationship in every way possible.

Four actions should be applied in order to reinforce and strengthen customers' relationship:

1. Identification of individual features, wishes of each customer.
2. Modelling of current and potential purchases.
3. Creation of business plans and strategies beginning with the most profitable projects.
4. Reorganisation of enterprise's activity is necessary for creating closer relations between the enterprise and a customer.

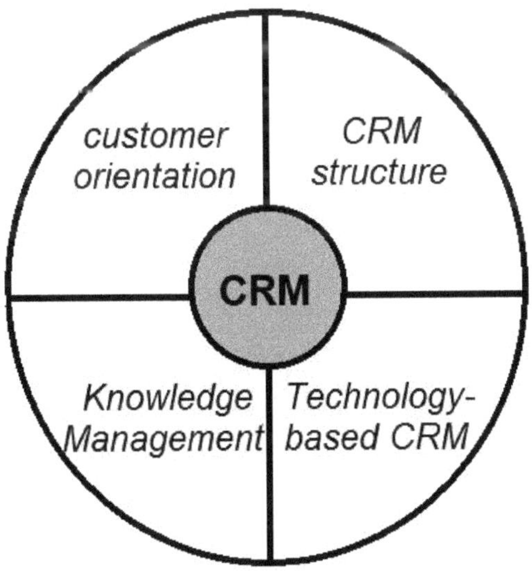

Figure: Four elements of CRM system

Summarising viewpoints of various authors, it would be possible to highlight that in order to successfully implement CRM, it is necessary to balance and integrate technologies, processes and people. These elements are closely related to enterprise's strategy, processes of technologies, and processes of integration of overlapping functions as well as orientation to basic customers.

When forming CRM system, the authors faced the dilemma how to appropriately choose structural elements of the system that would show the existence of the system, as well as it would guarantee its implementation. Thus, by constructing the theoretical model, first of all priorities of functionalism and implementation against the creation strategy were searched for, but of course by not eliminating the latter components.

Theoretical Model of CRM Implementation

Referring to standpoints of many authors on the creation of the customer management system, and having analysed the structure of CRM models presented by them, the following stages and elements of CRM model formation were chosen:

1. CRM strategy and evaluation of current situation within an enterprise: Before starting the implementation works of CRM, the audit of current situation should be performed, i.e. skills of the work with customers, wrong decisions and failures, competitors, partners, customers are analysed as well as enterprise's needs to establish CRM system are also identified.

The CRM strategy is the basis for the creation and implementation of customer relationship system, thus this element in the model is seen behind the borders of the system but not eliminated.

2. Formation of CRM system, customers, their segmentation: The task of each enterprise is qualitative cost-effectives and profitable service of customers. In order to attain the goal, it is necessary to pay more attention to such value - creating means related to customers' service as selling development, loyalty development, data collection, customers' segmentation, customers' service when the enterprise itself initiates it, etc.

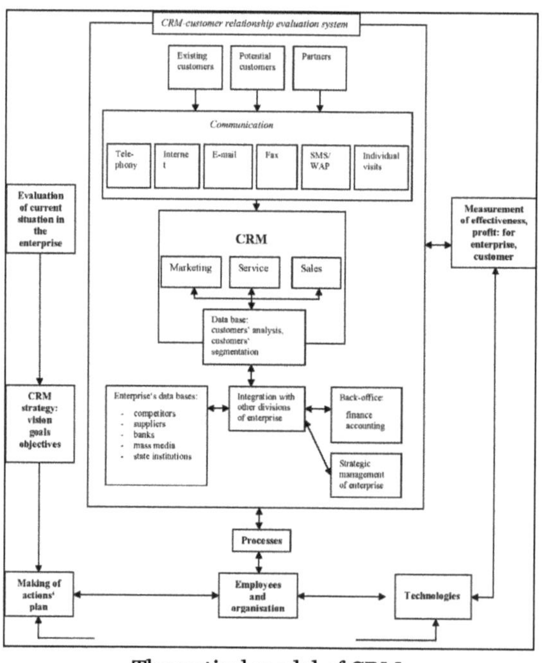

Theoretical model of CRM

In the model the customers' element is primary and the most important.

3. Communication channels of interaction: Information sources and data base. In the model they are secondary, but they guarantee technological functioning of CRM, as well as they allow proper analysis of the information and formation of customer's databases.

4. Employees and an organisation itself: CRM projects often are of huge degree and most frequently cause reorganisation of usual processes, the change of set goals and the way of customers' management. Having chosen CRM as strategic medium, it has to necessarily penetrate within a whole organisation and remain in the focus of attention in any activity of an organisation. Enterprise's employees also have to constantly give thought how everyone should behave in order to improve relationship with customers. In the model these components of CRM creation are shown as guaranteeing system's functioning where employees have to prepare the analysis of a situation, to formulate strategy, action plans as well as to control system's efficiency and efficacy

5. Processes: It is necessary to determine how enterprise's processes should function and what factors can influence successful results of an enterprise. CRM project is carried out for a whole organisation, thus it relates to a lot of current and new processes of an enterprise. Considering it also induces cultural changes, coordination to new circumstances, CRM project can be related to optimisation of organisation processes and management of changes. It is necessary to integrate CRM system into other processes of an enterprise. In other words, CRM system will not be useful till it is not related to other main systems of an enterprise. If CRM system is not inserted into the entirety, it will soon become a closed island. In the model it is shown as the basis for the interaction of the most important elements.

6. Information technologies: Fast and easy accessibility of accumulated information; accessibility of information from geographically remote locations, optimisation of work time use, decrease of negative impact of employees' change: by means of CRM system the maintenance of relationship between a customer and service operator is realised by any communication media. It can be post, e-mail, phone calls, the Internet, individual visits, etc. In the model these elements are very important both in economical and relationship marketing meaning. Fast and effective customer relationship management will depend on properly chosen technologies.

7. Investments and anticipated profit: Investments into CRM and future profit depends on a lot of factors, which are determined by different circumstances related to an enterprise (among them also readiness of an enterprise to implement CRM). The size of investments into CRM depends on the following factors:

- Investments into IT software and hardware.
- Investments into a new role the essence of which is CRM improvement and application, formation.
- Resources that will be necessary in managing changes (fixation project).
- Expenditure of CRM system consumers' education.
- Suppression of disturbances often occurring in an organisation when implementing a project.
- Implementation tasks of much broader extent and more complicated than expected.

It is rather difficult to carry out the real analysis of expenditure and profit. As such profit is more qualitative than quantitative. However real profit manifests so that possibilities of sales are better controlled and distributed more considering their importance (management of sales channels), more effective split by important data, better quality of the data, more attention is paid to "real customers", employees better understand customers, reports on sales and management are easier prepared.

In the model these elements are not directly shown, they will be the output of the CRM system. From the management viewpoint, an effectively functioning system has to give profit both for the enterprise and customers.

In figure presents theoretical model of CRM implementation; it was formed by having summarised all chosen stages and elements of customer management system formation.

Customer Loyalty and Satisfaction

Customer loyalty every supplier wants to create and retain a loyal customer who engages in continued profitable business with him. Customer Loyalty is the measure of success of the supplier in retaining a long term relationship with the customer. Thus customer loyalty is when a supplier receives the ultimate reward of his efforts in interacting with its customer. Customer loyalty tends the customer to voluntarily choose a particular product against another for his need. The loyalty may be product specific or it may be company specific. When a loyal customer has repetitive requirement of the same product, such customers may be described as being 'brand loyal'. On the other hand he may also require different products of the same manufacturer. That is to say he makes significant purchases direct from the same supplier and that counts as the company specific loyalty.

Loyalty also means that customer is sticking to the supplier on certain grounds though he may be having other options also. It may be possible that the supplier may not have the best product or the customer may be having some problems with the supplier in respect of his supply of the product but the customer likes to ignore other options and prefers to continue with the same supplier as the customer thinks the supplier provides him more value and benefit than others. Such loyal customers tend to spend more money buy more, buy longer and tell more people about the product or supplier. This type of long-term customer loyalty can only be created by making the customers feel that they are number one priority with the supplier.

Some customers are inherently predictable and loyal, irrespective of the supplier with which they are doing business. They simply prefer long-term relationships with him. Loyal customers are predisposed to stay with one product or supplier, resisting competitive offers and also recommend the supplier to others.

In case the business is done directly the relationship is direct so also the loyalty. But if the selling is through two or more intermediaries then the loyalty has to be measured at different levels. In that case the end customer loyalty is influenced by the loyalty of the intermediate customers. Then the supplier has to focus his loyalty retention plan accordingly and has to judge and analyze the loyalties of the intermediaries. This process depends on what amount of importance he gives to each of the intermediaries and how much to the ultimate customer. But it is certain that well-managed customer retention programs are sure to give the ultimate customer loyalty.

True, the customers who are targeted by a retention program demonstrate higher loyalty to a business. Therefore such customer retention programs should include regular communication with customers, and provide them opportunities to remain active and choosing to do business with the supplier.

Loyalty is demonstrated by the actions of the customer. But it doesn't mean that the customer satisfaction level can measure his loyalty. Customer loyalty is not customer satisfaction. Customer satisfaction is the basic entry point for a good business to start with. A customer can be very satisfied with the deal and still not be loyal. On the other hand a customer may not express satisfaction but wants to remain loyal to the supplier due to some reasons which keeps him benefited from that supplier. For the same degree of satisfaction, the loyalty level may also be different for different suppliers.

On the other hand, loyalty should not be considered as just an attitude. Customer loyalty should have a direct connection to a company's financial results. The supplier should be able to plan a clear and direct economic benefit of some kind, as the result of the strategies and tactics he employs to increase its customers' loyalty.

Measuring customer loyalty and developing a retention strategy are of great importance to an organization's success.

Most of the organizations have murkiness in considering customer loyalty and satisfaction. They feel that both are same and a satisfied customer is always loyal to them. But this is not true as the customer can be delightfully satisfied but he may be or may not be loyal. This is because satisfaction an emotional and slushy feeling over the job done. But loyalty is related to the action taken by the customer future. There can be following two combinations of aspect when satisfaction and loyalty are treated together:

- Satisfied but disloyal customers: A customer can be fully satisfied but may not be loyal due to following reasons-
    - Entrepreneur Customer: These types of customers like to experiment a lot and hence try to create various options for them to get more benefits. So even if they are satisfied they diverge to other options available in the market.
    - Pressure from Competitors: Due to the pressure in market the customer tends to follow the competitors path and divert from the existing supplier to remain sustain in the global marketplace.
    - Outdated Suppliers: The customer may be satisfied with the existing customers but sometimes feel that the product and services he is using are outdated in market. Due to the changing technology there is always a need to update the technical aspects and product features even if the old products and services are satisfactory. Focusing on these facets the customers normally go to other suppliers for his new requirements.
- Unsatisfied but loyal customers: The other abnormal situation is when the customer is loyal but is unsatisfied. The reasons for this are following-
    - Lack of available options: There can lack of options available for customers. This situation arises when the existing supplier is having a monopoly in a particular segment of

products or when all other competitors are worse than existing supplier. The customer feel trapped in this type of situation and is forced to be loyal to the supplier but at the end of the day he will be an unsatisfied customer.

- Improved Supplier: In another situation the suppliers may take the customers in confidence by convincing them to provide improved products and services in the coming future. This is an important tactic that supplier implement in their marketing strategy to become customer centric and to have customers stick to them and be loyal. To remain in a healthy relationship the customers also remain loyal but have a feeling of dissatisfaction beneath. But finally if the supplier continuously supply degraded products and services the customer could easily divert from them in search of better prospects.

- Customer Inertia: There are some customers who afraid to change the supplier. Even if they have bad experience with the supplier, they continue to have business with them. This may be due to the emotional and business attachments or bonding of customers with those particular suppliers. Their could be many others reason for this like, the customers' feel reluctant to face the complexity of the process of changing their way to other suppliers and prominently when they already have a long term relationship with their suppliers. Under this situation the customer tries to ignore the feelings of being unsatisfied and remain loyal to them.

For an organization to be in business and make profit it is a very important aspect for them to gain customer loyalty. Even if high satisfaction may not guarantee loyalty but it can be literally a prerequisite for it.

Drivers of Customer Loyalty

It is very important for an organization to identify the factors and facets which drive customer loyalty. These factors help the organization to manage customer loyalty in a better and efficient way. Following are the drivers of customer loyalty:

Attitude- A customer to bear on his loyalty can have following types of attitude:

- Emotional and sentimental: Some customers stick to a particular supplier due to the emotional and sentimental attachments with that supplier. This attachment may be due to the physical location of the supplier, product pattern provided by the supplier that exactly suits customer or may be due to the esteemed assistance and services provided by him. This type of bonding enhances customer loyalty and it is very difficult to break this bonding under any circumstances.

- Rational Type: Such type of customer makes purchase decision rationally. Before making any purchase they evaluate the suppliers and assess the profitability criteria.

- Entrepreneur Type: These types of customers have a habit to try new options. Their decision to choose supplier is normally irrational and can change their loyalty to other suppliers even if they are satisfied with existing customers. It's difficult for the supplier to retain or manage these types of customers as no situation could bind them.

- Product and services: Following are the important aspects of product and services that could substantially help in retaining loyalty of customers.

- Differentiated Products and Services: Differentiation in products and services help the organization to reduce competition in market and have substantial influence on customers' mindset.
- Multiple Products for the same customer: By manufacturing multiple products for the same customer enhances the relationship with customer which increases loyalty. If the customer is loyal towards any one brand then there are good chances to retain his loyalty for whole range of brands.
- High Service Component: The products having a high service component captures more customer loyalty. This is because the customer does not want to experiment with other products provided by different supplier. Hence they become loyal to the existing customer due to the provision of high service components.

Technology

The technological aspects of product manufactured by the supplier plays a vital role in customer loyalty. The more products are technologically sound, more is the loyalty.

Human Resources

Organizational human resource plays a vital role in marketing segments where customer comes in direct contact. In some consumer sectors like household and automobiles, the customer gets a chance to evaluate capability of organizational human assets. If the customer evaluates these human assets as useful and is influenced by the aspects then he develops a positive feeling against the supplier who possess these enhanced human assets.

Supplier's Culture

Supplier's culture is most important driver of customer loyalty. In consumer sector this culture means quality and in core sector it can be related to technology. For example, in US 'Friedrich' has ranked with good quality, enhanced design and user friendly features which have created brand loyalty. In Indian the supplier of almost all the dairy product called 'Amul' has pursued customer loyalty because of their overall culture. In core sector the image of the supplier is the biggest driver of loyalty. This image could add a status symbol for most of the customers. 'Mercedes' automobiles and 'RayBan' sun-glasses are example of this. The customers uses these products only for maintaining or enhancing their lifestyle and always be loyal to them.

Customer Loyalty Breakers

When customers end up his relationship with suppliers, he breaks the loyalty with him. Following are the reasons which are responsible for loyalty break ups:

- Customer dis-satisfaction: Customer dissatisfaction is the primary reason that results in breaking up the continued loyalty with the supplier. Most of the unsatisfied customers try to find more prominent alternatives which results in their migration. In most of the cases the customer does not even complain about the dissatisfaction and simply divert their way to other supplier.

- Tough competition and new options availability: Vivid competition also acts as a breaker of loyalty as it gives customers new options which are exposed in the market and are sometimes better than before. These new options results in enhancing expectations of customers which leads to accelerating break ups in relationship between supplier and customers. This happens because the existing customer's supplier is unable to fulfill their demands in an appropriate manner.

- Enhanced product features and advance technology: Due to the abrupt change in market conditions, inheritance of advanced technology in all ranges of products and service is inevitable. If the supplier is unable to follow the process of continuously updating technological related aspects of products and services he may lose customers as they divert in search of technological sound products and services. Apart from the advanced technology, if the customers get enhanced and user friendly product features then it acts like additional incentives for them to migrate.

- Customer expectation: Expectations of customers can go way beyond expectations of supplier which results in breaking loyalty. If supplier is not able to meet customers' expectations then obviously customers would look for better alternatives. These expectations can be related to cost, quality, product service, efficiency, durability or any other aspect. Many a times these expectations could be unrealistic or unreasonable due to the market scenario or some external business pressure. Under this kind of situation it is becomes very difficult for an organizations to meet all the expectations which result in sudden divert by breaking loyalty bond. Any supplier which comes close to these unrealistic and unreasonable expectations of customers could retain him easily.

- Customer attitude: Customer attitude plays a vital role in breaking up the loyalty with existing supplier. This is because some customers have a habit to try new options and change business tactics. Even if they are fully satisfied with the existing supplier they would attempt a change for the sake of getting new and better option or because of any change in business rules and tactics. These types of customers are experimental in nature and try to be innovative and creative by taking high business risks. These customers are supposed to be least loyal because they less likely to be attached with any sort of bond with single supplier. To retain these types of customers is a pain for all the suppliers and they generally try to change their attitude by inheriting some business tactics in their marketing strategies.

- Product services: Providing products with low or bad service components will result in ending up loyalty with customers. Customers not only use the products but also demands valuable and spontaneous service. Hence apart from manufacturing good and sound products it is very important for the supplier to provide enhanced service components along with the product which will act as a roadblock for customer to divert.

- Market recession: Some unrealistic situation in global market which affects the allover economy of a country could also be a reason in ending up loyalty bond with customers. Under this situation called 'recession', intense cash flow problem is seen. This leads customers to cut-off expenses incurred in business and may lead to divert to other suppliers in search of low cost but reliable products and services.

Tracking Customer Loyalty

For maintaining customers' loyalty it is very important by organizations to track their loyalty. Following are the two methods of tracking customer loyalty:

1. Loyalty tracking on time scale: Loyalty can be tracked on linear time scale. This includes preparing time scale graph which shows the loyalty trend of customers in accordance to time. The graph is normally created when the supplier evaluates that customer is showing less interest in buying and the time gap between each buy is gradually increasing. When the graph goes from secured to lost stage, it is important for the organization to identify corrective measures to retain the customer back to track. When the corrective measure works efficiently the graph again moves towards secured level in the coming future which indicates that the supplier is gaining customer loyalty again and there are fewer chances for the customer to divert to other options. This is a simple but powerful technique to track customer loyalty in-house without employing external resources. However this is not an accurate method to track customer loyalty but it shows the trend if the correctives measure taken to retain customer is working efficiently or not. Changes in the loyalty is normally seen after tracking loyalty on time scale but the details are not exactly focused and does not accurately provide the actually loyalty variation of the customer to supplier. This process is normally implemented in the initial stages after the supplier identifies that there are chances that customer can divert. If corrective measures are not taken at this stage then it becomes difficult for the supplier to retain the customer.

2. Loyalty tracking on Volume-Loyalty Matrix: Other way to track loyalty is on a matrix called volume-loyalty matrix. This kind of tracking includes determining the loyalty according to the pre-defined matrix quadrants so that the supplier could judge the customer value and accordingly engage corrective actions. The quadrant variable could be associated with values like 'premium', 'neglected', 'patrons' and 'pitfall'. If the customer value remains the same but the customer loyalty travels from neglected to premium quadrant then the customer loyalty is moving in the positive direction and there are chances that it may cause to increase customer value as well. If the customer value increases but the customer loyalty travels from premium to patron's level then it shows that the loyalty is declining and needs attention and corrective actions should be taken to improve customer loyalty. If the customer value increases rapidly but customer loyalty travels from premium to pitfall level then it indicates that the loyalty is declining rapidly and serious attention should be taken. Under this condition the loyalty bond gets weakened and customer can divert at any time. This is purposeful and powerful tracking method to track loyalty because end results are focused and the seriousness of whole scenario is clearly visible. This helps the supplier to make strong and focused strategic plans to reclaim customer loyalty. Normally this tracking process is implemented under adverse conditions to get satisfactory results. When the tracking on time scale graph does not work efficiently supplier implements volume-loyalty matrix to enhance customer loyalty in an efficient and efficacious manner.

   Tracking customer loyalty is very important process that all the organization should implement continuously to track customer buying trend and force them be loyal to them and increase business values and profits.

Increasing Customer Loyalty

It is necessarily required for an organization to interact and communicate with customers on a regular basis to increase customer loyalty. In these interactions and communications it is required to learn and determine all individual customer needs and respond accordingly.

Following are some important aspects which suppliers should always keep in mind to increase customer loyalty:

1. Emotional attachment: Emotional and sentimental attachment plays a vital role in increasing customer loyalty. Hence it is important for the suppliers to identify the factors which force the customers to get emotionally attached with them and should mound this information accordingly to enhance this emotional relationship. There can be a range of factors for customers that develop this emotional attachment with suppliers, some of which are discussed below:

- Many customers get emotionally attached because of the high name or good image of the supplier in the market. They feel highly elicited in status for having business deals with them which could also substantially upraise their image. This helps in increasing loyalty of customer with that particular supplier unless and until customer finds any other high named supplier who meets all his expectations.
- Some customers will get attached with supplier just because of the excellence in technical aspects of product which also includes best service and healthy organizational culture. These types of customers only believe in the fact that all the products and services work in accordance to them and in an efficacious and efficient way. This attachment results in customer to become loyal.
- Some customers get highly impressed with the overall behavior of supplier. Soft spoken and well-mannered executive is always a positive gain for the supplier to get the customers emotionally attached with him. This behavior could also include provision of spontaneous responses in an efficient way. All these aspects can increase customer loyalty to much higher levels.

2. Supplier's credibility: Supplier's credibility helps to elevate customer loyalty. Credibility provides confidence and comfort to the customers regarding the reliability, durability, quality and performance of products and services. In industrial sector, the products provided by suppliers are actually used by customers for production purpose. Hence unavailability, malfunctioning or low performance of these products could highly affect the profitability in business. By nullifying all these factors and providing high valued service and high end products which are available all the time develops a sense of credibility among the customers. In such case customers develop faith and belief in supplier which obviously increases customer loyalty.

3. Customer satisfaction: Customer satisfaction is the measure of how the needs and responses are collaborated and delivered to excel customer expectation. It can only be attained if the customer has an overall good relationship with the supplier. In today's competitive business marketplace, customer satisfaction is an important performance exponent and basic differentiator of business strategies. However, a satisfied customer may be or may not be loyal but an unsatisfied customer potentially seeks other options and may migrate easily. Hence it is important for the supplier

to identify dissatisfaction factors and develop corrective measures to cope up with. It is often seen that if these corrective measures are implemented successfully to improve satisfaction then satisfaction level increases to a much higher level as compared to a normal satisfied customer. A satisfied customer mostly tends to be a loyal customer hence customer satisfaction is an important factor that increases customer loyalty.

Customer Satisfaction

Business always starts and closes with customers and hence the customers must be treated as the King of the market. All the business enhancements, profit, status, image etc. of the organization depends on customers. Hence it is important for all the organizations to meet all the customers' expectations and identify that they are satisfied customer.

Customer satisfaction is the measure of how the needs and responses are collaborated and delivered to excel customer expectation. It can only be attained if the customer has an overall good relationship with the supplier. In today's competitive business marketplace, customer satisfaction is an important performance exponent and basic differentiator of business strategies. Hence, the more is customer satisfaction; more is the business and the bonding with customer.

Customer satisfaction is a part of customer's experience that exposes a supplier's behavior on customer's expectation. It also depends on how efficiently it is managed and how promptly services are provided. This satisfaction could be related to various business aspects like marketing, product manufacturing, engineering, quality of products and services, responses customer's problems and queries, completion of project, post delivery services, complaint management etc.

Customer satisfaction is the overall essence of the impression about the supplier by the customers. This impression which a customer makes regarding supplier is the sum total of all the process he goes through, right from communicating supplier before doing any marketing to post delivery options and services and managing queries or complaints post-delivery. During this process the customer comes across working environment of various departments and the type of strategies involved in the organization. This helps the customer to make strong opinion about the supplier which finally results in satisfaction or dissatisfaction.

Customer's perception on supplier helps the customer choose among the supplier on basis of money value and how well the delivered products suit all the requirements. The supplier's services never diminishes after the delivery as customer seeks high values post marketing services which could help them use and customize the delivered product more efficiently. If he is satisfied with the post marketing services then there are good chances for supplier to retain the customers to enhance repeated purchases and make good business profits.

It is necessarily required for an organization to interact and communicate with customers on a regular basis to increase customer satisfaction. In these interactions and communications it is required to learn and determine all individual customer needs and respond accordingly. Even if the products are identical in competing markets, satisfaction provides high retention rates. For example, shoppers and retailers are engaged with frequent shopping and credit cards to gain customer satisfaction, many high end retailers also provide membership cards and discount benefits on those cards so that the customer remain loyal to them.

Higher the satisfaction level, higher is the sentimental attachment of customers with the specific brand of product and also with the supplier. This helps in making a strong and healthy customer-supplier bonding. This bonding forces the customer to be tied up with that particular supplier and chances of defection very less. Hence customer satisfaction is very important panorama that every supplier should focus on to establish a renounced position in the global market and enhance business and profit.

Reasons of Dissatisfaction in Customers

When the suppliers are unable to entertain customers or their business strategies fail to build a good relationship with customers, they probably end up with customers' dissatisfaction. Their can be many reasons for the customers to become dissatisfied. Some of these reasons are:

1. Taking example of India, most of the population here are vegetarian. They do not require a bigger space in their refrigerator for deep freeze option. But still, following foreign trend of making refrigerators most of the manufacturers are providing huge capacity deep freezers. If the people are not able to use this space or option, it is waste for them. Obviously they feel dissatisfied with this.

2. Vacuum cleaner, one of the modest innovative equipment which was invented to reduce manual household works on just click of a button. It is a huge success in European countries where the environment is dusty as compared to other parts of the world and the cost for managing household work is pretty expensive. But in countries like United Stated where the environment is very different and dust free, there is no need for installing this equipment in house as it would be kept uselessly in house. In India the environment is lot dusty but the cost exempted for managing the household work is very cheap and affordable, so why people will go and buy a vacuum cleaner and invest a lot of money in that, if they can hire a manual cleaner boy without investing much. If they buy a vacuum cleaner and later on feel that it is turning out to be expensive and tedious deal then it brings dissatisfaction among them.

3. The eating tradition in India is very much different from other countries. In Europe, people usually eat continental food and they have habit of appetizing the main course with bread, so they usually keep a small plate (normally called quarter plate) in the left hand side so that the bread is available to eat in between with left hand. In India, people prefer 'Roti' (Indian version of bread) and they like to eat it with right hand so they want the small plate to be kept on right hand side. But in India, most of the good restaurants are influenced by European traditions and keep on serving the small plates on left hand side on the table. This creates uneasiness for the people to eat food which leads to dissatisfaction.

4. Problem also occurs when the customers get wrongly customized products. This is because of the communication gaps between supplier and customers and forcing the customer to become dissatisfied due to this.

5. Apart from delivering good and quality products it is equally important for the suppliers to provide excellent post deal services. For example, a customer bought a Fax machine from a supplier and suddenly something went wrong and the machine stopped sending fax at the time when there was an urgent fax to be sent. Customer called the supplier and asked

for urgent support but none of the executive at the supplier's side was available for fixing this issue. Customer finally took some local vendor's help to fix as it was very urgent. Such a situation can develop an irritating gesture for customers against the supplier and to his dissatisfaction.

Apart from the above examples many more similar reasons could lead to customer's dissatisfaction. It is very important for the supplier to concentrate on customer's needs and provide him the required products and services. If desired measures are not taken, customer's dissatisfaction could possibly build poor relationships between the two parties which could break anytime.

Measuring Customer Satisfaction

For improving customer satisfaction it is essential for the supplier to measure it. It is purely believed that if anything is not measurable then it is not authentic. Customers are the most important asset for any organization as they are only responsible to drives the business. Measuring customer satisfaction helps in identifying specific customer information which is needed to run business smoothly.

Following are the information and details that could be generated after measuring customers' satisfaction:

1. Business Related: Measuring customer satisfaction helps an organization to identify the efficiency of its business strategies and marketing tactics and encompasses if the organization is customer focused or not. It also provides analyzed details on how many numbers of customers have defected, how much loss the business has incurred and up to what extent the profit is decayed due to customer defect. A customer is usually dissatisfied when his expectations are not met or the commitments from supplier are not fulfilled reasonably and within the given time span. This becomes a serious issue for the customers as the delay will obvious affect their image too. The customer usually shares these problems and issues with other customers which hiders the business of the supplier. Some of these unsatisfied customers launch complaints but most of the other customers simply defect to other suppliers without even informing which creates a big void in the business processes of supplier because they did not get chance to analyze the reasons of customer defection. Loss of customers is directly proportionate to loss of business and profitability. If an organization is able to measure business related aspects of customer satisfaction then they become capable to bridge the gaps between them and customers to enhance more customer satisfaction among their peer customers.

2. Customer Related: By measuring customer related aspects of customer satisfaction following details can be entailed:

- How many total numbers of customers have defected?
- Specifically which customers have been defected?
- Reason why they have defected and where exactly they have defected?
- Measurement of customer satisfaction always helps a supplier to analyze appropriate reasons of lost of customers and take measures to avoid this. It also provides analyzed information about the business loss in the coming future. This actually helps the supplier to be

profitable because cost involved in acquiring a customer is comparatively higher then the cost involved in retaining an existing customer.

- It also helps the supplier to identify the value of their products and services according to the customers' perception. If customer is dissatisfied with products and services then there is a need for supplier to check the performance and quality of the product and services so that other customers could not complaint regarding the same.
- It can also analyze the exact need and requirement of customer so that measures are taken accordingly to satisfy each and every customer.

3. Suppliers Related: Following are the supplier's specific information that could be generated while measuring customer satisfaction:

- It helps the supplier to conclude about his own image, strength and weak points.
- It helps the supplier to identify his area of perfection and competency so that they flourish in monopoly of specific products and services.
- It helps in encompassing the organization's position according to the benchmark possessed in the market by competitors.

The best way to improve customer satisfaction is to first measure it and then apply methods to enhance it. It helps the supplier to always keep a check on allover business processes by identifying strong and weak aspects and creating strong bond with all their customers to enhance business.

Methods of Measuring Customer Satisfaction

Managing customers' satisfaction efficiently is one the biggest challenge an organization face. The tools or methods to measure customer satisfaction needs to be defined sophisticatedly to fulfill the desired norms.

There are following methods to measure customer satisfaction:

1. Direct Methods: Directly contacting customers and getting their valuable feedback is very important. Following are some of the ways by which customers could be directly tabbed:

- Getting customer feedback through third party agencies.
- Direct marketing, in-house call centers, complaint handling department could be treated as first point of contact for getting customer feedback. These feedbacks are compiled to analyze customers' perception.
- Getting customer feedback through face to face conversation or meeting.
- Feedback through complaint or appreciation letter.
- Direct customer feedback through surveys and questionnaires.

Organizations mostly employ external agencies to listen to their customers and provide dedicated feedback to them. These feedbacks needs to be sophisticated and in structured format so that conclusive results could be fetched out. Face to face meetings and complaint or appreciation letter engages immediate issues. The feedback received in this is not uniformed as different types of customers are addressed with different domains of questions. This hiders the analysis process to be performed accurately and consistently. Hence the best way is to implement a proper survey which consists of uniformed questionnaire to get customer feedback from well segmented customers. The design of the prepared questionnaire is an important aspect and should enclose all the essential factors of business. The questions asked should be in a way that the customer is encouraged to respond in a obvious way. These feedback could received by the organizations can be treated as one of the best way to measure customer satisfaction.

Apart from the above methods there is another very popular direct method which is surprise market visit. By this, information regarding different segment of products and services provided to the customers could be obtained in an efficient manner. It becomes easy for the supplier to know the weak and strong aspects of products and services.

2. Indirect Method: The major drawback of direct methods is that it turns out to be very costly and requires a lot of pre compiled preparations to implement. For getting the valuable feedbacks the supplier totally depends on the customer due to which they looses options and chances to take corrective measure at correct time. Hence there are other following indirect methods of getting feedback regarding customer satisfaction:

- Customer Complaints: Customer's complaints are the issues and problems reported by the customer to supplier with regards to any specific product or related service. These complaints can be classified under different segments according to the severity and department. If the complaints under a particular segment go high in a specific period of time then the performance of the organization is degrading in that specific area or segment. But if the complaints diminish in a specific period of time then that means the organization is performing well and customer satisfaction level is also higher.
- Customer Loyalty: It is necessarily required for an organization to interact and communicate with customers on a regular basis to increase customer loyalty. In these interactions and communications it is required to learn and determine all individual customer needs and respond accordingly. A customer is said to be loyal if he revisits supplier on regular basis for purchases. These loyal customers are the satisfied ones and hence they are bounded with a relationship with the supplier. Hence by obtaining the customer loyalty index, suppliers can indirectly measure customer satisfaction.

Factors affecting Customer Satisfaction

Customer satisfaction is the overall impression of customer about the supplier and the products and services delivered by the supplier. Following are the important factors that could affect customer satisfaction:

- Department wise capability of the supplier.
- Technological and engineering or re-engineering aspects of products and services.
- Type and quality of response provided by the supplier.

- Supplier's capability to commit on deadlines and how efficiently they are met.
- Customer service provided by the supplier.
- Complaint management.
- Cost, quality, performance and efficiency of the product.
- Supplier's personal facets like etiquettes and friendliness.
- Supplier's ability to manage whole customer life cycle.

The above factors could be widely classified under two categories i.e. suppliers behavior and performance of product and services. The supplier's behavior mostly depends on the behavior of its senior subordinates, managers and internal employees. All the functional activities like customer response, direct product and maintenance services, complaint management etc. are the factors that rely on how skillful and trained the internal and human resources of the supplier are. The second category is regarding all the products and services. This depends on the capability of supplier to how to nurture the products and service efficiently and how skilled the employees are. It's all about how the skills are implemented to demonstrate engineering, re-engineering and technological aspects of the products and services. The quality and efficaciousness of the products is also an important factor that enables compatible and hassle free functions and operations. This bears to lower maintenance and higher life of the product which is highly admired by the customers.

If the product is having some problem or compatibility issues and requires frequent maintenance and support than the customers could get irritated and possibilities of sudden divert is there which lead to supplier's financial loss. In the same way if the product is expecting huge amount of financial and manual resources then customers could get a feeling of dissatisfaction and worry. However, if these aspects are handled efficiently by giving class services and dealing with complaints effectively then dissatisfied customers could be converted into long time satisfied customers and retaining them becomes easy.

It is practically impossible for the supplier to provide all the above explained features. There are always some positive as well as negative features in products and services which could lead to delight or irritate customers. The final opinion is the sum of overall experiences which a customer percept. But it is also true that more the positive aspects, the more the customer is satisfied. Hence the aim of the supplier should be always to enhance these positive feelings among all the customers to increase customer satisfaction. The supplier must identify how to enhance these positive aspects to maximum level by analyzing the customer's data and information using CRM system. The individual liking and disliking of customers differ from customer to customer. It is hence required to target a customer and identify individual requirement to make them satisfied.

Having discussed the above factors that affect customer satisfaction we can say that higher the satisfaction level, higher is the sentimental attachment of customers with the specific brand of product and also with the supplier. This helps in making a strong and healthy customer-supplier bonding. This bonding forces the customer to be tied up with that particular supplier and chances of defection are very less. Hence customer satisfaction is very important panorama that every supplier should focus on to establish a renounced position in the global market and enhance business and profit.

Customers Response

Customer response is the reaction by the organization to the queries and activities of the customer. Dealing with these queries intelligently is very important as small misunderstandings could convey unalike perceptions. Success totally depends on understanding and interpreting these queries and then working out to provide the best solution. During this situation if the supplier wins to satisfy the customer by properly answering to his queries, he succeeds in explicating a professional and emotional relationship with him.

Responses have numerous combinations of features and aspects by which questionnaires can be easily produced.

Following are the situations a customer can fall into after they get responses:

1. Customers can be totally satisfied by the type of response with a positive feeling towards the respondent.
2. They can be totally satisfied but without any sort of strong feeling towards the respondent.
3. Slightly satisfied with the responses but with or without any feelings towards the respondent, depending on the efforts and type of responses provided by the respondent.
4. They can also be totally dissatisfied by the responses but no hard feelings towards the respondent as the respondent could have delivered the things correctly and efficiently.
5. They can also be totally dissatisfied by the responses and with negative feelings towards the respondent as the respondent could have messed everything.

The customer can fall under any of these situations and develops a perception in his mind regarding the organization depending on the quality and types of responses he gets from the respondent. If the organization succeeds in satisfying the customer then he wins in developing and maintaining a relationship with that customer and can easily retain him. Contrarily, if the customers find the quality of responses as low and unsatisfactory and supplier's attitude as unfamiliar and negative then they will surely diverge their way to other organization for better alternatives. By this the organization could finally loose the business with that customer. Hence, customer response is very important aspect for all organizations to create business relationship and good customer satisfaction and loyalty with their customers. In the same way, for customers it's a very essential way to judge their suppliers and determine if they can be good suppliers for them or not.

Good customer response is an essential asset for an organization and directly or indirectly always helps them to grow substantially in business. For example, a customer buys toothpaste from a shop. After opening it he finds the tube half empty from inside. He immediately sends a notification to the manufacturer by launching a complaint. The company in turn promptly sends an apology letter with a new tube of toothpaste. The customer will obviously become happy and satisfied with the prompt response and the fruitful service provided by the manufacturer. This satisfied customer will propagate the concern shown by the manufacturer for even this small deal to all his friends and family. By this quick and positive response the manufacturer turned that customer to a business ambassador to increase the sales and productivity of business.

Before developing the strategies for customer responses it is important to understand the master plan which indicates how the responses should be modeled according to customer's attitude which is different in different situations. Giving the right response at right time is the only key factor for successfully building the relationships with customers and influencing them to have long-term business deals.

Measuring Customer Response

After emphasizing on customer response and its advantages it is also important to know how to measure these responses and what can be achieved after accurate measurement. For this it is necessary for an organization to incorporate following performance indicators:

1. Productive Performance Indicator: The productive performance indicator determines the number of customer orders processed per human-hour. This order processing must be done is such a way that the time taken for processing is minimal to increase the productivity. Strategies used in customer service automation can bring immediate improvements in call center automation, internet ordering, contact management automation, EDI's etc. Web integrated customer response systems cuts off the need to hire more employees as everything is automated.
2. Financial Performance Indicator: The key financial performance indicator is *Total Response Cost* (TRC). By the use of TRC organization can easily compute the cost incurred for customer responses workflow, assets used, infrastructure used within organization, medium charges like internet and phone, income of executives etc. Some extended use of TRC is also to indicate the profitable aspects like which response was profitable and which was not. It can also compute which customers are profitable for the organization and which are not and which are they who can continue to give more profit in future. Total response cost is a powerful system which helps improving the financial aspects of organization by limiting the investments made by the organization and always keeps a check on customer response to enhance financial features.
3. Quality Performance Indicator: The Primary quality performance indicator is *Order Entry* Accuracy (OEA) and First Time Fill Rate (FTFR). OEA is formulated as specific orders produced by customers per total order produced. FTFR is calculated by total products delivered per total products requested. There are many other indicators which help measuring quality performance of customer responses like Invoice Accuracy and Order Status communication accuracy. Invoice accuracy tool keeps a regular check on Invoice automation system and measure the accuracy of them. It is generally formulated as the total invoices with accurate match of items, prices and quantities etc per total invoices received. More the percentage produced by these tools more is the customer response value. It is necessary to measure quality performance so that the customers receive best services and customer satisfaction index always remain on top.
4. Response Cycle Time Indicator: Response cycle time indicator is indicated by *Order Processing Time* (OPT). This calculates the time taken for the order; from time it was entered till the time it is delivered. One more important indicator called Order Entry Time (OET) is also installed which calculates the time taken from intimation of order until the order is captured or entered in the CRM system. This shows the time elapsed in the telephonic conversation or internet. By this the overall entry time taken by the executive to enter the details in the systems can be calculated. This is an important factor and can be used for increasing

the productivity and for trying to reduce the time taken for order processing. Lesser the time taken to process the orders and entering the relevant information in the system, more are the chances to consume large number of customers in a given specific interval of time.

With the help of above discussed indicators or measurement tools customer response can efficiently be measured. Without having the knowledge of how the processes are performing and understanding which functional areas is lagging behind, improvement and enhancement cannot be done. Hence we can say that measuring customer response is the best strategy to improve it.

Medium of Customer Responses

The responses can be provided through any of the following media:

1. Face to Face Interaction: Face to face interaction is the most efficient medium and provides the probability to judge the emotions and body language of the respondent. When a customer visits the supplier's premises and supplier receives him respectfully and spends some time with him, giving him all the attention, listing patiently for the purpose of his visit and determining feasible actions, then the customer feels high and confident towards the supplier's gesture. Hence it is important that the supplier should pay full attention towards the customer. If in between he receives any call or indulges himself in other works, then it creates an indication to the customer that he is unwanted or the supplier does not want to attend him efficiently. Such a thing creates negative or wrong feelings in customer's mindset towards the supplier and acts as a staggering block in future business relationship. It is also seen that most of the senior members of the organization does not find any time to interact with the customers face to face which is not the correct approach as customers are the key revenue generators of business and attention should always be given to them to understand their needs and make them satisfied. The way the suppliers present themselves during a face to face conversation or interaction reflects their sincerity and commitment to the customers. In case they fail to provide such interaction, they may have to pay a heavy price both in short as well in long run.

2. Telephone Communication: Telephone communication is also effective and plays an important role. A telephone call should always be answered when a customer calls, and if by any chance it is missed a return call should always be made. Sometimes the supplier does not want to entertain the calls from aggressive and irritating types of customers. This could also happen when the supplier has any sort of commitment with the customer which he is not fulfilling due to some unrealistic reasons. By doing this the situation does not tend to solve but aggravates in course time. The key is to talk to them and explain the actual situation and reasons by taking them into confidence. By doing this the customer will always think that supplier is promptly attending his calls and is concerned about him. It is also important to interpret the purpose of the caller, what the customer is actually asking for and then after patiently listening and analyzing the facts a correct and satisfied response must be provided. If the details asked by the customer over a call are not answerable instantly, then the call can be hung up by telling that details will be provided to him as soon as possible. Thereafter it is necessary to take those points of customer's queries into consideration and analyze those to come up with exact details. These details should be provided to him by calling him again. Efficient telephonic interaction always pays off when responses are given effectively.

3. Writing Communication (Post, Fax, Email): The writing communication should always be acknowledged immediately and should be replied in detailed format. The advantage of written communication over face to face and telephonic communication is that it is least misinterpreted as it is saved and can be read many times. But the disadvantage is that it lacks in total communication. Hence it is always important to send the written response in details so that any of the relevant point is not omitted in the response.

Qualities of a Good Response

An organization should understand that response is the key towards creating quality relationship with customers and nurturing the future business depending upon the customer's perception and senses determined from the response. Response creates a channel of interaction that can enhance business relationship which will be mutually beneficial. This is only possible when the responses from supplier bring forth positive and strong feelings and emotions within customer's mindset which will help in building a positive image of supplier and in plunging linkage and bonding with customer.

Following are the qualities which a good response should possess:

1. Fast
2. Approachable
3. Informative
4. Positive
5. Comprehensive
6. Create Bond
7. Confidence Builder
8. Comfort Provider

If a customer gives a phone call or sends a notification or message to a call center of an organization and the respondent returns the call effectively or sends even a tiny acknowledgment, there is a chance of establishing positive relationship and customer acquires the comfort and confidence that he is safe in reliable hands. While acknowledging a customer it is important for the supplier to understand the actual subject line or the exact need which the customer is referring to and then provide responses.

It is obvious sometimes that in attempting to provide the response fast the executives' responses may become tangential. Take an example of a Bank customer; he did some shopping on his bank debit card after the bank provided the offer of 5% cash back. After doing the shopping he waited for the bank statement and after receiving it he found that there was no cash back on the shopping he did. So he sent a formal complaint stating the whole issue to the manager of the bank where he has an account. The response came after 10 days which astonished the customer. The bank thanked the customer for informing the change in the address and assured that they have updated the details accordingly in the database. The matter of cash back was not included in the response. It is easy to imagine customer's mental condition on this response. This could have happened when the bank staff would have mismatched the complaints or in hurry would have sent the acknowledgment differently.

The response was worse and would have created the following impressions in customer's mind:

1. The bank manger is least bothered about the complaints and feedback he gets.
2. The bank staff is not bothered to read the message properly or due to negligence would have misinterpreted.
3. There is no systematic approach of the processes followed within.
4. The bank is not focusing on the services provided to the valuable customers.
5. Degraded systems installed in the bank.

The customer will soon realize that he is not banking under safe hands and will think of quitting the bank as soon as possible. Contrarily, if the bank would have received the complained efficiently and perceived it quickly to determine the actually problem, then they would have transferred the cash back amount instantly into customers account and sent an apology letter for the inconvenience caused due to them to the customer. This would have retained the customer's faith over the bank and would have made him to continue a long term satisfied relationship with the bank.

It is hence very important to collect the message or feedback intelligently from the customer, analyze the problem effectively and then respond to them. If the complaint or any question is not feasible or is not clear then a frank face to face interaction should be preferred where the situation can be examined and explained sufficiently. Hence good response always keeps the customers intact and satisfied. It helps to bring up good relationship and business deals with them.

Response in Consumer Sector

In consumer sector, suppliers most probably come in contact with distributors or middle-men rather than directly to customers. For them, distributors are the actual customers and had to be in contact with them at all the business stages. The direct contact with customer happens very rarely and only in extraordinary situations like extreme complaint or due to some urgency the customer opts to contact suppliers directly. Hence, fast and comprehensive response to customer is very important as the communication happens rarely under urgent circumstances and emotionally charged situations. If the responses are not managed properly the customers have the right and potential to cause damages to supplier in regards to deal and relationship. But inversely, if the responses are efficient and useful then the customers are prone to become business ambassador of the supplier.

Efficient consumer response (ECR) is the key strategy to handle responses and do business in consumer segment. ECR is the technique to work together to understand and deliver consumer's needs efficiently, faster and at low cost.

There are two basic principles of ECR:

1. Consumer Focus: For business success, consumer must be provided with demanded and expected products and services. Without focusing on consumers, valid responses cannot be

provided. For example, if a consumer deals with pharmaceutical products then the supplier should have in depth knowledge of pharmaceutical domain. If the supplier fails to respond to any of the query or is not able to handle the situation then consumers would rather prefer to divert as they feel unsafe. It is also important to interact with consumers on a regular basis so that they have the feeling of confidence and will feel proud to get supplier's focus.

2. Working Together: Various departments opting to work together as a team within an organization yield best consumer value. By working together it becomes easy to overcome all the barriers that are hindering efficiency and effectiveness of the organization. Issues and complaints can be easily interpreted and resolved by working as a team. The strategies and business plan should be shared within all the departments of the organization so as to get feedback on each and every aspect and best and quality response could be provided to consumers.

Efficient consumer response encompasses a supply chain management system. It is a managerial strategy which primarily focuses on consumer demands and follows the whole supply chain process for responding efficiently to that demand. ECR not only deals with responses and operational areas of retail marketing but also provide ways in which suppliers, retailers and third party distributors work together. There are basically two levels of activities that are performed in ECR. The first level is specifically concerned with our topic of discussion i.e. consumer demand and responses. The second level is associated with product supply management. The measure of success of this system is the level of efficiency achieved in customer satisfaction.

The communication between the two parties could happen in any of the three modes i.e. face to face, telephonic and email/fax but it is important for the supplier to judge the responses on quality and comprehensiveness in all the three modes. Hence, the main objective here is always to enhance customer satisfaction and reduce total business cost. Good consumer response is an essential asset for an organization and directly or indirectly helps them to grow substantially in business.

Customer's Response in Core Sector

In Core sector the interaction happens directly between supplier and customers due to type of work and the reason of building total relationship with customers.

There are following three stages in core sector in which customer raises their queries and in turn get different type of responses:

1. Pre-deal stage: In this stage, the customers try to find out business with suppliers by exploring business opportunities. At this stage the discussion is basically on implementing the project economically so the customer wants supplier to provide as much response as possible. The supplier must provide responses for following issues during pre-deal stage:

- Determine and provide detailed and comprehensive data.
- Must analyze and inform customer about the various types of assessments regarding different opinions.
- Must inform the customer about recent technological facets and the developments which are predicted in the near future.

- Must suggest the customer on maintenance and support requirements of each of his opinion.
- Provide information and pros and cons of similar kinds of projects executing at various places.

The communication between the two parties could happen in any of the three modes i.e. face to face, telephonic and email/fax but it is important for the supplier to judge the responses on quality and comprehensiveness in all the three modes. The customers are intelligent enough to come up to the final opinion even in pre-deal stage. It's crucial for suppliers to gain confidence of customers in this stage which will help them to strengthen their relationship in the further two stages.

2. Operational stage: In this stage the customer gives the supplier the project contract and passes it on to the operation people of the organization to analyze further developmental aspects of the projects. He obviously revalidates all the opinions he made in pre-deal stage. It is often that these operational people are among the busiest people of the organization and are more oriented towards their day to day work rather than customers. But the customer still wants them address the following issue while they respond to them:

- Regular progress of the project with all details implications if any.
- Relevant and actual information on status of technology, engineering, manufacturing etc.
- Plan of actual delays in project if any.
- Possibilities of any change in any of the project module or the predicted changes after the first version of the product.
- Testing strategies and quality check constraints.

Customer is again responsible for making new set of opinions on the operational stage of the project. This is the stage when the supplier needs to be more cautious as a lot of cost and resources are being used in this stage and they have the opportunity to convert this stage into final deal. The response and interaction with customers in this stage are very rare but it is the duty of the organization to keep the customers well informed by giving proper responses on each operation stage to keep the suppliers in confidence and collect more information if needed.

3. Post-deal Stage: This is the stage when supplier has delivered the final product and the customer is analyzing the product at their end. During this stage there are not much interaction between supplier and customers as long as the product works fine and the customer is satisfied. But in case there are defects in the product or it is not working as expected, then the situation worsens and communication between the two increases. The following are the key responses that the customer must expect during this stage.

- Prompt reply on any abnormal functioning of product.
- Quick attention regarding any faults.
- Priority on repairing these faults.

- Dedicated expert team for quick error handling.
- Managing the product with less capacity and higher efficiency.
- Supply of spares or any asset required at actual price.
- Training from supplier's side to end users.
- Best maintenance and services, post deal.

The final opinion of customers about the suppliers is the sum of responses received at each of the above discussed stages.

Customer Relationship Management and Internet

While CRM is not a technology within itself, it is often used with technological tools to build stronger relationships with customers. The Internet has become an important part of CRM. As more people begin conducting business over the Internet, it has become necessary for CRM vendors to create applications that are web based.

There are a number of Internet technologies that are directly connected to CRM and one of these is online chat tools. Internet chat is a communications tool that has existed for a number of years. However, many companies are just now seeing the benefits of using it in a way that can allow them to effectively communicate with their customers.

When Customer relationship management systems were first introduced, they were developed with client-server tools. Because of the rapid popularity of the Internet, more vendors are creating CRM solutions that are web based. They are typically used by call centers and technical support departments.

A number of companies are now using chat software to facilitate better communications with their clients. It is important to realize that text based chat programs predate the World Wide Web by a number of years. However, combining this technology with the Internet has allowed it to be user-friendly. In addition to this, the latest chat programs have functions such as video and audio.

There are a number of benefits a company can gain by adding chat functions in their CRM programs. Perhaps one of the most powerful benefits is that many customers are already familiar with chat programs, especially those that use the Internet frequently.

Even though new forms of technology are typically challenged by many people, chat programs have become widely popular since their introduction. A number of statistics indicate that millions of people are logging into online chat rooms on a regular basis.

Some of these chat rooms are dedicated to specific subjects, and the members will frequently log in to chat about them. Chat rooms can allow customer service representatives to serve multiple clients at one time. In addition to this, setting up an online chat room is much cheaper than establishing a call center.

In traditional call centers, it is not uncommon for customers to wait 15 minutes or more before they can speak to a live customer service representative. Not only is this annoying, but it is expensive for the company to maintain.

Long wait times are especially a problem at the call centers of large corporations. With chat software, a customer can get service as soon as they sign in. Chat software has become an important part of CRM that responsible companies will want to look into. Another impressive thing about chat software is that it can automatically record the conversation that takes place.

Perhaps one of the most powerful advantages of chat software is the cost. A small to medium sized business can set up a customer support department that is entirely comprised of chat programs, and they can provide their customers with faster service than they would find in most call centers.

The Internet has allowed small businesses to compete at a very high level. While most small businesses could not afford the costs involved with setting up a call center, online chat programs have allowed them to achieve the same objectives for a lower price. Some have even said that it is very likely that chat programs may eventually make call centers obsolete.

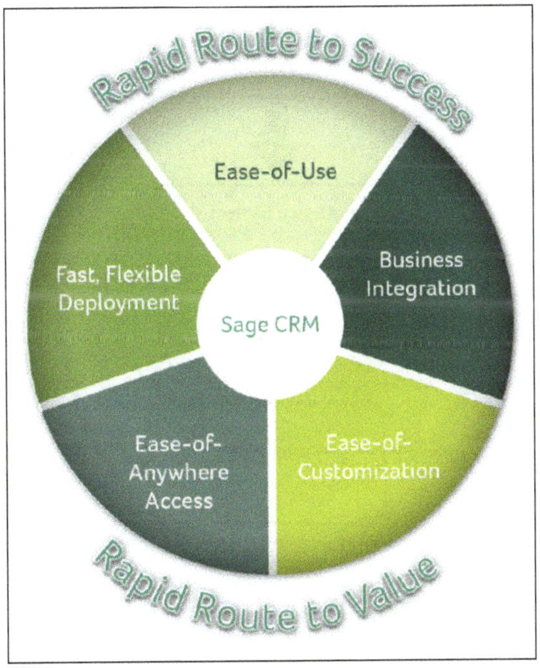

The emergence of the internet heralded a new opportunity for customer relationship building. For one thing, search engine made it easier for customer to find online merchant and interact with them. And, once found, those merchant offered customer more streamlined ways of ordering and receiving product and services.

Moreover the internet simplified bidirectional communication, for the first time offering a better way for consumer to relay personal information to the merchant. Instead of waiting to be mailed a form to open an account or order a phone line, a prospective customer needed only to send an application through cyberspace, resulting in shorter delivery time, improved accuracy, and quite often a higher positive perception. In fact the internet is an environment of zero latency, offering real-time information and often on demand product delivery.

Internet users appreciate not having to go out of their way to buy what they want, and the simpler the process, the higher the potential for customer satisfaction indeed, the web offered customer options they hadn't had with other delivery channels, namely:

(a) 24-hour access,

(b) Up to minute information(on, for example, stock levels, product feature, and prices),

(c) Online customer support,

(d) Online self service,

(e) Personalized content,

(f) The ability to research a product or merchant during a shopping trip.

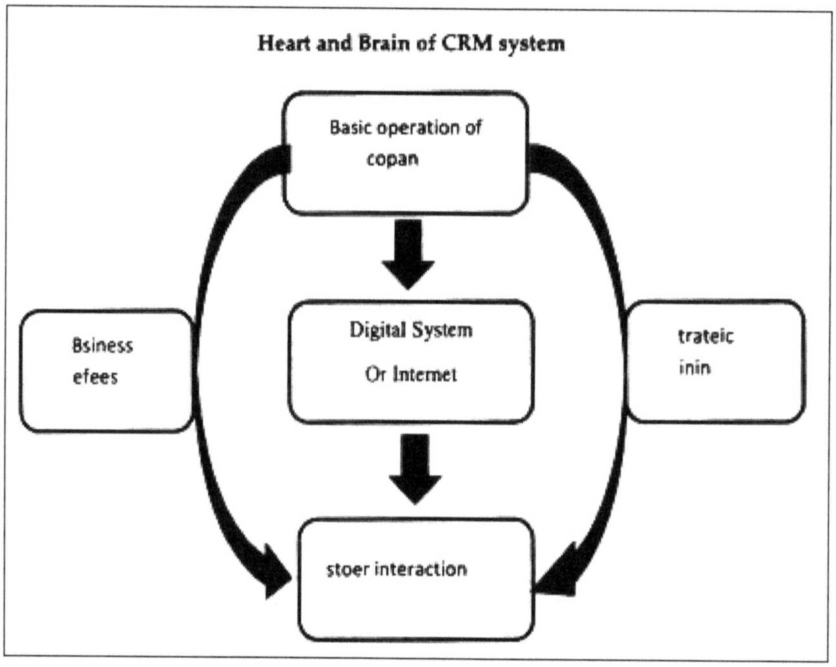

What CRM does through Internet?

1. Tracking and monitoring customer needs.
2. Providing customized products/services matching with customer expectations.
3. Converting customer micro-information for market targeting and decision making.
4. Conveying information about customer to other departments in meaningful form integration of other departments through information and to deliver quality products and services.
5. Reducing order processing time.
6. Improving receipts/payment from customers.
7. Tapping customer feedback for strategy and differentiation.

Open-Source CRM

In CRM (customer relationship management) open source CRM (open source customer relationship management) is the phrase to describe an open CRM solution: That is the CRM system uses open source programs in which the source code is available to the public for use and modification from its original design free of charge (i.e., open). Open CRM gives organizations control over the CRM solution and can further develop the open source CRM software to best meet its own business goals.

Open-source is a software development philosophy in which source code is made freely and openly available to the general public. Any interested party can download the code, modify it to their heart's content, use it how they see fit and, if they wish, distribute their modified version for others to use.

Large amounts of openly available code can make it easier to start developing complex applications. A lot of the heavy lifting has already been done, and development teams just need to tweak the code for their purposes. Most software, even privately developed programs, are built on at least some code from open-source libraries.

Like other developers, CRM vendors also take advantage of the open-source libraries. Some CRM is developed completely as open-source, while some is a hybrid of open-source and privately developed code. While there are some compelling reasons to choose open-source CRM, there are also some considerable limitations. Understanding both is crucial when deciding between open-source and proprietary CRM.

Advantages of Open-source

Open-source CRM offers several benefits that you may be able to take advantage of. Of course, these are only advantages if you have the resources to exploit them.

1. Free or Low-Cost: Most open-source applications are available to you at no cost. Some developers offer higher levels of support with a paid fee, but the basic code is yours for nothing. If you have the time and the talent to modify the code for your needs, you can save a lot on licensing fees.

2. Customizable: Open-source code is meant to be torn apart, tinkered with, and rebuilt. Your team can take the source code and turn it into whatever you need it to be. If you know exactly what you're looking for, and don't want a lot of extraneous parts, then open-source CRM may be for you.

3. No Commitment: Commercial CRM vendors typically require a licensing commitment of at least a few months. This could leave you paying for a system that you don't like or don't use. With open-source CRM, there are not time commitments. You can use it for as long as you like, and quit using it without any fear of penalties.

4. Disadvantages of Open Source: Every CRM system is going to have its limitations. Open-source CRM has limitations that are particular to its underlying design philosophy.

5. Limited Support: Open-source CRM vendors don't offer much support for their free versions. While there are some options for paid support, you might as well buy the CRM if you're going to go that route. With open-source, most of your support is going to come from developer forums that might not respond quickly or accurately.
6. Fewer Functions: If you're looking for all of the bells and whistles, open-source CRM may not be your best bet. A lot of the development is conducted by people during their spare time, so the focus is more on critical functions than slick GUIs and robust integrations.
7. Perfection Paralysis: Assuming that you have onsite devs who can tweak your open-source CRM, there's a chance that they'll always be tweaking it. At some point, you need a system that works, and fills the majority of your needs. If your dev team is constantly "fixing" things, the system is never really complete, and your employees may be constantly adapting to the latest "fixes." Worse yet, your employees may start bugging the dev team for new functions and features that weren't on your list, further delaying completion.

Examples:

There are more than a few open-source CRM vendors on the market today; here are some of the better-known ones:

1. SugarCRM – SugarCRM is one of the, if not the, most popular open-source CRM solutions available. Their community edition is free, has a wide variety of features, and is supported by a large community of professional and amatuer developers.
2. Vtiger – Built on a variety of open-source software and licenses, Vtiger has been downloaded more than three million times. Priced at just twelve dollars per month per user, Vtiger includes direct support, as well as developer forums.
3. Zurmo – Zurmo is an open-source CRM system that uses aspects of gamification to promote end user engagement. In short, they try to make it fun- or at least interesting- to use CRM. They offer free and paid versions with improved support and features for paying subscribers.
4. SuiteCRM – SuiteCRM is a free, open-source alternative aimed at enterprise-level subscribers. A software fork of SugarCRM, SuiteCRM is meant to compete directly with Microsoft Dynamics CRM, Salesforce, and paid editions of SugarCRM.

Who Benefits from open-Source?

Open-source CRM can benefit any company, but there are some situations that would probably enhance its utility. Small companies and startups may not need all the bells and whistles as much as they need to save capital. For those businesses, free or low-cost open-source CRM may be a good way to get critical functionality without paying for all of the trimmings.

On the other hand, businesses that have a robust development team on site could benefit from the ability to fully customize an open-source CRM solution. However, you should keep in mind that not all development experience is the same. Experience developing apps for your customers may not translate into an ability to develop CRM for your company. Also, an in-house team does run the risk of facing perfection paralysis.

Time Sink or Saver

Like any CRM system, you should have well-defined criteria for what you expect from the software. You should have clear reasons for why you want CRM, what you expect the benefits to be, and how success will be measured. Treat open-source CRM with the same care you would give any large software implementation and it will offer real solutions for your business.

Open-source CRM is only a pet project if you treat it as one. Even if it's free, open-source CRM will likely require a large commitment of time and energy. If that time and energy isn't properly focused, then it will be as wasted as if it had been spent on a pet project.

CRM for Small Business

Customer relationship management (CRM) often transforms a small business into a strong, vibrant and rapidly growing one. That may come as a surprise if you thought CRM was just for big corporations with huge sales teams, but the truth is that you don't have to be big to benefit from CRM.

Simple and Scalable Customer Management

In the early stages of a company's growth, your contacts book is one of your most valuable assets. There are prospects out there to be found and converted to customers, alongside existing customers who can give you an essential steady stream of repeat business.

At the very beginning, a small business might have little more than a list of prospects that they hope to turn into customers. These prospects may be stored on a handful of business cards or in a list of names and phone numbers on a spreadsheet or document.

The next step is a contact management application. This does the basics: it stores names and other personal details, along with notes about previous and future contact dates and times, what was said, and what needs to be done.

But a CRM platform takes this further and enables true customer management. It doesn't just make it easy for you to stay in contact with your customers; it actually helps you do business with them, supporting your business and delivering the speed and scalability that a fast-growing enterprise needs.

A CRM system is like a map and compass for your small business. It helps you understand exactly where you are with your customers, what direction you need to take to keep them happy, and what obstacles you'll need to navigate around to close the deals with them.

More Effective Selling

Imagine the power of having a comprehensive view of every customer at the touch of a button – being able to see a record of all of their previous interactions with you, the status of their orders and invoices pending, their transaction history and everything you need to make the right pitch at the right time. With CRM this ability isn't limited to huge companies with enormous budgets – it's available to small business too.

In practical terms a good CRM tool does much more than store contact information for you to act on. It can help you qualify your leads so your efforts can be directed most effectively, and it can automatically prompt you at appropriate times to ensure that your planned contact programmed is fulfilled. That means no more failing to call someone as promised or forgetting to check up on the progress of a deal.

Not every prospect can be turned into a sale of course, but a CRM tool can also help you learn from every outcome so you can improve your sales strategies. That's because an effective CRM system lets you collate and analyse the data that it stores, allowing you to continually improve and hone your activities towards optimum effectiveness.

Simplified it Infrastructure

As your organisation grows, your IT requirements grow too: you'll need to share your CRM data with colleagues, collaborate on sales initiatives, and access the latest information while you're on the move from a tablet, smartphone or other mobile device.

Running software systems in-house that can achieve all this is challenging for a large organisation with a dedicated IT department. For a small business? It doesn't bear thinking about.

But with a platform that helps you to develop mobile apps for your business as well as your customers, you can take advantage of 'micro-moments' of productivity throughout the day. By building employee smartphone apps targeted at specific tasks, companies worldwide are seeing huge efficiency savings – replacing a paper-based vehicle condition check with an app, for example, or approving a customer quote on a smartphone.

Social Media-aware Customer Service

At some point in the growth story of almost every small business business, keeping up with customer service becomes an issue. Thanks to the power of the cloud, you can connect your CRM to other cloud-based services. For example, with today's social CRM systems even a small business can gain a thorough and comprehensive overview of customer and prospect activity on networks such as Facebook, Twitter and LinkedIn.

As well as responding directly on these platforms, you can use these insights to predict future trends and patterns – anticipating questions and finding solutions before they become a cause for complaint. When problems do arise, modern CRM allows you to deliver customer service directly via social media, making for a far smoother, more agreeable experience for all involved.

Desk.com, the out of the box customer support app from Salesforce, is used by leading small business and small businesses to help customers, increase satisfaction and grow fast.

Flexible Growth

As your company grows, the CRM platform you use needs to grow too. Think about how important that is. Naturally, many small businesses use 'small business tools', but as they outgrow them they're forced to change software systems, alter their business processes and retrain their staff to use the new setup – with all the disruption and risk that this entails.

That's why it's important that your CRM platform is scalable and extensible, with extra apps and features you can bolt on to provide the extra tools you need as you grow. The good news is that CRM runs best in the cloud.

That means it can be accessed easily from anywhere, and everyone in your business has the most up-to-date information about customers and deals at their fingertips. Best of all, no-one has to worry about installing, managing and updating software, because there is no software to worry about.

Salesforce Sales Cloud gives you multiple ways to build a platform for your company's growth. The Salesforce App Exchange contains thousands of free and paid-for apps you can easily add to your CRM, providing extra capabilities such as invoicing, document signing and integration with popular applications such as Outlook. You can also create your own custom apps on the Salesforce Platform.

Mobile CRM

Mobile CRM is also called M CRM. Bertrand Bathelot, associate professor of marketing and founder of the website definition-marketing.com, explains it refers to "all applications, services and content created and optimized for mobile devices, and intended to optimize and improve Customer Relationship".

Mobile CRM covers a great range of mobile applications. In order to make their offer even more complete, some publishers offer access to their CRM solution from mobile devices (smartphones and tablets). However, these mobile CRM applications do not have to be a perfect replica of the full software. By becoming mobile, these CRM must also become lighter for a simpler and more ergonomic use.

Importance of Mobile CRM

"Real-time"- a powerful creator of expectations. Long gone are the days when the professional sphere was limited strictly to the four walls of the office. Now, we can access everything, all the time. We are connected everywhere, to everything, in every moment. Our office fits in the palm of our hand. We cannot imagine doing without one, and in France, 73% of the population has one: a smartphone of course. To the question "what devices do you use most often to go on the Internet", 42% of French answered "a smartphone", compared to only 38% for computers and a meager 7% for tablets.

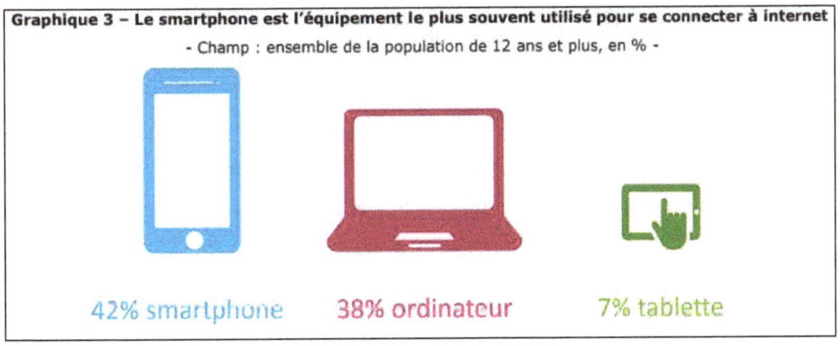

Information is only one click away, and is updated in real time. As a result, our expectations too, are heightened. We expect information to be available and up-to-date in real time. In short, we want more reactivity.

Mobile CRM for a more Agile CRM

Having up-to-date, easily accessible data from anywhere and at any time is a true competitive advantage for companies. Particularly so for sales teams who often work on the move. This distance from the head office sometimes generates problems in the flow of information, both upstream and downstream, which, in turn, is detrimental for business. Therefore, your sales force needs a powerful tool a mobile CRM.

With a mobile CRM, they can update, synchronize and share information with all the departments of the company, and vice versa. With a mobile CRM, they can be as efficient on the go with a tablet or a smartphone as if they were in the office. In addition to saving time for your sales force, it ensures increased productivity, performance and quality for sales management.

Mobile Sales: A key Driver of Sales Effectiveness

The leading Mobile CRM applications all feature a number of common decisive advantages, such as options to:

- View and edit contacts in real time.
- Scan business cards to seamlessly upload them to the CRM.
- Create and manage business opportunities remotely.
- Notifications and reminders to organize tasks and prioritize actions.
- Synchronize files and their calendar.
- Geolocation to plan their itinerary to their next sales appointment.
- Access to dashboards and reports.

This list, which is far from exhaustive, highlights the most common features of mobile CRM solutions. Of course, if you need other features, ask your publisher if they can set it up for you. After all, nothing ventured, nothing gained.

Mobile CRM: What you need to Remember?

Mobile CRM meets the expectations of immediacy and need for real-time information, at the same time it simplifies the work of remote sales forces. It enables them to access customer data, manage their business opportunities, prioritize their actions, share their calendar in real time, relocate their customers and always be up-to-date with new documents made available to them.

Lastly, remember that a mobile CRM is of little value if it is not synchronized. This is key to offer a unified experience to your customers on the one hand, and to simplify internal processes within the company on the other.

And before we go, here's a quick tip for you: before choosing your CRM publisher, and if you need a mobile app, first check whether it is available on the Apple Store and Google Play to make sure it is compatible with all mobile operating systems.

Social Customer Relationship Management

Social CRM or social customer relationship management is the integration of social media channels into Customer Relationship Management (CRM) platforms. Increasingly, CRM platforms support social media alongside traditional channels so customers can interact with businesses via their preferred channels. This means better customer service and greater marketing insight gathered from customer social media data.

Why do Businesses need Social CRM?

Social CRM makes it possible for a business to communicate with customers using the channel of their choice—whether by phone, text, chat, email or social media (e.g. Facebook or Twitter). Off the back of these interactions, a social CRM system helps businesses gather richer, actionable insight about customer sentiment on their company, their brand, and specific products or services.

The best CRM systems are able to take this dynamic customer profile and put it to good use by disseminating that information across different teams, including customer service, marketing and sales.

Using Social CRM for Customer Service

Social CRM is used by businesses looking to optimise service levels and the multi-channel customer experience. It can help businesses get the basics of customer service right, responding seamlessly in the way that suits the customer best.

Today's consumer expects the same great service from a business regardless of channel.

Customer Expectations are Rising

Consumers expect to be able to move easily between channels of communication and for the business to respond promptly and personally in any of them. If the business can remember them so they don't have to explain themselves again, even better.

This is especially important as customers increasingly see social media as the easiest way to raise a service query—telecoms giant BT says that 40% of their feedback from customers originates on Twitter, for example.

With social CRM, when a customer chooses to contact a business via a social channel, that interaction can be tracked and managed in as much detail as a traditional CRM system can track a telephone or email enquiry.

Business Benefit

Businesses are able to act more quickly, respond better, and even anticipate customers' upcoming needs. By enabling businesses to track social interactions with customers using the same sophisticated tools as they use for other touch points, companies can deliver faster, more complete resolutions to customer service cases from across the whole business, resulting in happier customers.

Social interactions take place on a one-to-one-to-many basis, meaning the way in which the interaction is resolved can impact directly on brand sentiment.

A customer service agent dealing directly with a customer on Facebook is engaging in a personal interaction with a public audience. It's easy and logical for customers to want to share socially about their service experience afterward, too.

Using Social CRM for Marketing

Social CRM helps businesses make customer engagement a two-way street. Instead of a passive audience, customers become active participants in the story of a brand, and in turn, they get to see a brand value them as a customer.

A marketing team may be producing great content – blogs, Facebook posts, YouTube videos, Instagram accounts and snappy tweets – but that part of the conversation is one-way. By using monitoring and tracking tools to see who's engaging in conversation with the business, social CRM can help businesses to identify and reward brand advocates and influencers, encouraging them to spread the word still further.

Benefits of Social CRM

For the marketing, sales and customer service departments, social CRM can help generate more leads that turn into happier, satisfied customers who go on to become brand ambassadors for an organisation. It can change the understanding of brand reach and perception while providing access to a raft of new information about customer behaviour and opinions.

Key benefits of social CRM are that it enables a business to:

1. Deliver customer support in the online platforms customers use.
2. Interact and engage with customers in real time.
3. Resolve issues speedily by monitoring social media for complaints.
4. Find and reward brand advocates and customers who help others.
5. Get greater exposure in the places where audiences spend their time.
6. Increase engagement and deepen relationships with customers.

The Business case for Social CRM

Social CRM has the potential to deliver returns across and between several core business functions.

Customer Service

By tracking and managing customer contacts across channels and business functions, customer service teams can deliver dramatically better service and markedly improve resolution times.

Some 79% of Salesforce customers reported improved customer service, and 63% increased customer retention – demonstrating that social CRM delivers real commercial benefits.

Sales

Track each prospect's progress and location within the sales funnel using a social CRM. Sales teams can create a personalised experience for specialised users, rather than using the traditional CRM blanket approach.

Beyond individualisation, sales teams can expect to see an improvement in retained and referred business as customers become recommenders and advocates; and that leads to increased revenue. In a survey of Salesforce customers, 55% reported increased customer loyalty and 54% increased sales revenues.

Marketing

Increased reach and visibility, lower costs- Marketers can use social CRM to increase reach while improving customer tracking and measurement. This can feed back into other marketing tactics and help drive lead generation and sales.

In one Social Media Examiner survey, 89% of respondents said social media increased their brand's exposure, while nearly half reported that spending just 6 hours a week on social media activity reduced overall marketing costs.

Role of Social Media in Customer Engagement

Any business owner knows that effectively engaging with customers is a vital factor when it comes to business success. Without customers, businesses would have no purpose, which is why it is so important to value them. Proper communication and engagement is a must for any business, both large and small. Finding ways to communicate with customers on a personal level was very difficult in years gone by. However, technological advancements have made this far easier over recent years, enabling businesses to build a rapport with customers.

As we know, the internet now plays a huge part in our daily lives, both on a personal and a business level. Over recent years, social media platforms have emerged and are now used across the world by both personal and business users. On a personal level, these platforms allow us to communicate with friends and family, share media, and keep up with what's going on. On a business level, they play a huge part in customer engagement and communication, making them invaluable to businesses of all sizes.

How Social Media helps with Customer Engagement and Satisfaction

Social media platforms are able to help with customer satisfaction levels and engagement in a number of ways. This is why they have become enormously popular among businesses around the world. In addition to effective engagement and communication, social media also makes it far easier to market your brand, even if you are on a strict budget.

Some of the ways in which these social media platforms can help when it comes to this type of activity include:

- Build a rapport with followers: When you use social media, you can build a rapport with audiences, which is something you cannot do with traditional advertising. In short, you put faces to names and reinforce your company image when you are able to connect with your audience on a more personal level.
- You can make your followers feel special: Social media is a great way to make your audience feel special by offering special deals and promotions. For instance, if you run a payday loans company, you can offer a special rate for a limited time to followers. This can even help you win more followers as well as make the existing ones feel that you are giving them exclusive benefits.
- Engage with audiences: The key benefit of social media is that you can engage with your audience. By ensuring your posts are of a high caliber and are relevant, you can get a positive reaction from your audience and in turn, engage with them. This can work wonders for your business image, as it makes customer realize that you are more than just a name or logo.
- Improve communication: Efficient and effective communication with customers is extremely important for your business. Poor customer service and response can have a seriously damaging effect on your reputation. With social media, you can provide fast and efficient responses to customers by giving them the option to contact you via this platform. This can help to speed things up at your end too, so it benefits both your business and your customers.

These are some of the main benefits that you can look forward to in terms of customer engagement and communication.

Key Benefits for your Business

It is not just your audience and customers that will benefit from your decision to use social media platforms. Your business can benefit from a wide variety of ways by doing this as well. So, what are the benefits for your business? Let's take a look:

- Ability to build your customer base and audience: By using interesting and relevant posts, you have the ability to quickly build up your audience and customer base. Your existing followers are more likely to share your posts which mean that you can effectively benefit from growth without having to spend a fortune on marketing.
- Being able to boost your reputation: Customers like to deal with companies that have a 'face' rather than some nondescript company they know nothing about. Engaging with them via social media will enable you to portray an image rather than just a name. This will help to boost your reputation and make your communication with your audience far more meaningful.

- A speedy, cost-effective means of marketing: While you are engaging with your customers via social media, you are also marketing your brand without even realizing it. Simply having a social media presence and engaging with your audience regularly will promote your brand and business. When you imagine the amount of money you might spend on other forms of marketing, this is definitely a huge bonus.
- Saves you time and money on communications: Traditional forms of communication can be time-consuming or costly. Phone calls and letters can cost money; even sending emails can take up time. However, with social media communication, you can send fast, instant responses to customers, which will keep them happy and save you time and money at the same time.
- As you can see, there are various benefits that you can enjoy by using social media, and this is just a handful of them.

Customer Relationship Measurement and Research

Customers are the most important part of business. There cannot be any business without them. Only satisfied customers will be interested in buying and they will also refer other customers to buy. By measuring customer satisfaction a supplier can maintain a quality and long term relationship with customers and secure their future business and financial assets. This measurement is essential for suppliers to understand that their strategies are in right direction.

Market research or market survey is the tool that can be implemented to measure customer relationship, customer satisfaction and customer loyalty. This tool is capable to furnish accurate information on the following main facets of customer relationship - 1) Loyalty 2) Satisfaction 3) Customer Behavior 4) Response 5) Service 6) Customer Compensation 7) Customer Needs.

This tool furnishes the above related information not only with accuracy but also with their future aspects which is a very important asset for business perspectives. By knowing the future perspectives of customers it becomes easy and efficacious for suppliers to build a medium term or even long term relationships with customers. These future perspectives of customers are related to following factors:

1. Present customer needs: By analyzing current needs of customers the suppliers can determine the trend of buying of customers. How the present needs of customers can change in past can also be predicted by these sophisticated research and analytical tools by deriving some important trend variables of these customers.
2. Suppliers influence on products and services: How the suppliers are influencing the customers by their products and services is an important factor for this research.
3. Competitors influence on products and services: Competitors are also the important factor for analyzing future needs of customers. If competitors are making more prominent impression of products and services then it is important for suppliers to mould their business strategies to meet future needs of customers and to attract them to have business with them.

4. Environmental or market effects: By predicting the current market trend suppliers can analyze how the market is going to perform in the coming future. This research includes deep analysis of the financial and economic conditions.

Market research is a strong tool that renders the customers with important and unique data on customers' needs which helps them to create business strategies and come up with considerable business decisions. It helps the organization to encapsulate future business by determining business goals and objectives to meet business targets. It also helps providing feedback regarding image and performance of the organization so that they could leverage the strategies to meet the targets. It helps them to be always on top.

Building relationship with customers in current market trends is the most important aspect that an organization should focus on. Today distinction and eminence are the most sustainable approaches for which developing good relationship with customers is essential. Hence incorporating techniques which could measure the relations with customers are very important for all the organizations so that they remain in this bonding forever. Every business unit uses different approaches according to the business they posses to measure their relationship with customers. Also, these approaches of measuring customer relationships are associated differently to different types of customers according to their individual importance. By doing this the organizations are able to decide which area requires application of resources to get best business impact.

Market Research and CRM

One of the best applications of Market research is in the area of customer relationship management. It helps an organization to get an accurate and sharp feedback on their performance and through different customer opinions helps them to understand what customers feel about them.

The following are some subjects in which market research could give valuable feedbacks:

1. Getting useful information for future market growth.
2. Getting an idea on new product feasibility and acceptance by customers in market before making investment on testing and producing the product.
3. Assessing cost sensitivity of customers.
4. Finding new features of products which can attract customers and knowing what advantages and benefits they could provide.
5. Finding the hidden aspects what a product possesses and how to leverage those aspects to bring them in front of customers.
6. Assessing level of customer's satisfaction with the organization specifically in the fields of performance, technology, quality service cost and completion schedule.
7. Determining strong aspects for leveraging and weak aspects for making improvements to finally increase satisfaction level in customers.
8. Creating database on information of competitors and treating this database as the reference point or benchmark as per feedback from customers.

9. Identifying main areas in which the organization is leading the competitors and areas in which they are lagging behind with them.

10. Identifying market trends and reasons for these trends.

11. Identifying reasons for poor business and determining which areas are mostly affected with this.

12. Providing business solutions for typical problems in all the aspects.

13. Determining purchasing channels which the customers prefer. Do they prefer online purchase or human contact?

14. Identifying future perspectives.

In many organizations the officials and executives are most of the times face to face with customers. The customers rarely provide any negative feedback being face to face as it may be embarrassing for them to do so. In the same manner they also hesitate in giving positive feedback because they are afraid that by doing so they could weaken the negotiation power with the suppliers. It is therefore very important for the organization to perform market surveys and analyze the actual feedback which they are unable to get it revealed from the customers.

In other cases where customers are not face to face, the suppliers do not get the chance to get feedback from them directly. They only get indirect feedbacks from agents or middlemen which are rarely atomistic and do not perceive the actual meaning. Business results and conclusions require more detailed and analytical information. Hence, there is always an essential need for accurate market research or survey to be performed to get proper and reliable customer feedback.

In CRM system, this market research is embedded like market intelligence which is based on real-time customer information. This information is integrated in such a way that it is accessible centrally with the organization irrespective of departments. But it is also validated so that the confidential information is not accessed by the department which does not have the rights to see it. For example, notifications for late payment by customers should only be visible to accounting department and not to customer service departments which are exposed to customers. All the information is stored centrally in one CRM system but is integrated and customized in this intelligent way.

Integration of market research and CRM has turned out to be very efficient as it saves time for analysis and gives more accurate and authentic results as compared to the tradition market research tools.

Stages in Market Research Process

The market research process involves a round of separate stages of data interpretation, organization and collection. These stages could be considered as a benchmark of market research, but it depends on an organization how they have encapsulated their strategies to follow this process. Hence some of the interlinked stages could be conducted repeatedly and some of the stages can also be omitted.

Given below is a typical market research process which is depicted stage-wise:

1. Defining the Problem or Need: The starting phase is always identifying the reason or problem for which research is to be conducted. This includes collecting of relevant initial information and how this information will affect decision making process. It also includes defining problems after discussing with decision makers of the organization. Once the problem is defined precisely and the need of research is discussed, the further process could be conducted in an efficient manner.

2. Determining who will do the research: Once the initial stage of defining the problem and the need of research is done, it is important to determine who will do the research and what will be the approaches to resolve these problems. This involves creating a problem solving framework and analytical models after discussing it organization experts. In this sample case studies are created according to the defined framework by enforcing the relevant information and secondary data.

3. Picking out the appropriate methodology: A specific methodology is entailed by the research professional after identifying the specific needs and exploring the case studies. It may include a combination of specific approaches like telephone survey, web or email survey, one-to-one interviews, secondary research etc.

   This methodology acts as a blueprint of research process and following basic steps:

   - Methods for collecting and preparing quantitative information.
   - Determining the need of this information.
   - Scaling and measuring procedures.
   - Designing sample Questionnaire.
   - Formulating case studies and sampling process.
   - Planning information analysis.

4. Data Collection Process: This process includes field work and desk work for collecting all relevant data and information. Field work includes interviewing the personals by interacting them face to face by visiting them in home or offices or arranging group meetings at any preferred place. Desk work includes contacting personals over telephone or via series of emails and web meetings. This could take comparatively more time as compared to the field work. Involving experienced and trained executive for this helps in reducing data collection errors.

5. Data Preparation, tabulation and analysis of results: After the data collecting stage the collected data is edited, corrected if required and validated. This process is the most important process in the research as the results are generated on the basis of data preparation. So it is required for an organization to verify the authenticity of the collected data and edit or correct it if needed. The final data is then segmented according to the business standards and inserted into the CRM database in a more tabulated form so that search or combination could be made easily.

6. Presentation and report generation: The entire process is properly documented with respect to organizational standards so that it can be referred in future for decision making process or to change or modify any specific process or module. This document contains overall architecture of the project depicting all the processes with the help of tables, graphs and figures to provoke impact and clarity.

   Market Research undeniably plays a vital role in exploring the business. The above process if conducted in an efficient manner could help predicting and correlating customer needs and then modeling or modifying the business strategies accordingly.

Desk Research - Methodology and Techniques

As depicted by name Desk Research is the research technique which is mainly acquired by sitting at a desk. Desk research is basically involved in collecting data from existing resources hence it is often considered a low cost technique as compared to field research, as the main cost is involved in executive's time, telephone charges and directories. However, it could also be a complete waste of time and money if the researcher does not have the proper knowledge of how the research in performed.

Desk research is very effective and can be conducted in starting phase of market research as it is quite quick and cheap and most of the basic information could be easily fetched which can be used as benchmark in the research process.

There are basically two types of desk research techniques:

1. Internal Desk Research: Internal desk research can be treated as the most reasonable starting point of research for any organization. Much Information could be generated internally within the organization as a course of normal process. Account related information which indicates what type of products are sold, in how much quantity and at what cost, sold to which type of customers including their geographical location and so on. The main advantage here in performing internal desk research is that it involves internal and existing organizational resources to organize the collected data in such a way that it is not only efficient but also usable. Internal desk research is comparatively very cheap and effective as internal recourses are deputed and the expenditure in getting data from outside is less.

2. External Desk Research: External Desk Research involves research done outside the organizational boundaries and collecting relevant information.

   These outside resources are described below:

   - Online Desk Research: There is incredible amount of data available online on internet. It's important for organization to be information specific while fetching out this information as there are billions of pages available on internet. There could be two approaches for digging out the relevant information from internet, one is directly browsing the specific information from industrial, marketing or business sites and extracting the information out from sites. Secondly, using the various search engines like www.abc.com, www.xyz.com, www.xyz.go.com, etc. for modulated searching. The important aspect here is to refine the searching techniques in such a way that results are promising and relevant. For this it is necessary that the researcher should know the importance of the research and follow the guideline intellectually to reduce the efforts made and time consumed in searching.

- Government published data: Government usually publishes a great extent of data online that can be used in the research process. This data is related to social, financial and economic aspects. The government websites are mostly free to access and contains most prominent information. Thus, this could be the cheapest medium of gathering the information.

- Customer desk research: One of the best and most prominent ways of extracting information for research is directly communicating with existing or prospect customer. Customers are the one who are considered the most informed as they are actually using products and services and are aware of the current market trends more than any other. Hence the feedback and information provided by customers is the most accurate and useful data which can be used most effectively in the further process of research.

Field Research and Important Sources

Field Research deals with creation and collection of actual and authentic information by field of operation in any organization. The process involves determining what precise data is necessary and from where this information needs to be obtained. After determining this information the data is actually gathered. Thus this research technique is treated as the primary research approach because the determined data is specific to the purpose of gathering that data.

Field research is generally performed in person, telephonic or by electronic media like teleconferencing, web - meetings and emails. Many of the big organizations involve outside vendors or companies to perform this task which they usually refer as outsourcing, but small organizations or new companies do this themselves by involving their internal resources. The outsourcing depends on the type and amount of information to be gathered in the research. If the required data is less and limited to some small and specific modules then big organization also prefer to do this task in-house.

Field research is expensive and involves more and experienced resources as compared to desk research which is not as accurate as field research. Being expensive it is required to perform the research in efficient manner and obtain or determine only specific information and answer only particular questions as irrelevant data is a waste and will be of no use for further research processes.

The following are the importance sources for field research:

1. Customers: These can be existing customer or prospect customers. Customers are the most important and efficient sources for field research process and can provide following useful information:

    - Useful information regarding competitors and new strategies they are going to implement.

- Present market trend.
- Actual and innovative market requirement.
- Market distribution channels.
- Production and consumption channels and product usefulness.

2. Competitors: It is difficult to fetch out information from own competitors but if this is possible then competitors are the basic and useful source of information and provide information regarding:
   - Newer and upcoming technologies and software.
   - Types of product which prominent and mostly preferred by customers.
   - Efficient and affordable pricing strategies.
   - Promotional efforts that could turn around the marketing strategies.
   - Information of other ruling competitors.
3. Industrialists or marketing experts: These are the most knowledgeable personals who could provide in depth information regarding:
   - The future trend of market.
   - Economical imbalances regarding particular segments of products.
   - New range of raw materials available in the market.
   - New research and marketing methodologies and application of vibrant technologies.
4. Distributors and Suppliers: Distributors and suppliers are also very good source of information. They can provide information like:
   - Availability of raw materials in market.
   - Pricing details and negotiation techniques.
   - Best distributing channels.
   - New marketing processes.
   - How to deal with compliance issues.

There are many other less prominent sources like interviews, trade shows, and promotional programs etc. and much of the relevant information could be gathered from these sources as well. All the information gathered from the above sources is then manipulated and segmented. As in field research most of the information is relevant as it is actually gathered for a particular purpose, so regular round of work around on the data is not required. After validating the information it is then fetched into the CRM system and is converted into intelligent data which can be accessed on real time.

Data Analysis and Compilation

After gathering the information from desk and field research the raw data must be compiled so that the taxonomic analysis can be performed and data can be broken up into respective parts and segments. This can be achieved in the following manner:

1. Keeping on revisiting and focusing on the ultimate objective of the research and modeling all the processes accordingly.

2. Dividing the actual objectives into sections and emphasizing on divided sections separately by involving analytical techniques.

3. Arranging the questions in the questionnaire properly so that the analysis can be done efficiently.

4. Putting the questions from the questionnaire to each of these sections to get analytical replies. It is possible that questions in the questionnaire could be multiple times assigned to the segments so that it appears at more than one place.

5. Grouping up the answers in numerical format for all the questions in a predefined scale. For example if the questions is 'How will you rate the services offered by the company' and the answer or response is 6 points on the scale then putting it as it is. Normally big organizations have large data to be analyzed and the scale substantially goes to 10 or 12 digits. It can be reduced to a scale of 3 to 5 digits to reduce the complexity and time taken in analysis. But accuracy on the other hand will be reduced as the figures need to be rounded off in case the scale is reduced.

6. The survey questionnaire may contain the comparative responses with other competitors. In this case the responses can be arranged accordingly by analyzing the responses and calculating the weighted average of the response and comparing the average with benchmark figures. This helps the organization to determine which division or service need to be leveraged.

Data analysis and compilation also includes data cleaning strategy before the further analysis is performed. This cleaning is basically validating the data for any error or irrelevant data. It's a separate process for data cleaning performed before the analysis which is very important to fetch desirable results. This process also includes determining the missing values and inputting the most appropriate values in place. It is also important to maintain the quality of the analysis and compilation for which the ideal key is use reliable measurement techniques. Data sampling is also one more distinguished approach to decrease probability of repetitive data elements. It includes creating subsets of information according to a specific variable value and managing them as a whole. More the data is relevant the more accurate the results are.

An organization must define all the objectives in accordance to market requirement. The results from the compilation and analysis of data and information are very important and significant for the organization and shows success factors. The result of the process also depicts the trend of the organization by determining weak and strong points and how they stand stood in the market. Hence, every organization should have an organized and sophisticated way of compiling and analyzing the information.

Report Preparation - Characteristics of a Good Report

The market research is normally outsourced to third party agencies by organizations and in turn they create a professional report to the organization. These reports are preferably provided to senior officials who are the critical decision makers of the organization. Hence these reports need to be exclusively efficient and well formatted and the matter should be limpid, analytical and directive.

The actual facts must be depicted clearly and it is desirable that the data and results are furnished in graphical or tabular format which could create a substantially good impression and is unambiguous to understand. The reports must be essentially capable to compare related information in the report so that conclusions can be derived potentially and easily.

It is necessary for a report to contain following details to be called a good report:

1. Information collected in the report must be relevant and focused to derive desired results. Pictorial and graphical presentation of data and related information help to understand the details easily. There is a possibility that the collected data in the report needs to be represented at many places in different formats to fulfill the report goals. The ultimate goal is to determine all the issue and make suitable strategies to cope up with these issue or problems.

2. Report should follow the exact predefined goals and objectives. If there is any sort of divergence of related information which does not match the goals then the results are of no use. In fact there is a probability of landing up in making negative or out of focus strategies, which will be very dangerous.

3. The report should always contain the executive summary of the work. This is generally kept before the actual report starts as it shows the summary of the desired business plan.

4. Apart from the actual analysis the report should also depict the reasons of making this report and what advantages and profit it can provide after successful implementation of business plans described inside the report.

5. It should also contain the methodology of the research which shows the overall process adopted to create the report.

6. It is important that the report contains the possibility of errors in any of the module or process so that immediate measures could be taken to cope up with these errors.

7. The report should contain the description of the questionnaires used in analysis and the way it has been prepared.

8. The methodology used in the interviews should also be elaborated and what was achieved in this should also be described.

9. If the information show that some aspects needs to predict the future trends then the reports should depict that prediction. This prediction should have scale of success so that the accuracy could be judged efficaciously. The report should also define each and every variable and element used in creating these predictive analyses.

10. The report should be flexible enough to be changed accordingly. The analytical information described inside the report should be maintained in such a way that there is no extra effort labored if any strategy or process it to be changed in future. It should necessarily mould the changes without changing the structure of the report.

The analytical report creation is very important phase of market research which acts as a blueprint of the business plan which is to be executed. By following the above guidelines while report generation process can be efficiently taken care of.

Action Plan in Report Preparation Process

Describing the action plan in the report preparation process is very important as it concludes the report by defining the final actions to be taken care of. An ideal action plan consists of all abnormal behavior in findings to motivate the organization to focus on these aspects and determine desirable strategies tackle these situations.

Typically an action plan should show the following aspects in the report:

Positive Aspects

It should describe the fields in which organization is doing better than expectation of customers and competitors. The actual report contains description of questionnaire and interviews and the respective responses are scaled accordingly. The responses are analyzed with respect to market benchmarks. If the figures are above expectation it means the organization is doing good in those aspects and strategies could be determined to continue to serve in the same manner or enhance them more. Action plan depicts this information to give straightforward outcomes to show the leadership aspects of the organization.

Negative Aspects

It should also describe the fields in which organization is not doing so well as compared to other competitors and is not meeting the customer expectations. It also shows the areas where organization is meeting customer expectations but is not catching up with competitors and is lagging behind them. This information will help the organization to define enhanced strategies to improve related processes and try to do better in these aspects and remain competitive for others.

Customer Satisfaction and Loyalty

Action plan shows the level of customer satisfaction and loyalty according to the analyzed report. This describes in which fields the organization needs improvement and how, what are the reasons for the downfall and what strategies to follow cope up with this to improve customer satisfaction and loyalty.

Apart from the above aspects there are many other information that is provided by action plans like providing analyzed information regarding what type of products are being preferred by customers in the current market scenario, what technologies basically are used in implementing these products so that they serve in more efficient way. The action plans also give other useful information. The entire process is properly documented with respect to organizational standards so that it can be referred in future for decision making process or to change or modify any specific process or module. This report contains overall architecture of the project depicting all the processes with the help of tables, graphs and figures to provoke impact and clarity.

An organization must define all the objectives in accordance to action plan. The results from this information are very important and significant for the organization and show success factors also which depict the trend of the organization by determining weak and strong points and how they stand stood in the market.

The organizations can totally rely on action plans as far as they are created and analyzed in an efficient way. The analysis report could improve the overall functionality and analysis of an organization and hence it is necessary to indulge professionals in performing these analysis processes on a regular basic and before kicking off any new project. The information analyzed in the report is dominantly inserted into CRM system to automate the final process of implementation. The information gets more prominent after being manipulated in a CRM system and can be used efficiently to derive more desirable results.

References

- Customer-relations: smallbusiness.chron.com, Retrieved 2 February, 2019
- What-is-crm: managementstudyguide.com, Retrieved 12 June, 2019
- The-Model-of-Creation-of-Customer-Relationship-Management, CRM-System: researchgate.net, Retrieved 17 January, 2019
- Customer-loyalty: managementstudyguide.com, Retrieved 7 March, 2019
- Customer-response: managementstudyguide.com, Retrieved 9 July, 2019
- Internet-and-its-effect-on-crm, internet: businessmanagementideas.com, Retrieved 29 April, 2019
- Open-source-crm-pros-and-cons, crm-value: crmswitch.com, Retrieved 6 March, 2019
- Crm-for-small-business: salesforce.com, Retrieved 18 August, 2019
- Mobile-crm-definition-issues-features: efficy.com, Retrieved 26 January, 2019
- Social-crm: salesforce.com, Retrieved 1 April, 2019
- The-role-of-social-media-in-customer-engagement: socialnomics.net, Retrieved 3 February, 2019
- Customer-relationship-measurement: managementstudyguide.com, Retrieved 28 May, 2019

2

Customer Relationship Models

A framework which seeks to improve the relationship between a business and the customer is known as a customer relationship model. There are a number of models which detail the different actions and processes which can be used for effective customer relations. The topics elaborated in this chapter will help in gaining a better perspective about the different models such as IDIC model and Gartner's CRM model.

Businesses small and large depend on customers for survival. Customers drive new trends and provide profits for current and future operations and investments. The use of a customer relationship model can help small businesses identify new opportunities and cater to the needs of their customers and clients.

A customer relationship model, also commonly referred to as customer relationship management, seeks to improve the relationship between a business and the customer. When companies, including small businesses, can better identify the needs and desires of their consumers they can increase loyalty and grow the customer base. With this knowledge, small businesses can better distribute products and services and take advantage of new trends in the marketplace. Useful information and knowledge can stem from identifying and analyzing purchasing trends in specific market segments, such as those based on geographical location or customer demographics, such as age, income and family size.

Methods

Taking advantage of the benefits related to a customer relationship model requires data collection and analysis. Data can come from a number of sources. Customer relationship models can collect data from an analytical or behavioral standpoint. Analytical models utilize data collected from customers, such as location, amount of purchase and email addresses. Behavioral data collection stems from focus groups and surveys and has more to do with what drives consumer behavior.

Potential Benefits

Small businesses can put information gleaned from customer relationship models to work. They can use the data to operate a loyalty rewards program, customize sales and promotions to specific customer groups and develop ongoing relationships with customers. Another benefit includes the ability to cross-sell. Cross-selling involves suggesting a complimentary item, such as a cushion for a patio chair, at the point-of-sale. This increases profits, brand exposure and helps develop a personal relationship with the customer.

Customer relationship models seek to acquire, develop and retain customers. Small businesses must remain vigilant when it comes to managing customer data and strike a balance between offering valuable promotions and offers and inundating customers with unsolicited mail. Businesses should obtain permission from customers before sending offers via email or mail to help create an atmosphere of mutual respect.

IDIC Model of Customer Relationship Management

The IDIC (identify, differentiate, interact, customise) is a model developed by Peppers & Rogers. The model helps to assess the expectation of customers and their value to the business.

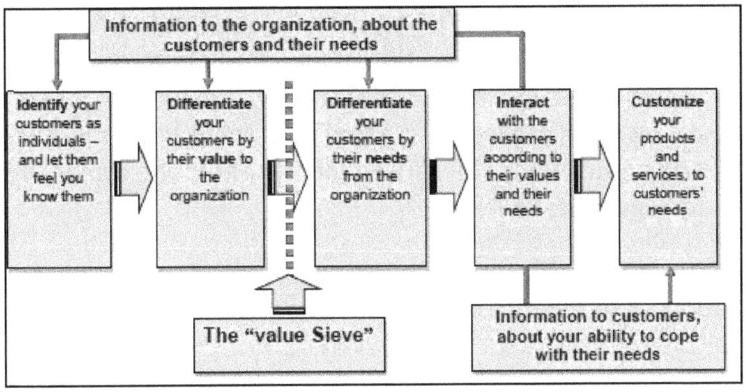

Figure: IDIC Model of customer relationship management

Identify Customer Expectations

A business working towards customer relationship management has to first identify its customer needs, wants and preferences. This helps to curate new products and strategies oriented towards customers. For instance, in terms of identification, Nestle conducted a market survey to identify the customer base for their coffee by assessing the nations where caffeine intake was high. It found that Western countries had a more positive outlook towards coffee drinks while Eastern nations preferred tea as their caffeine drink. The company then established its coffee brand, Nescafe, in the Western countries. The brand also offered coffee flavoured candies in Eastern countries to gauge reaction to the flavour.

Differentiate Customer Expectations

To meet customer expectations it is important to differentiate customer base into value and need. This differentiation helps to prepare strategies that meet company goals and customer expectations for strong customer relations.

Differentiation by value helps to identify customers that are loyal and should be focused on. Their feedback can be valuable for product line extension, increased efficacy and performance, as well as revenue generation.

Differentiating existing customers on the basis of their needs helps to strategise promotions. For instance, apart from analyzing the customers who add value to the company's brand image, DuPont made it a point to understand that other customers needed effective customer service to address their needs individually.

Customer Interaction

Customer interactions help to understand customer expectations and how they relate to the business products and services. The interaction, based on customer value and needs, provides a chance to collect feedback, opinions and wants. Unilever always has its sales representatives and customer care executives ready to discuss possible improvements they can make on their product line or take feedback for improvements. This has helped them develop customer-oriented products.

Customizations to meet Customer Expectations

After identifying, differentiating and interacting with the customers a fair idea can be drawn for new strategies and product customizations. For instance, market research firms like McKinsey realized the need for customizations from the feedbacks of customers. Their customers expected increased customizations on their requests. This will help them in taking their own strategic decisions based on the reports of McKinsey. McKinsey incorporated the clause of providing a percentage of customization leverage in its reports.

The IDIC model provides a sound framework through which businesses can tread through customer engagement and work to meet their expectations.

Gartner's CRM Model

The Customer Relationship Model (CRM) model developed by the market research and consulting firm, Gartner Inc. is known as the Gartner's CRM model.

Gartner created the Eight Building Blocks of CRM — a framework to help enterprises see the big picture, make their business cases and plan their implementation. The framework can be used for internal education and debate in developing the CRM vision and strategies. It can also be the basis of an assessment of the enterprise's existing and required CRM capabilities, to help understand its current position and future strategy.

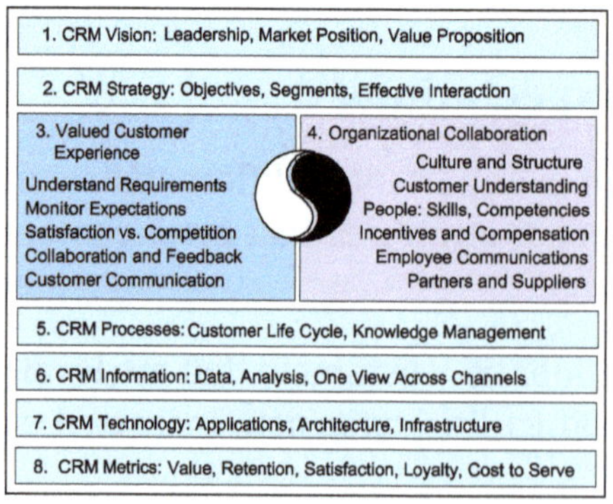

Figure: The Eight Building Blocks of CRM

The framework emphasizes the need to create a balance between the requirements of the enterprise and the customer. The two central building blocks in figure (valued customer experience and organizational collaboration) are joined by a yin and yang motif to emphasize that this is where people meet, build relationships and provide value to each other. Through 2005, 90 percent of successful CRM initiatives will have balanced the needs of improved customer experience with improved organizational collaboration (0.8 probability). Too many CRM initiatives suffer from an inward focus on the enterprise, whereas the point of CRM is to achieve a balance between value to shareholders or stakeholders and value to customers for mutually beneficial relationships.

We drill down into the Eight Building Blocks of CRM — vision, strategy, valued customer experience, organizational collaboration, processes, information, technology and metrics — providing more detail and fleshing out the framework.

1. Vision: Successful CRM demands a clear vision so that a strategy and implementation can be developed to achieve it. The CRM vision is how the customer-centric enterprise wants to look and feel to its customers and prospects — the customer value proposition (CVP) and the corporate brand values are key to the CRM vision. Without a CRM vision, the enterprise will not stand out from the competition, target customers will not know what to expect from it and employees will not know what to deliver in terms of external customer experience. A successful CRM vision is the cornerstone to motivating staff, generating customer loyalty and gaining a greater market share. "Creating a CRM Vision" defines a CRM vision, outlines the key steps and challenges in creating it and discusses its role in creating a successful CRM program.

2. Strategy: A CRM strategy is not an implementation plan or road map. A real CRM strategy takes the direction and financial goals of the business strategy and sets out how the enterprise is going to build customer loyalty — that "feel-good factor" of customer connection with an enterprise that means customers stay longer, buy more, recommend the enterprise to others and are more willing to pay a premium price. The objectives of a CRM strategy are to target, acquire, develop and retain valuable customers to achieve corporate goals. "Developing a CRM Strategy" discusses the steps involved in the development of the CRM strategy.

3. Valued Customer Experience: Customers' experiences when interacting with the enterprise play a key role in shaping their perception of the enterprise — the value it provides and the importance it places on the customer relationship. Good customer experiences drive satisfaction, trust and long-term loyalty. Poor customer experiences have the opposite effect and, because bad news travels faster and further than good news, they harm the enterprise's ability to create new relationships with prospects. No amount of internal "second guessing" can simulate what it's really like to be a customer. "Customer Experience: The Voice of the Customer" focuses on the need to seek and act on customer feedback to create and maintain a successful customer experience.

4. Organizational Collaboration: Many enterprises believe that implementing CRM technologies makes them a customer-centric organization. They forget, ignore or deliberately avoid the necessary changes to the enterprise itself. True CRM means that individuals, teams and the whole enterprise must become more focused on the needs and wants of the customer. The term "organizational collaboration," described in "True CRM Requires Organizational Collaboration", highlights the many facets of the customer-centric internal change needed to deliver the required and desired external customer experience. As a critical part of a CRM program, it will involve changing organizational structures, incentives and compensation, skills and even the enterprise culture. Ongoing change management will be key.

5. Processes: Past efforts to re-engineer processes were primarily driven by the desire to improve the efficiency of an enterprise and reduce costs. The beneficiary was the enterprise, not its customers. The rise in CRM has led to a focus on reworking key processes that touch the customer and asking customers which processes matter to them. We call this customer process re-engineering. Enterprises frequently do not realize that their functionally fragmented processes often mean that the customer has a poor experience and receives less than the expected value. Successful re-engineering should create processes that not only meet customers' expectations, but also support the customer value proposition, provide competitive differentiation and contribute to the desired customer experience.

6. Information: Successful CRM requires a flow of customer information around the organization and tight integration between operational and analytical systems. Having the right information at the right time is fundamental to successful CRM strategies, providing customer insight and allowing effective interaction across any channel. Unfortunately, most enterprises' CRM information capabilities are poor — the result of numerous and fragmented departments, initiatives, databases and systems. Enterprises that establish a business plan for sourcing, managing and leveraging their customer information assets are more likely to achieve their CRM goals and objectives and gain a competitive advantage.

7. Technology: For most technologists, CRM is all about technology. CRM technologies are an essential enabler for any modern CRM business strategy, but they are just one piece of the puzzle. Gartner has a wealth of ongoing research into CRM technology issues and "Technology Decisions are Key to Enabling CRM Strategies" looks at the key decisions that enterprises have to take in three areas: CRM applications, architectural issues and integration. In many CRM projects, integration issues start as a relatively low priority, and then rise in prominence (cost and time) as enterprises realize that true CRM requires seamless customer-centric processes, supported by integrated technology across the enterprise and its supply chain.

8. Metrics: The other seven building blocks depend on performance targets and metrics to gauge their success, and enterprises must set measurable CRM objectives and monitor CRM indicators to successfully turn customers into assets. Without performance management, a CRM strategy and associated program is destined to fail. "Getting the best out of CRM Performance Metrics" introduces a framework for measuring an enterprise's success with CRM by creating a hierarchy of performance metrics with four levels, namely: corporate, customer strategic, operational and process, and infrastructure input metrics. These metrics have an internal and an external focus and link operations to strategy and corporate financial benefits. Each enterprise will have a unique set of metrics applicable to their situation.

Payne's Five Process Model

Payne's Five Processes Model helps to improve Customer Relationship Management (CRM) which makes acquisition and retention of customers a priority. It includes processes that can help to build and maintain relationships with customers. The model was established by Adrian Payne and Pennie Frow in 2005 to identify and assess processes relevant to CRM.

The model discusses the relevance of various processes, namely (Payne & Frow):

- Strategy development process,
- Value creation process,
- Multichannel integration process,
- Performance assessment process, and
- Information management or analytical process in CRM.

Each of the above is a cross-sectional, process-oriented approach and interlinked. They have their own role and function for increased success with CRM implementation. Payne and Frow extensively reviewed literature, along with field-based interactions, to develop a comprehensive process that would aid in developing a sound CRM strategy. Through their research, Payne and Frow stressed the importance of having CRM at strategic level.

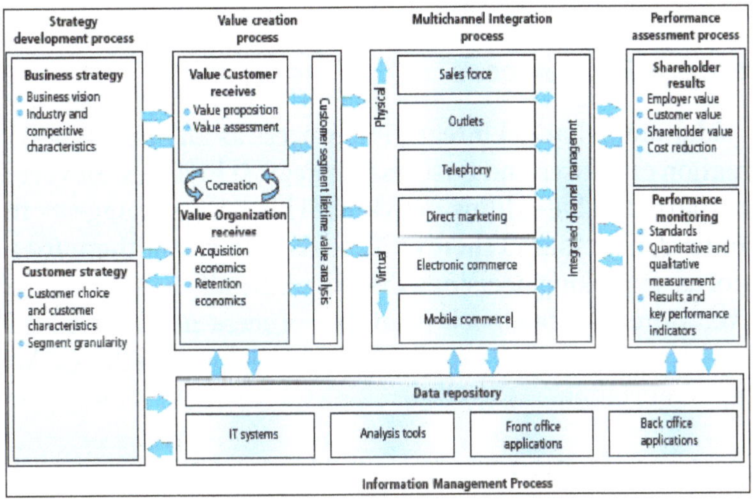

Figure: Payne's Five Process Model

Strategy development and value creation process are a part of strategic CRM. The multichannel integration process is a part of operational CRM. Information management and performance assessment processes are a part of analytical CRM.

Strategy Development in Payne's Five Processes Model

The strategy development process is further divided into two parts; business strategy and customer strategy. For business strategy, a business needs to develop a vision in relation to its offerings. The purpose is to create a goal to establish itself as a key player in the industry.

This model suggests that invariably:

- Business strategy paves the way for understanding,
- How customer strategy needs to be shaped and,
- How it should change over time in conjunction with the changing needs of the customers.

It involves understanding the choice of customers and their characteristics for developing effective products and services. According to Payne and Frow, it is important to examine both current and potential customer base as a part of customer strategy. It helps with appropriate segmentation and identify future actions to tackle different customer needs.

Value Creation Process

The value creation process of Payne's Five Processes model involves identifying the value of a customer to the business and vice-versa. The business needs to understand which customers are valuable through the process of value proposition and value assessment. This process, as per the model, needs to be transformative as per the results received from the strategy development so that value is extracted and transformed into meaningful propositions. Payne's Five Processes model explains that there are 3 aspects of effective value creation. Firstly, the organization needs to determine which processes can create value for the customer. Secondly, identify customers who can add value to the organization. Thirdly, identify how to maximize value in desirable customer segments for a successful exchange of values.

Multichannel Integration Process

Payne and Frow consider multichannel integration process as an important process as it works on inputs from value creation processes and business strategy. It involves converting the insights from these processes to outputs in value-adding activities. This process suggests the business conduct tasks to engage customers, understand their perspective and retain them for a longer duration. It helps businesses to focus on making decisions that integrate all channels and ensure the customer experience is positive. Moreover, feedback from this process needs to be taken into account to further evaluate both strategy and value proposition. This helps in better CRM implementation for greater success of the organization.

Performance Assessment Process

Performance assessment is very important to understand how well the value proposition of the business is and whether the customer's interest is leading to better business performance. Payne and Frow suggest an understanding of the performance through shareholder value, customer engagement scenario, profit margins, and returns through dividends. According to the Payne's Five Processes model, performance assessment of business should also include monitoring of customer satisfaction and analysis of Key Performance Indicators (KPIs). Doing so shall help to assess the extent of success of the implementation of the CRM processes.

Information Management or Analytical Process

Information management is the analytical part of the model. It is a support to the other processes. Payne's Five Process model suggests collecting, organizing and using information related to customers helps with insights on consumer behaviour. It helps businesses to create appropriate marketing responses and improve value propositions. To manage such activities, businesses should develop a data repository system with data analysis tools. These applications can help keep the CRM process a comprehensive one for quantitative and qualitative measurement of market competitiveness.

- Application of Payne's Five Process Model of CRM in an e-commerce Business.

E-retailers have majorly benefitted from this model. Integrating Payne's Five Process model is very important to provide a customer-based value proposition. E-retailers work to build CRM strategy by engaging customers, offering value propositions as discounts, loyalty privileges and priority shipping. Multi-channel integration can also be included from customer reviews, customer service, e-mail support as well as return policies. Performance of the CRM process can also be assessed from the online traffic, time spent on browsing and surfing habits. Assessing what factors trigger purchase intention can help create better value propositions.

Payne's Five Process model evaluated the correlation between business processes, prospects and customers. The various processes encompass the spectrum of CRM, right from the strategic point of view to assessing the performance of customer engagement. Every process supports itself and other processes, with each task being interdependent for success.

CRM Value Chain

The CRM value chain is a proven model which businesses can follow when developing and implementing their CRM strategies. It has been five years in development and has been piloted in a number of business-to- business and business-to-consumer settings, with both large companies and SMEs: IT, software, telecoms, financial services, retail, media, manufacturing, and construction. The model is grounded on strong theoretical principles and the practical requirements of business.

The ultimate purpose of the CRM value chain process is to ensure that the company builds long-term mutually-beneficial relationships with its strategically-significant customers. Not all customers are strategically significant. Indeed some customers are simply too expensive to acquire and service. They buy little and infrequently; they pay late or default; they make extraordinary demands on customer service and sales resources; they demand expensive, short-run, customised output; and then they defect to competitors.

What is a Strategically Significant Customer?

We've identified four types of strategically significant customer (SSC). Self- evidently, the high life-time value customer is a key SSC. These must be the focus of customer retention efforts. Life-time value potential is the present- day value of all future margins that might be earned in a relationship.

Tempting as it may be to believe, not all high volume customers have high LTV. If they demand JIT, customised delivery, or are in other ways costly to serve, their value may be significantly reduced. We know of one company that applied activity-based costing disciplines in order to trace process costs to its customer base. They found that 2 of their 3 biggest customers were in fact unprofitable. As a consequence the company re-engineered its manufacturing and logistics processes, and salespeople negotiated price increases.

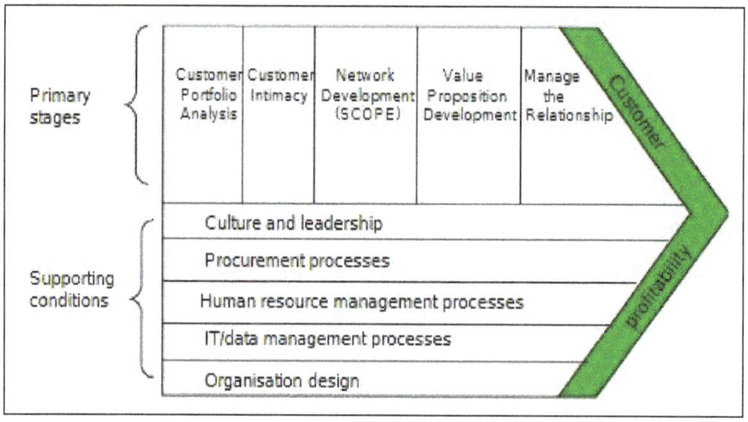

CRM value chain

A second group of strategically significant customers we call 'benchmarks'. These are customers that other customers copy. A manufacturer of vending machine equipment is prepared to do business with Coca Cola at breakeven. Why? Because they can tell other customers that they are supplying to the world's biggest vending operation.

The third group of SSCs is 'inspirations', customers who inspire change in the supplying company. These may be customers who find new applications, come up with new product ideas, find ways of improving quality or reducing cost. They may be the most demanding of customers, or frequent complainers, and, though their own LTV potential is low, they offer other significant sources of value. One insurance company modified its claims process to satisfy one particular car fleet operator; this process eventually became the company's default standard.

The final group of strategically significant customers we call 'cost magnets'. There are customers who absorb a disproportionately high volume of fixed cost, thus enabling other, smaller customers to become profitable. One oil- seed processor, for example, has two major customers, a manufacturer of snack foods which buys oil in bulk and a retail multiple which buys consumer packs. Although they account for 60% of oil-seed processing time, they absorb 85% of fixed costs between them.

Five Steps to Profitable Relationships

The five steps in the CRM value chain are customer portfolio analysis, customer intimacy, network development, value proposition development and managing the relationship at each stage of the value chain there are concepts, tools and processes to help create and implement successful strategy.

Very briefly, the CPA step analyses the customer base to identify customers to target with different value propositions. The second step involves the business in getting to know the selected customers as segments or individuals and building a customer data-base which is accessible to all those whose decisions or activities impact upon customer attitude and behaviour. Step three involves building a strong network of relationships with employees, suppliers, partners and investors who understand the requirements of the chosen customers. Step four involves developing, with the network's compliance, propositions which create value jointly for the customer and company. The fifth and final stage is to manage the customer relationship.

The focus here is on both structure and process. From observation of failure it is clear that CRM solutions cannot be transplanted into any organisation in the absolute certainty that the business will flourish. For success to happen, CRM needs a supportive culture: it's unlikely to yield dividends in companies which only pay lip service to customer focus. Neither will it succeed in organisations wedded to product-based structures or reward systems based on sales volume. Similarly, if IT, human resources and procurement processes are not aligned with the CRM agenda, it's unlikely to flourish. For example, we know one IT company which is trying to implement CRM strategy whilst still recruiting up-and-at-'em salespeople who are quota driven. Another company is in the throes of a cost-reduction programme and procures least cost inputs to its manufacturing process without due regard to the impact on customer satisfaction and buying behaviour.

Customer Portfolio Analysis

CPA, the first step in the CRM value chain acknowledges that not all customers have equal value to the company. CPA asks the question: 'who are our SSCs?' The answer can be pitched at sector (e.g. food retailing), segment (e.g. food retail multiples) or individual (e.g. Tesco) levels.

Companies which have no customer history on which to base their analysis can use segmentation approaches to identify potential SSCs. When CPA has sorted the actual or potential customer base into different groups, they can be taegeted with different value propositions. An important consideration is to analyse and sort by profit potential, not by volume, whether that is by sector, segment or individual.

One CPA tool sorts customers into 4 strategic groups: sack, re-engineer, nurture and invest. Sackable customers are those who have no present or future profit potential or life-time value.The 'invest' group contains customers who are both valuable currently and have significant future potential. The 'reengineer' group contains customers who are not presently profitable but who could become so if the relationship were re-engineered. Options may include reducing the level of customer service, disintermediation, or telesales, rather than face-to-face sales representation. The final segment 'nurture' contains those customers who are currently profitable but have little future potential. The task here is to address, possibly in consultation with those customers the reasons for pessimism. It may be that they can jointly find solutions which suggest a more profitable future relationship.

Customer Intimacy

Choosing customers to serve is one thing. Getting to know them well is altogether different. Most companies collect customer data. Some industries are overwhelmed with information – scanner data, loyalty card data, complaints files, market research, geodemographic data. The challenge is to use the data to better understand the who, what, why, where, when and how of customer behaviour. Mining data intelligently is, of course, a source of huge competitive advantage, and it enables a more refined CPA to be undertaken.

Develop the Network

Company does not compete against company. Network competes against network. For example, Sainsbury does not compete against Tesco. Their respective networks compete. Tesco's network, which includes partners such as Royal Bank of Scotland (for its retail banking offer) and Privilege Insurance (for its insurance offer) currently seems to be performing better than Sainsbury's. A company's network position i.e. its connectedness to other parties who co-operate in delivering value to the chosen customer, is a source of great competitive advantage. An innovative software house partnering with IBM, for example, enhances its network position. IBM also benefits, as well as their joint customers.

Networks consist of partners like these, employees, suppliers and owners/investors. CRM is not a quick fix; it requires owners and investors who will commit to the long-term investment in the people, processes and technology to implement CRM strategies. Employees will probably need reorienting and reskilling, if not redeployment. There is clear evidence that employee performance in moments of truth with customers influences customer satisfaction and purchasing intention. It only takes a short leap of faith to link employee satisfaction to customer satisfaction to business performance. Suppliers also need to understand who the customer is trying to serve. According to the consultants A T Kearney, companies are going to continue vendor reduction programmes over the next several years, as they try to build closer relationships with fewer partner vendors. CRM is becoming twinned with SRM, supplier relationship management. Kearney reckons 20% of current in-suppliers will be de-listed by 2003. For CRM to succeed, the network of suppliers, employees, owners/investors and partners must be aligned and managed to meet the needs of the chosen customers.

Value Proposition Development

By the fourth step of the CRM value chain, you will know who you want to serve and will have built, or be in the process of building, the network. Now the network has to work together to create and deliver the chosen value(s) to the selected customers. Great value is found more effective and more efficient solutions of customer problems. Although it is traditional to focus on the product as the main source of value, many companies are finding that people, process and service offer more competitive advantage as products become more commoditised. How things are done with and for customers - process - is particularly important. There may be small processes, such as how complaints are handled; or big processes, such as how new products are jointly developed with customers. The value star illustrates sources of customer value in a retailing context.

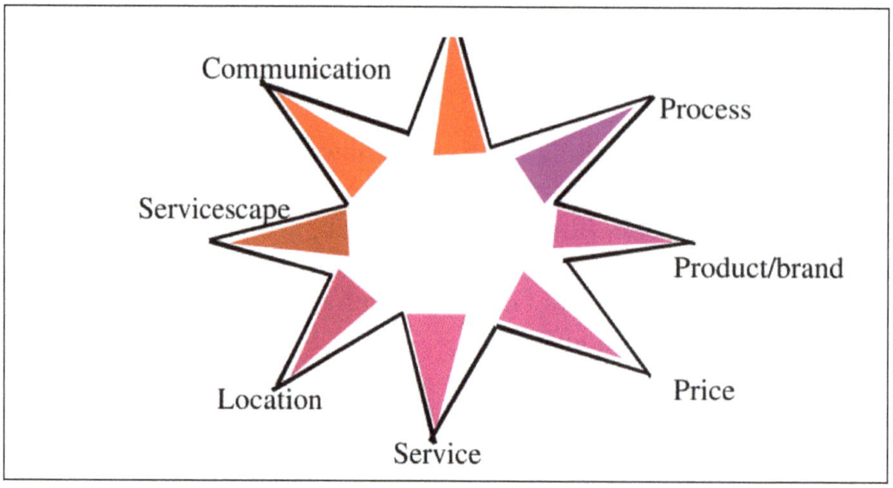

The value star (retail example)

Managing the Relationship

For relationships to succeed with strategically significant customers, companies are having to re-invent structures and process. On the way out are hierarchical structures and product managers. Replacing them are flatter organisations with empowered front-lines and customer or market managers. We encourage companies to replace their single marketing strategy with a trio made up of a Customer Acquisition Plan, Customer Retention Plan and Customer Development Plan. Each of these has different metrics from those found in run-of-the-mill marketing strategies. New measures include customer acquisition costs, customer retention rates, share-of-customer and customer development targets alongside more conventional measures such as customer satisfaction and sales volume, and additional measures relating to the performance of network members.

Quality Competitive Index Model

The Quality Competitive Index (QCI) model is a type of customer management model. According to this model, a business needs to perform certain tasks that help in acquiring new customers and retain old customers. The model is very different from other CRM models as it focuses on customer 'management' rather than relationship building. 'Customer management' means giving importance to impulse buyers.

They do not want a long-term association with the company but are nevertheless important for revenue generation. The QCI model helps to review the current practices and create a quantitative approach to improve customer management process.

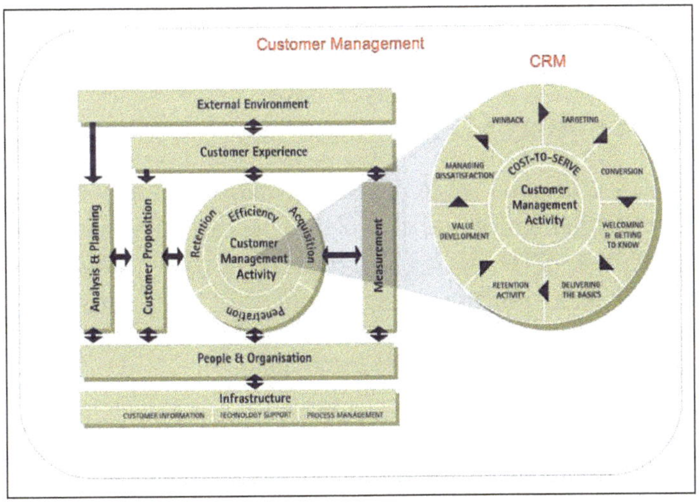

QCI model

The model is made up of eight elements:

- Analysis and planning,
- Information technology,
- Proposition,

- People and organization,
- Process management,
- Customer management activities,
- Customer experience and,
- Measurement of effect.

The core element of this model is its customer management activities, which include acquisition, penetration, and retention. The supporting elements are people and organization, while these are affected by customer experience and external environment.

Analysis and Planning

The process of customer management starts with an analysis of customer behaviour and planning to develop the value of the company. The business can then plan to design customer management activities for engagement. The analysis and planning is based on the REAP of customer management activities, which is Retention, Efficiency, Acquisition, and penetration.

Proposition

The 'analysis and planning' is the base of customers and their needs, leading to effective planning. The next element of the QCI model is coming up with the 'proposition'. Proposition includes processes that can attract new customers, which depends upon the evaluation of the needs of the customers in the previous step. The segmentation of customer needs to form the base for different propositions. This further helps to derive enhanced customer experience and engagement strategies.

Information and Technology (IT)

Information and technology is an enabler in managing customers as well as customer-related data. Technology helps deliver critical information related to the customers to the organization and vice-versa. Thus Information and Technology systems need to be updated constantly to effectively manage customers and people, as per the changing needs of both entities.

This element includes important sub-processes such as:

- Sourcing customer information,
- Planning and analyzing information,
- Management of quality and review of technology systems for replacement and renewal.

People and Organization

A business cannot manage customers without a robust team of customer relationship executives. As per the QCI model, the business needs to develop and maintain a responsible team for:

- Managing customer requests,

- Feedbacks,
- Queries and concerns.

Also, businesses need to establish a system for role identification, task segregation, and conduction of gap analysis for training.

Process Management

Coordinating marketing, sales, and customer support are essential for customer management, as per the QCI model. According to this model, a consistent process which provides continuous management support to customers and identifies shortcomings is important. This is the importance of 'process management' element.

Customer Management Activity

This element of the QCI model has three sub-categories of activities, governed by efficiency in all:

- Acquisition: It includes targeting of customers and getting to know their needs for developing products/services. The execution of this activity involves effectively putting across the business's propositions after identifying the customers and their needs.
- Penetration: This sub-activity includes understanding the customers through the collection of information, which can be then processed to understand how to best create a valuable customer base. The activities involve simple messages to welcome customers to the organization, provide an understanding of the business activities and helping customers connect with the business goals.
- Retention: This can be done through value development, as well as through win-back strategy. This strategy serves as a retention process and an acquisition process.

Measuring the Effect

This element involves assessment of the process to ensure continuous improvement of the customer management process. The measurement also helps understand the level of performance of individuals and teams on their roles and creates benchmarking on customer management success.

Customer Experience

Addition of customer experience to the customer management mix provides an additional layer of measurement. It bridges gaps in customer perception and customer enhancement processes.

The QCI model provides a detailed process of how to establish a connection with customers, cordially interact with them, and customer management. The model also accepts the role of external environment in impacting customer experience and provides an understanding of how to counteract any negative aspects by making sure the foundation of the CRM processes.

Forrester Model of CRM

Forrester defines CRM as the set of business processes and supporting technologies used to acquire, retain and enhance customer relationships. CRM encompasses the activities organizations use to understand, target, deliver, and respond to customers across marketing, sales, and service, as well as among external demand chain partners. The phenomenon of the social Web – which Forrester calls Social Computing – is forcing business process professionals to expand their thinking beyond the goal of optimizing a two-way relationship between an enterprise and customer to also include the simultaneous interactions that customers have among themselves. CRM is evolving from its traditional focus on optimizing customer-facing transactional processes to include the strategies and technologies to develop collaborative and social connections with customers, suppliers, and even competitors.

Notwithstanding this emerging trend, one challenge remains constant. Organizations still struggle to define the right CRM strategies and effectively acquire and deploy the right CRM technology solutions that will meet their needs. In 2010, when we surveyed business and IT executives at 99 organizations who are responsible for CRM initiatives, well under 50% fully agreed that the "applications really improved the end user's productivity" and "business results anticipated from the implementation were met or exceeded." Complicating the situation, business process professionals are often confused about which customer management technology solutions have the strongest track record for delivering results. We have found that while social CRM is capturing the imagination of decision-makers at many organizations, it is the tried-and-true technologies that offer the most certain return on investment. Disappointment with CRM is usually the result of poorly conceived strategies that lack a laser focus on improving a specific set of business capabilities to increase revenues or reduce costs.

To avoid wasting your time and money on ill-conceived CRM programs, beware of the two most common pitfalls of CRM plans:

1. No strategic focus on business value: Many companies have a grand vision to become "more customer-focused," but the implementation of this vision often lacks practical focus and recognition of the typical constraints (e.g., time, money, and politics) that must be taken into account to make the vision a reality. A CRM program should be tightly linked to business goals, focused on customer benefits, clearly identify the processes and constituencies that will be affected, and specify the associated information and functionality needs.

2. Lack of attention to business process and people issues: In some organizations, CRM initiatives have degenerated into technology-centric projects aimed at basic process automation. While automation projects may well lead to cost savings, the sheer complexity and size of these initiatives has led to a blurring of the target value. Complexity and a lack of clear objectives divert resources from the important tasks of redesigning underlying processes and architecting how employees will work effectively within these processes. The potential of CRM lies not in technology itself, but in the process of using technology alongside an in-depth understanding of the customer to drive unique, valuable customer interactions.

The most successful CRM initiatives are framed in terms of their overall impact across the organization and the customer but are implemented in focused, incremental steps.

Four Key Elements of a successful CRM Strategy

Forrester's Best Practices Framework For CRM defines the critical capabilities necessary for building high-quality customer relationships. The framework distills findings from our interviews with 101 user companies, analysis of 33 CRM vendor solutions, and insight from discussions with 29 CRM professional services organizations. It also incorporates our recent experience in applying the framework to help more than 30 Forrester clients define their CRM strategies and establish a road map for the future. The framework includes 11 sets of capabilities across four categories — comprising more than 150 best practices, including social CRM capabilities

1. Strategy: Your customer strategy identifies the customers the organization intends to serve and articulates the desired customer experience to be delivered.
2. Process: Business processes are comprised of the practices associated with major customer facing business functions in the organization. For example, marketing, e Commerce, direct sales, partner sales, customer service, and field service.
3. Technology: Your technology environment plays an important role in enabling the CRM business processes and is comprised of customer analytics, customer data management, and technology infrastructure.
4. People: How people are organized and led has a large role in determining success with CRM. You must pay attention to the organization's corporate culture, leadership practices, collaboration methods, training programs, and performance measurement approaches.

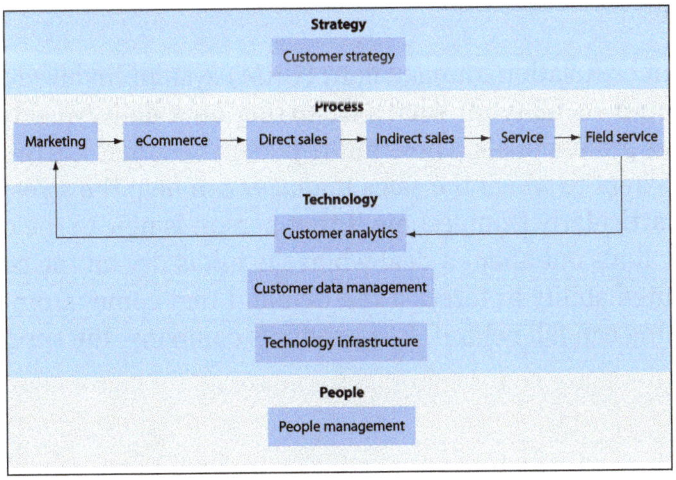

Forrester's

CRM Maturity Model

The CRM Maturity Model is a high-level blueprint for defining which level you are at in the customer relationship management lifecycle and what tools and strategies you need to get to the next level. From an organizational standpoint, stepping up a level in the CRM Maturity Model is a big deal. With each level comes a more detailed set of processes, a defined sales pipeline with centralized data and tools that allow different departments to synchronize and create a 360 degree view of the customer lifecycle. In essence, each level will likely create more leads, deepen relationships and increase the likelihood of future business, all the while consuming less of your time.

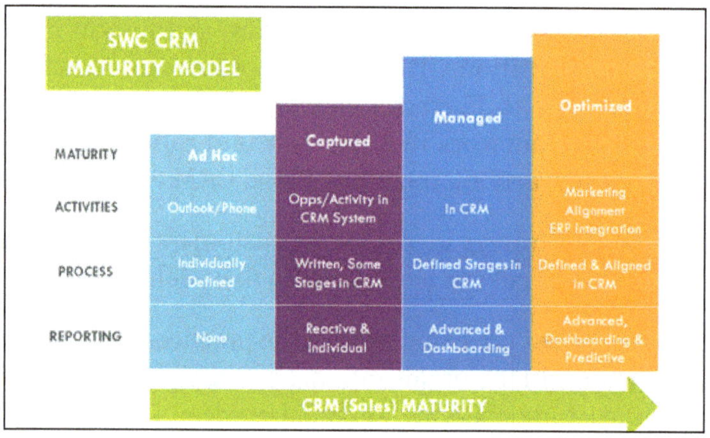

Level 1: Ad Hoc

At Level 1, sales professionals typically use offline tools to manage their accounts, leads, opportunities and sales tasks. Many times these "tools" are a large yellow notepad. The sales professional manages their contacts in Outlook which syncs up with their smartphone. At this level, each sales professional has their own sales process that loosely follows an organization's process.

- No CRM System:

There is no true Customer Relation Management (CRM) system involved in Level 1. This means sales management has no visibility on what's occurring on a daily/weekly basis without having meetings or calling sales professionals. These multi-person meetings are time consuming. The lack of visibility limits the extent to which the sales manager can help the sales professional deal with roadblocks, which is particularly troublesome if that person is new to the organization. The sales manager typically only finds out about a deal when the ink is dry on the contract. The rest of the organization has a limited ability to forecast the demand that comes from closed deals. In a services company, recruiting can fall behind. In a products company, the supply chain and assembly line falls behind.

Level 2: Captured

Organizations at Level 2 maturity have a CRM system where sales professionals are uploading their leads, opportunities and activities. Basic sales stages are being identified and team-based selling is starting to coalesce around the system. Data is now centralized; it's not walking out the door when there is turnover. Sales managers can see a sales pipeline, trends and begin to help sales professionals with leads.

- Value to sales professional – familiar tools become more powerful:

With Level 2 maturity, there is Outlook and CRM integration. Sales professionals create opportunities or contacts in Outlook and link it to their CRM with one click there is no need to go into a web browser. Using their phone or tablet client, the sales professional can use voice-to-text to quickly add opportunities and notes that will be created in CRM.

Level 3: Managed

Organizations typically at Level 3 maturity are using CRM's workflow and rules-based engine to drive the sales process. The organization's sales process typically has stages. Each stage has a set number of rules and data points that are required before moving to the next stage. One stage may require an NDA to be signed, for example. The qualifying stage may require the sales professional to confirm the budget or purchasing timeline.

- Value to Sales Professional – Guided Process Reduces Sales Cycle.

Every organization has processes, but when these processes are vaguely defined and loosely enforced, they can be the root of frustration and inefficiencies. Without these processes, for example, a sales professional may be told to go back and ask the potential customer for something they missed. Having the process clearly defined creates efficiency and transparency; the sales professional knows exactly what to do because they are guided through it all. This level of maturity leads to a decrease in the sales cycle.

Level 4: Optimize

When an organization has reached Level 4 maturity, they typically have implemented one or more of the following:

1. Marketing and Sales Alignment: Marketing and sales alignment occurs when you can make a connection from a marketing activity (e.g. email campaign), to a lead, to a qualified opportunity and finally to a closed deal. By implementing this alignment, the organization can quantify the value of its marketing investments and sales can be directly tied back to marketing activity.

    - Value To Sales Professional – Alignment Visibility.

Now the sales professional can see how much marketing activity contributed to their sales. For example, CRM would show that a certain sales professional had 10 leads generated from a marketing campaign. The professional qualified the 10 leads to four opportunities. Two of those opportunities lead to a proposal of which the professional was able to win one deal. Those are tangible results that leads the sales professional to supporting future marketing efforts.

2. ERP Integration: An organization at Level 4 typically integrates CRM and Enterprise Resource Planning (ERP) to pull pricing data into CRM. This reduces the risk of incorrect pricing and lost revenue. CRM pushes orders into the ERP which initiates production or allocation of resources. In this situation, sales is helping the organization forecast demand. Forecasting demand is a powerful organizational tool that is a constant challenge. Being able to forecast demand has an impact on the recruiting process (services company) and production (product company) in a manufacturing plant. The increase in efficiency leads to a stronger bottom line for the organization.

    - Value to Sales Professional – Faster Sales Cycle.

Organizations often lose business because they can't move fast enough to answer customers. When a sales professional has always up-to-date pricing and doesn't need to wait on other departments for information, the sales cycle decreases. Level 4 maturity leads to less stress on the sales professional as they have more time to work the sales cycle.

3. Customer Service Integration:

   In most organizations, there is some synergy between the marketing and sales departments. However, there can be little communication between the sales and customer service departments. That all changes with Level 4 maturity. Many CRM systems including Salesforce and Microsoft Dynamics CRM have customer service capabilities. Imagine a world where marketing, sales and customer service work in tangent to manage the entire customer lifecycle. Marketing starts by nurturing the potential customer. Then, sales qualifies, understands the problem and proposes a solution. Lastly, customer service ensures the customer is happy and getting answers to their questions. This is true organizational alignment.

   - Value to Professional – 360 Degree View.

In many organizations, the sales professional looks to the future because they don't have visibility into how their accounts are being serviced.

With Level 4 maturity, the sales professional gets to look at one pane of glass (their CRM website) for a particular customer that shows opportunities, recent activities, past marketing campaigns (nurture),and service tickets (current requests and issues). A 360 degree view allows the sales professional to deepen relationships, proactively address issues, and ultimately increase the likelihood of future business.

The CRM Maturity Model is essential for assessing and optimizing your sales processes, but to go from one level to the next requires the right software, tools and experience.

Customer Value Model

A customer value model (CVM) is a data-driven representation of the value, in which the company is doing business. Customer value models are used primarily in B2B markets where the choice of a given product, service, or offering is primarily based on customer value.

Customer value is defined as,

Value = Benefits – Price

Thus, customer benefits are quantified in a CVM – product features and capabilities are translated into dollars. Customer value models are different from customer lifetime value models, which seek to quantify the value of a customer to its suppliers.

Uses of Customer Value Models

1. New product and service development and refinement: The relationship and the customer

is one of the most important features of the market. This on-site interaction can be used to define and define features and functionality. Often a key is to focus on product or service capabilities rather than on features. Successful CVM endeavors to change the basis of the customer-supplier product conversation from features and functions and toward problems, benefits, and value.

2. Sales tools: CVMs can serve as a quantified statement of value and benefits for a customer that is used by the salesperson as a salesperson to a new account and grow current customer. CVMs also can help the firms to determine the more rational promotion cost.

Customer Value Model Methods

There are several methods and approaches used to create customer value models. All of these approaches appear to depend on a large number of customer interactions and on-site interviews and observations of customers. The CVMs are of varying complexity. P & Ls (profit and loss statements) to establish a clear connection between the product benefits and the bottom-line customer.

References

- Customer-relationship-model: smallbusiness.chron.com, Retrieved 7 May, 2019
- Customer-relationship-management: projectguru.in, Retrieved 23 July, 2019
- Paynes-five-process-model-crm-strategy: projectguru.in, Retrieved 25 February, 2019
- The-CRM-value-chain: researchgate.net, Retrieved 28 June, 2019
- Different-elements-qci-model: projectguru.in, Retrieved 8 March, 2019
- Crm-maturity-model, customer-relationship-management: swc.com, Retrieved 19 August, 2019
- Customer-value-model: clickandsave.eu, Retrieved 15 January, 2019

3

Strategic Customer Relationship Management

Strategic customer relationship management deals with the development of a business culture which is focused on customers. One of the tools by which B2B companies develop profitable customer relationships is through customer portfolio. The chapter closely examines these key concepts of strategic CRM to provide an extensive understanding of the subject.

Strategic CRM

The aim of strategic CRM is to concentrate and enhance the knowledge about customers and use this knowledge to improve and customize the interactions with customers to maintain a long-term relationship with them.

Determining and development of CRM strategies involves following steps:

1. Amplify commitment: Strategic CRM involves almost all the departments of an organization e.g. finance, sales, manufacturing, distribution, marketing etc. Hence it is essential to get support and use their important feedback while determining strategies. For this each and every department should be kept informed about all the developments and implementation of processes carried out or performed. Everyone should also be emphasized about the positive approaches and end results of the strategies.

2. Building valuable project team: After organizational commitment is secured the next important stage in developing CRM strategies is building a determined and valuable project team. Each and every member of this team should be experiences and dedicated professional as these members will be the key decision makers in the whole process. They will be responsible to communicate all the related details and benefits of the CRM strategies to all the members of the organization. These members should be from following work groups to ensure all the aspects of strategies are addressed efficiently:

   a. Management: Management professionals are responsible to provide motivation, leadership and management at every strategic development step especially when a change in business process or organizational structure is expected.

   b. Technical: Automation of CRM strategies are important and must involve experienced technical hands. Also technical professional provide their useful contribution in building and managing software application and determining their compatibility with existing software features.

c. Sales and Marketing: These are final users of CRM system once the strategies are determined and implemented. The applied strategies are supposed to be successful once these users fell comfortable and satisfied by using all the CRM features. Being the end users these people are also responsible to provide useful feedbacks on efficiency and effectiveness while the strategies are in development phase.

d. Financial: The CRM strategies must also be gone through or evaluated under financial aspects. The financial professionals of the team can provide crucial analysis on assessment of enhanced productivity, evaluation of operational and production cost and final estimated cost of the project. They also help in assessing the investment cost per module or segment so that the product is delivered inside the budget.

e. External Experts: Many times some external consultants and other CRM vendors are substantially helpful in strategy development. These are people who are generally hired or outsourced for second fruitful opinion or if the organization is lacking with sufficient CRM experts. These professionals have vast experience in the same field and helps analyzing organization's actual business needs, work with other professional to review and approve complex business structure and even helps in formulating the team members according to the expertise they posses.

3. Requirement Analysis: CRM strategies should always focus and concentrate on the actual business requirements. This process involves a series surveys and questionnaires with top level sales, marketing and financial managers to gather the actual expectations regarding the strategies to be implemented and what results these strategies will throw in the final stage. This is a very crucial factor in the development of an effective CRM system because if the results are not matching the actual requirement or if they diverge from focus points, then that means it's not achieving the desired goals.

CRM Strategy

A customer relationship management (CRM) strategy is a company's plan to use CRM software to help grow sales and improve customer service. It incorporates an overall business strategy with input from sales, marketing, and customer service, identifying all potential touch points that occur during the customer journey.

It's a good idea to include throughout the strategy process, marketing, customer service, and any other departments that will be using the CRM.

Create an overall Business Strategy

Creating an effective CRM strategy starts with understanding your company's overall strategy. The strategy you choose attempts to answer key questions like where, what, who and how you will operate in your market. The answers will help form the backbone of your sales strategy. The following are some of the elements of a business strategy you'll need to know before creating a sales strategy.

Understand Business Goals

Setting the right business goals will inform how you approach the other elements of your customer relationship management strategy. Doing this will set you apart from the majority of your competitors as more than 80% of small business owners, according to Staples' National Small Business Survey, don't even monitor their goal setting.

The following are high-level examples of business goals:

- Improve the efficiency of my customer service team.
- Increase the margins on all new business by 5%.
- Implement a volunteer program for my employees.
- Boost yearly revenue by another 25%.

Develop a Unique Selling Proposition

A unique selling proposition (USP) defines the factors that make your product or service different from and better than your competition. Knowing your USP gives you one high-level tool when asked: "how are you different from the other company?" The USP also becomes the marketing trunk from which you hang the marketing limbs.

"We GUARANTEE -
Fresh hot pizza, delivered in 30 minutes or less or it's FREE!"

Value Proposition

A value proposition is a statement of the specific results a customer will get, and the value they will receive if they use your product or service. Being able to articulate this to a prospect will get the sales conversation started (and keep it from ending too soon) and differentiate you from your competition.

Here are a few examples of what a value proposition is not:

- "We provide cheap long distance phone services to small businesses."
- "Our solution will reduce your accounting stress and help you sleep better."
- "Our software helps attorneys draft legal documents."

Here's an example of value proposition from sales expert.

We help large companies reduce the cost of their employee benefits programs without impacting benefit levels. With the spiraling costs of healthcare today, this is a critical issue for most businesses. One of our recent clients, a large manufacturing company similar to yours, was struggling with how to reduce spending in this area. We saved them more than.

Know your Customers with Buyer Personas

A key foundational element for any business is understanding and its potential buyers. This helps determine who and how you will be marketing, selling, and servicing them. It also helps you better position your business with the needs and goals of these buyers in mind. These fictional customer representations are called buyer personas.

Most businesses have more than one persona, but not so many — less than five — that each one becomes too granular and your marketing gets diluted because you are trying to cover too many messaging bases. Personas typically address the following areas: Demographics, which include age, location, gender, marital status, education, job title, and income; and psychographics, which include goals, challenges, interests, values, and personality.

Once you know what ask, the next step is asking. Here are the most common and effective ways to gather information for developing buyer personas.

Interview your Employees

Employees, particularly those that interact with clients, possess a wealth of information. For example, a customer service representative talks to clients every day. They hear the challenges, goals, and even how they prefer to do their shopping.

Interview Current and Past Clients

The best way to learn about your ideal clients is to interview actual clients, current and past. Think about your best client, the one that represents the type you would like more of. Tell them you are trying to learn more about how to grow your business and would like to ask them some questions. These interviews are invaluable because you often hear things you didn't want to hear but glad you did. Keep the interviews short, no more than 20 minutes.

Conduct Surveys

Surveys are a great way to get answers about your potential buyers particularly if you have a lot of customers and prospects. A survey can streamline the process of gathering the data yet provide a clear picture of who's your buyers are and what's important to them.

Understand the Competitive Landscape

If you don't know who your competitors are and how your company fits into the space, you'll be at a costly disadvantage. Knowing the competitive landscape allows you to spot industry trends, understand how your competitors are marketing and selling, and ultimately know how and if your company will keep its differentiators to maintain its competitive advantage.

There are many ways to compare the competition so you'll have to decide what's most important.

	VersaTables.com	IKEA	HermanMiller	Office DEPOT	Steelcase	HAWORTH
Lifetime Warranty	✓		SOME PRODUCTS	SOME PRODUCTS	SOME PRODUCTS	SOME PRODUCTS
Made in the USA	✓		✓	SOME PRODUCTS	SOME PRODUCTS	SOME PRODUCTS
Free Shipping	✓		SOME PRODUCTS	SOME PRODUCTS	SOME PRODUCTS	SOME PRODUCTS
Green Manufacturing	✓	✓	✓	SOME	✓	✓
Customer Service	EXCELLENT	BAD	GOOD	OKAY	GOOD	GOOD
Ease of Return	EXCELLENT	DIFFICULT	OKAY	BAD	OKAY	OKAY
Product Recalls	✓ NONE	YES	✓ NONE	YES	YES	✓ NONE

Map the Customer Journey

The customer journey map is a roadmap showing how a customer or prospect interacts with your company with all of the experiences they have along the way. This encompasses your operations, marketing, sales, service, and support — any aspect of your business — and any way that these teams may "touch" a prospect or customer.

Some example touch points include the following:

- Your website
- Social media mentions
- Yelp reviews
- Email marketing
- Paid ads.

Ultimately, these people have goals, and you're trying to help them achieve those goals whether it's educating a prospect on how your software differs from your competitors or showing a customer how to use a particular feature of the software. Like buyer personas, these maps are *fictional* representations of how these interactions will transpire. The steps and actions taken are dynamic, and that's OK.

Website Customer Journey Analysis For SaaS Business

Search	Evaluate	Experiment	Purchase	Retain
How are prospects finding you? Where are they originating outside of your site	What are the details of your solution? How do they compare with other solutions?	How can prospects engage with solution before spending money?	What are the steps to payment? Do customers start with a free trial period?	How do customers get ongoing support?
Customer goals				
Locate a solution	Asses if this solution is the best option/fit for needs	Decide if this solution is worth paying for	Get access to all features and benefits according to chosen plan	Get ongoing support and customer service when needed
Touchpoints				
Google	Case studies	Trial registration	Cart page	Help pages
Twitter LinkedIn	FAQ page Pricing page Blog posts	Account creation Product tour	Checkout	Customer support contact

Cite specific URLs once you're ready to make recommendations for testing.

Basic customer journey map for SaaS company.

Identify Current Challenges

With the stages of your journey map outlined, review each stage to determine what issues and challenges you have for each one. For example, if your conversion rate after a software trial is low, determine why it's low. Once a prospect signs up, are they using the trial? Do you provide enough information to get them started? Do you provide them with a company point of contact to answer questions? Do you have an online support community?

Create a Content Plan

Each touchpoint in the customer journey will require content to support different stages. The types of content for prospects will differ from but also cross over to those of customers. For example, content for a prospect may include an asset like an educational e-book showing how a particular pain point can be resolved using a certain type of tactic. More specifically, a guide "How to Develop an Influencer Marketing Strategy" may be created by a marketing agency.

On the customer side, content can be assets like guides on how to use a product, instructional webinars, and paid ads for new or complementary products. These examples can also be used on the prospect side. You can see examples of content as touch points in the example customer journey map above.

Establish Sales Channels and Sales Process

The channels you sell your products and solutions will likely already have been decided unless you are just starting out. For example, if you own a residential roofing company, you are selling directly to the consumer. But if you're a business-to-business (B2B) software start-up, you have a number of possible sales channels to consider. What you sell and to who will determine what your sales process looks like, and how that integrates with your CRM strategy.

Sell Direct to Customers

As the name implies, you're selling directly to a consumer or another business if you're a B2B company. As in the roofing and software examples, you may offer a service that will be marketed and sold without involving any other selling layers. You have the most control over this process. However, for a company that needs to scale quickly, as in the software example, it can also be the slowest.

Sell using a Distributor or Reseller

When you sell your products through a distributor or reseller, you are giving up both the one-on-one interaction with the customer and control of the sales process. You are also leaving the entire experience from branding to quality control to this "middleman." Your profit margins will also be thinner.

But for some businesses, these sales channels can mean the difference between growth and closing the doors. You can combine these with your current sales model like selling direct to maximize opportunities for growth.

Here are some of the benefits of using a distributor or reseller:

- Instant access to established businesses and their clients, allowing for faster and larger rates of growth.
- Access to the sales experience of a reseller used to selling similar products.
- Lower potential barriers to entry.
- A competitive advantage over those not using these channels.

Understanding the Sales Process

Creating a sales process is a sometimes overlooked part of a CRM strategy. However, it's crucial, especially if you plan on growing your sales team and business. The more complex your sales and the longer your sales cycle, the more detailed your process should be. Start by identifying the pipeline stages. These are the steps in your sales process needed to move someone from a prospect to a customer. They will be tracked in your CRM.

Example of CRM pipeline stages

The stages in the process are sequential actions such as prospecting, initial contact, demo, proposal review, won, and lost. For each step, write out what's involved and what the expected outcomes.

Understand Organizational Dynamics

Whether implementing a CRM for the first time or switching to another platform, you'll need to know who will have access to the CRM and understand how the change may affect your team. Include relevant employees in all stages of your customer relationship management strategy from goal setting to technology considerations to selecting the CRM software. Employees with a voice in the process will be more likely to embrace the new technology.

Evaluate Cultural Readiness

If your team is not already using a CRM, it's a good idea to take the pulse of everyone who will be using it. Identify who these users are and let them know you're going to be implementing a CRM. What's your team's CRM experience? Which platforms have they used? What did they like or dislike about those platforms or CRMs in general? How did it help them perform their jobs better?

Identify CRM Roles

Not everyone in an organization will need to have access to the CRM. Determine who needs access and what levels of access each team member will have. You also may want to name a CRM admin, which is the person that understands both the technology of the platform and all the business processes. For small businesses, this could be an office manager, IT person, or even the business owner.

Another position to consider is a CRM strategist. These professionals, often consultants, develop, implement and manage CRM strategies on either a temporary or permanent basis for businesses.

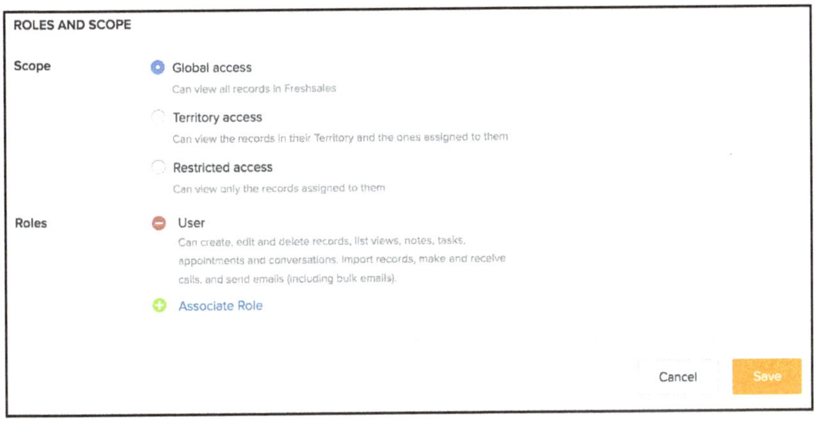

Align Sales, Marketing and Service

The departments that use a CRM the most are typically sales, marketing, and service. Bring these teams together to understand better how each one will use the tool and what existing tools, if any, each department is already using. For example, a marketing manager is using Mailchimp to send weekly promotional emails and keeps 20 GB of marketing collateral in Dropbox, which is not accessible by anyone else.

Knowing these details will help when it comes time to identify CRM requirements. If you continue to use Mailchimp, you want a CRM that integrates with it. You also may want a CRM with high or no storage limits if you plan to house marketing collateral in the software for easier access for everyone.

Team Goals

To evaluate the performance of your team, set goals for each group — such as sales — that will be using the CRM. These goals should tie in with your overall business objectives. Knowing these goals will not only set employee expectations, but they will also inform the requirements needed for the CRM.

For example, a software company's goal may be to close 80% of the demos it provides; however, it's only closing 60%. The company determines that part of this gap results from inadequate post-demo follow up. Thus they will want a CRM that can send automated follow up emails for better engagement post demo. The effectiveness of these emails can then be tracked with a CRM that has this capability.

Set Smart Goals to Track Performance Effectively

As you define your goals, make sure each one is SMART, which stands for Specific, Measurable, Attainable, Relevant, and Time-bound. There are variations of each letter so you might see achievable for attainable, but they're defining the same thing.

- Specific: Sell $150,000 in new business in the Northwest region this quarter.
- Measurable: Tracking and measuring progress towards goals was one of the reasons CRMs were created. Whether you're managing yourself or a sales rep., you need to know at any time how an individual or region is performing. The CRM should track progress towards the sales goal showing sales achieved to quota at any point during the quarter.
- Attainable: Is $150,000 based on a whim or is it backed up by past performance or another objective indicator? Either way, it has to be believed to be attainable by the person setting the goal and the one tasked with achieving it or else it will never happen.
- Relevant: Does the goal align with other sales goals in relation to the overall growth goals of the company? If not, it needs to be adjusted or rethought.
- Time-bound: The goal needs to have time parameters in place that puts the goal into perspective. If you have a quarter to close $150,000, you won't expect to close all of that business in the first week. The target date instead allows you to work backward from that date to determine everything you'll need to do to achieve it such as setting five meetings a week to close one deal a week.

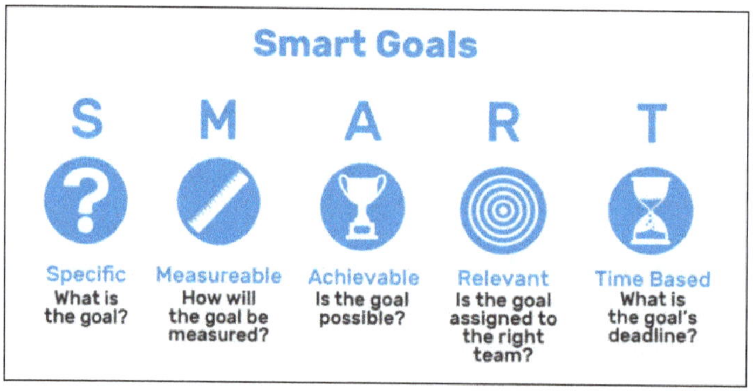

Establish Key Performance Indicators

Key performance indicators (KPIs) are simply metrics used to measure the performance of a person, team, and organization as they relate to their goals. The KPIs selected should tie directly to your company's overall goals and strategy. KPIs can be tracked with different CRM analytics like "close by lead type," "month-to-date sales vs. quota," and so on.

At the top level of a company, KPIs are typically broad like increasing revenue by 25% each month. At the mid-level, a sales team might have a departmental goal of increasing product demos by 20%. KPIs at this level help both goal achievement and building team cohesion. For an individual salesperson, it could be more specific to the success of that person as it relates to their specific targets.

For example, a salesperson with a $150,000 quarterly sales quota will need to set up 30 meetings each month to close on average five customers. In this case, the 30 monthly meetings are a KPI because it ties back to their quarterly sales quota. These metrics can be tracked and measured with a CRM easily.

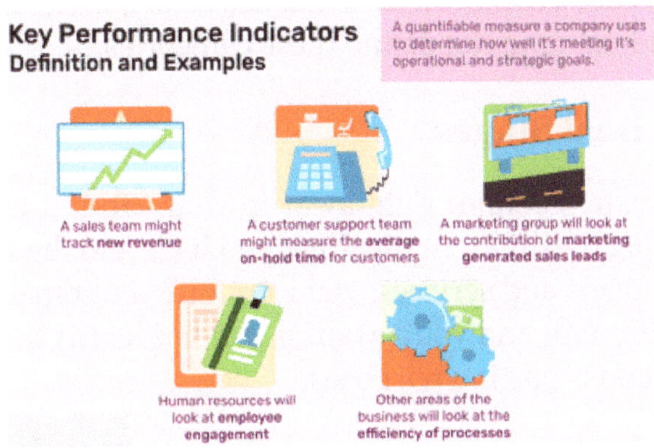

CRM Components

This is the more granular stage of the CRM strategy where you define the who, what, and how. It includes defining contacts, creating pipelines and deal stages, identifying requirements and selecting any additional software necessary for a successful sales team. These actions don't have to be created in the CRM initially, though it may help to visualize everything. If you haven't selected a platform yet, create these steps in writing until you do.

Contacts, Leads, Prospects and Opportunities

If you've used a CRM before you know how quickly it can get over-stuffed with contacts from various sources. Because not all of these need to be in your CRM, define what makes a good contact. At a minimum, it should be someone with a full name, email, and phone number. Some CRMs even require all of these before you can create a contact.

A lead may be someone who downloaded an ebook from your site. A prospect is someone who has the types of challenges that your company solves, which you may know because you met them at a tradeshow. An opportunity can be someone who has a challenge you can solve and is considering your company to help them solve it.

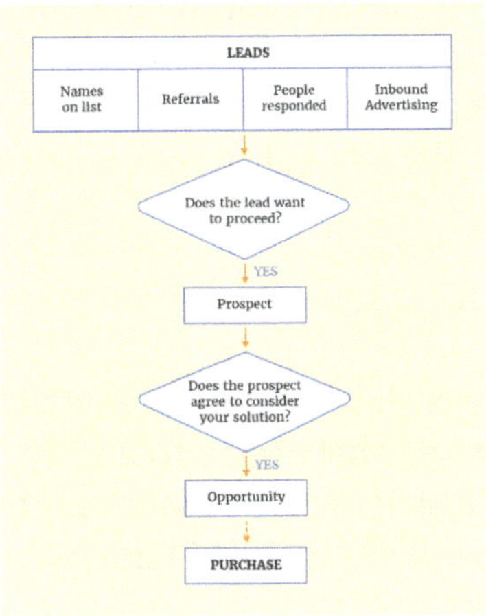

The best CRM software let you customize how you categorize a contact with the use of properties. In other words, you can identify them as a lead, prospect, opportunity or whatever label you want to use. Keep in mind, however, that some CRMs have different definitions for all of these. For example, some platforms consider a contact a lead that has been qualified. Depending on which CRM you use, you may have to adjust how you define these categories.

Create Pipelines and Deal Stages

While you don't need to create pipelines right away in your CRM, it may help to see them "live." More important is identifying the different pipelines you have and the stages involved in each one. For example, if you sell products and services, you want different pipelines for each. The stages in the sales process will be different, and you'll want a way to identify and track these separately in the CRM for management and reporting purposes.

Within each pipeline, list all of the steps necessary to take a contact from lead to customer. These are things like first contact, discovery call, demo, proposal review, and so on. If you've created a sales process, these should be easy to plug in.

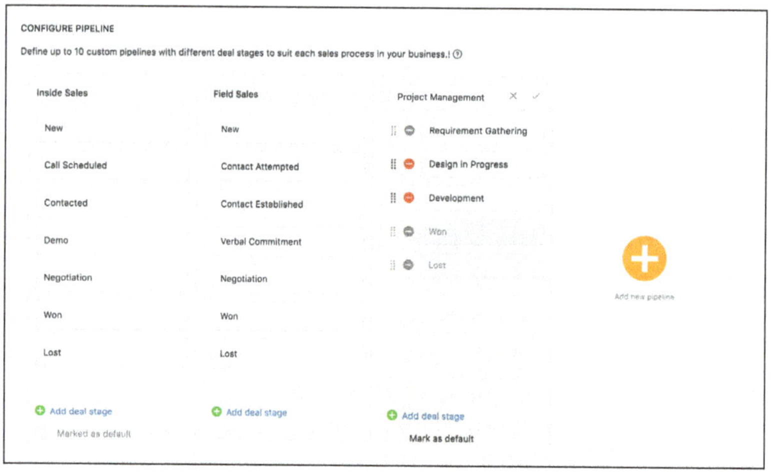

Creating multiple pipelines with different deal stages

Identify the Software Requirements

Identify the requirements you'll need for the CRM by meeting with the sales, marketing, and service teams. What software are these teams using currently? Do they need to integrate with the CRM? Are they looking for new capabilities? For example, sales might need Gmail integration capability, as they would like the ability to send simple, automated emails to follow up with demo customers.

Selecting the Right CRM Software

There are dozens of CRM platforms each with their strengths and weaknesses with varying costs. For a small business CRM, expect to pay between $10 and $50 a month per user. Some are more specifically designed for specific industries while others have tools like social media integration or marketing automation built in. Understand the capabilities you need by discussing with your sales, marketing, and service teams.

Review and Research Requirements

For example, to learn more about how a CRM differs from marketing automation visit "The Difference between CRM vs. Marketing Automation." Review the requirements from the previous stage on building your system. Are there specific must-haves you need such as integration with Outlook or data integration requirements? Make a list of these. Then use sites like Fitsmallbusiness.com to compare the different features, use cases, and user reviews.

Test Drive CRMs

Once you've narrowed down a handful of CRMs that meet your requirements, review all the features, costs, and upgrade capabilities. Most offer 30-day free trials. Sign up for a few of these to get initial impressions. Then request a demo with the company and be sure to include department managers so they can ask questions.

Customer Portfolio

A customer portfolio is a tool for B2B companies to develop customer relationships that are profitable and sustainable. The process starts by identifying all your company's customers and evaluating them using meaningful criteria.

To analyze your company's customers and customer relationships, you'll first have to define the evaluation criteria. The criteria should cover the most important aspects that tell you whether a customer relationship is worth pursuing.

Here is, for example, a list of criteria you might consider:

Basic Information of the Customer

- Name of the company.
- Customer's business–investor, governmental organization, municipal organization, manufacturer, contractor, consultant, etc.
- Persons who are involved in the relationship on your customer's and on your company's side.

Evaluation Criteria

- Type of the customer relationship–a partnership, recurring, occasional, or endangered.
- Customer service needs–total service, specialized, or basic service.
- Customer's decision criteria when selecting suppliers–price of purchase, total lifecycle cost, ease of purchase, trust, quality of the supplier, etc.
- Our portion of the customer's related purchases–small, medium, large.

- Customer profitability—high, moderate, low (if you have actual figures of the profitability, use them).
- Potential of additional sales—high, moderate, low, none.
- Ease of collaboration with the customer—easy, average, challenging.
- Customer's own business prospects—failing, stabile, growing.
- R&D collaboration with the customer—ongoing, emerging, none.
- Learning opportunities for us—high, moderate, low.

Financial Information

- Billings—total billing or billing broken down to service categories.
- Change in billings—billing compared to the previous year and projection for the next 12 months.

The Evaluation

Once you have all the information in one place, you can do various types of analysis. The purpose of the analysis is to discover differences and similarities among different customers. This helps determine your business strategy, customer portfolio, and customer relationship plan.

When analyzing their customer portfolio companies, it can often be seen how a small number of customers are actually creating the profits. On the other hand, less profitable customers can be necessary for other reasons.

Most companies lose 45 to 50 percent of their customers in five years. Acquiring new customers can cost 20 times more than does retaining the existing ones. A five percent increase in customer retention can increase the companies' profits by 25 to 85 percent. It is therefore important to carefully analyze if and how low-performance customer relationships could be improved.

If you finally conclude that some customer relationships are never going to be valuable, make a clear decision to break them off. Underperforming customer relationships steal time and money from more productive business endeavors. They are not good for the customer either. When you are not able and willing to give your fullest to customers, they will notice.

Customer Portfolio Management

Customer portfolio management (CPM) aims to optimize business performance – whether that means sales growth, enhanced customer profitability, or something else – across the entire customer base. It does this by offering differentiated value propositions to different segments of customers. For example, the UK-based NatWest Bank manages its business customers on a portfolio basis. It has split customers into three segments based upon their size, lifetime value and creditworthiness.

Basic Disciplines for CPM

In this section, you'll read about a number of basic disciplines that can be useful during CPM. These include market segmentation, sales forecasting, activity-based costing, customer lifetime value estimation and data mining.

Market Segmentation

CPM can make use of a discipline that is routinely employed by marketing management: market segmentation. Market segmentation can be defined as Market Segmentation is the process of dividing up a market into more-or-less homogenous subsets for which it is possible to create different value propositions.

At the end of the process the company can decide which segment(s) it wants to serve. If it chooses, each segment can be served with a different value proposition and managed in a different way. Market segmentation processes can be used during CPM for two main purposes. They can be used to segment potential markets to identify which customers to acquire, and to cluster current customers with a view to offering differentiated value propositions supported by different relationship management strategies.

We'll focus on the application of market segmentation processes to identify which customers to acquire. What distinguishes market segmentation for this CRM purpose is its very clear focus on customer value. The outcome of the process should be the identification of the value potential of each identified segment. Companies will want to identify and target customers that can generate profit in the future: these will be those customers that the company and its network are better placed to serve and satisfy than their competitors.

Market segmentation in many companies is highly intuitive. The marketing team will develop profiles of customer groups based upon their insight and experience. This is then used to guide the development of marketing strategies across the segments. In a CRM context, market segmentation is highly data dependent. The data might be generated internally or sourced externally. Internal data from marketing, sales and finance records are often enhanced with additional data from external sources such as marketing research companies, partner organizations in the company's network and data specialists.

- Intuitive
    - Brain-storm segmentation variables
- Age, gender, lifestyle,
- SIC, size, location,
    - Produce word-profiles,
    - Compute sizes of segments,
    - Assess company/segment fit,
    - Make targeting decision.

- One/several/all segments.
- Data-based:
    - Obtain customer data Internal and external,
    - Analyse customer data,
    - Identify high/medium/low-value customer segments,
    - Profile customers within segments age, gender, lifestyle.
- SIC, size, location:
    - Assess company/segment fit,
    - Make targeting decision one/several/all segments.

The market segmentation process can be broken down into a number of steps:

- Identify the business you are in,
- Identify relevant segmentation variables,
- Analyse the market using these variables,
- Assess the value of the market segments,
- Select target markets to serve.

Identify the Business

This is an important strategic question to which many, but not all, companies have an answer. Ted Levitt's classic article, 'Marketing Myopia' warned companies of the dangers of thinking only in terms of product-oriented answers. He wrote of a nineteenth century company that defined itself as being in the buggy-whip industry. It has not survived. It is important to consider the answer from the customer point of view. For example, is Blockbuster in the video-rental business or some other business, perhaps home entertainment or retailing? Is a manufacturer of kitchen cabinets in the timber processing industry, or the home-improvement business?

A customer-oriented answer to the question will enable companies to move through the market segmentation process because it helps identify the boundaries of the market served, it defines the benefits customers seek, and it picks out the company's competitors.

Let's assume that the kitchen furniture company has defined its business from the customer's perspective. It believes it is in the home value improvement business. It knows from research that customers buy its products for one major reason: they are home owners who want to enhance the value of their properties. The company is now in a position to identify its markets and competitors at three levels:

1. Benefit competitors: Other companies delivering the same benefit to customers. These might include window replacement companies, heating and air-conditioning companies and bathroom renovation companies.

2. Product competitors: Other companies marketing kitchens to customers seeking the same benefit.
3. Geographic competitors: These are benefit and product competitors operating in the same geographic territory.

Identify Relevant Segmentation Variables and Analyse the Market

There are many variables that are used to segment consumer and organizational markets. Companies can enjoy competitive advantage through innovations in market segmentation. For example, before Häagen-Dazs, it was known that ice-cream was a seasonally sold product aimed primarily at children. Häagen-Dazs upset this logic by targeting an adult consumer group with a different, luxurious product, and all-year- round purchasing potential. We'll look at consumer markets first.

Consumer Markets

Consumers can be clustered according to a number of shared characteristics. These can be grouped into user attributes and usage attributes.

In recent years there has been a trend away from simply using demographic attributes to segment consumer markets. The concern has been that there is too much variance within each of the demographic clusters to regard all members of the segment as more-or-less homogenous. For example, some 30–40 year olds have families and mortgaged homes; others live in rented apartments and go clubbing at weekends. Some members of religious groups are traditionalists; others are progressives.

User Attributes

Demographic attributes: age, gender, occupational status, household size, marital status, terminal educational age, household income, stage of family lifecycle, religion, ethnic origin, nationality. Geographica attributes: country, region, TV region, city, city size, postcode, residential neighbourhood Psychographic attributes: lifestyle, personality.

Usage Attributes

1. Benefits sought, volume consumed, share of category spend:

   The family lifecycle (FLC) idea has been particularly threatened. The FLC traces the development of a person's life along a path from young and single, to married with no children, married with young children, married couples with older children, older married couples with no children at home, empty nesters still in employment, retired empty nester couples, to sole survivor working or not working. Life for many, if not most people, does not follow this path. It fails to take account of the many and varied life choices that people make: some people never marry, others marry late, there are also childless couples, gay and lesbian partnerships, extended families, single-parent households and divorced couples.

   Let's look at some of the variables that can be used to define market segments. Occupational status is widely used to classify people into social grades. Systems vary around the world.

In the UK, the JICNARS social grading system is employed. This allocates households to one of six categories (A, B, C1, C2, D and E) depending on the job of the head of household. Higher managerial occupations are ranked A; casual, unskilled workers are ranked E. Media owners often use the JICNARS scale to profile their audiences.

A number of data analysis companies have developed geodemographic classification schemes. CACI, for example, has developed ACORN which allocates individuals, households and postcodes to one of the five categories shown in Figure, and beyond into 17 groups and 56 types. ACORN data suggest that clusters of like households exhibit similar buying behaviours. This clustering outcome is based on data covering over 400 variables, from online behaviour to housing type, education and family structure.

Lifestyle research became popular in the 1980s. Rather than using a single descriptive category to classify customers as had been the case with demographics, it uses multivariate analysis to cluster customers. Lifestyle analysts collect data about people's activities, interests and opinions. A lifestyle survey instrument may require answers to 400 or 500 questions, taking several hours to complete. Using analytical processes such as factor analysis and cluster analysis, the researchers are able to produce lifestyle or psychographic profiles. The assertion is made that we buy products because of their fi t with our chosen lifestyles. Lifestyle studies have been done in many countries, as well as across national boundaries. A number of companies conduct lifestyle research on a commercial basis and sell the results to their clients.

1. Wealthy achievers	25.4%
2. Urban prosperity	11.5%
3. Comfortably off	27.4%
4. Moderate means	13.8%
5. Hard pressed	21.2%
6. Unclassified	0.7%

2. The number represents the % of UK households falling into each category:

Usage attributes can be particularly useful for CRM purposes. Benefit segmentation has become a standard tool for marketing managers. It is axiomatic that customers buy products for the benefits they deliver, not for the products themselves. Nobody has ever bought a 5 mm drill bit because they want a 5 mm drill bit. They buy because of what the drill bit can deliver: a 5 mm hole. CRM practitioners need to understand the benefits that are sought by the markets they serve. The market for toothpaste, for example, can be segmented along benefit lines. There are three major benefit segments: white teeth, fresh breath, and healthy teeth and gums. When it comes to creating value propositions for the chosen customers, benefit segmentation becomes very important.

The other two usage attributes, volume consumed and share of category spend, are also useful from a CRM perspective. Many companies classify their customers according to the volume of business they produce. For example, in the B2C context, McDonald's USA found that 77 percent of their sales are to males aged 18 to 34 who eat at McDonald's three to five times per week, despite the company's mission to be the world's favourite family restaurant. Assuming that they contribute in equal proportion to the bottom line, these are customers that the company must not lose. The volume they provide allows the company to operate very cost-effectively, keeping unit costs low.

Companies that rank customers into tiers according to volume, and are then able to identify which customers fall into each tier, may be able to develop customer migration plans to move lower volume customers higher up the ladder from first-time customer to repeat customer, majority customer, loyal customer, and onwards to advocate status. This only makes sense when the lower volume customers present an opportunity. The key question is whether they buy product from other suppliers in the category. For example, customer Jones buys five pairs of shoes a year. She only buys one of those pairs from 'Shoes4less' retail outlets. She therefore presents a greater opportunity than customer

3. Smith who buys two pairs a year, but both of them from Shoes4less:

Shoes4less has the opportunity to win four more sales from Jones, but none from Smith. This does not necessarily mean that Jones is more valuable than Smith. That depends on the answers to other questions. First, how much will it cost to switch Jones from her current shoe retailer, and what will it cost to retain Smith's business? Secondly, what are the margins earned from these customers? If Jones is very committed to her other supplier, it may not be worth trying to switch her. If Smith buys high margin fashion and leisure footwear and Jones buys low margin footwear, then Smith might be the better opportunity despite the lower volume of sales.

Most segmentation programmes employ more than one variable. For example, a chain of bars may define its customers on the basis of geography, age and music preference. Figure shows how the market for chocolate can be segmented by usage occasion and satisfaction. Four major segments emerge from this bivariate segmentation of the market.

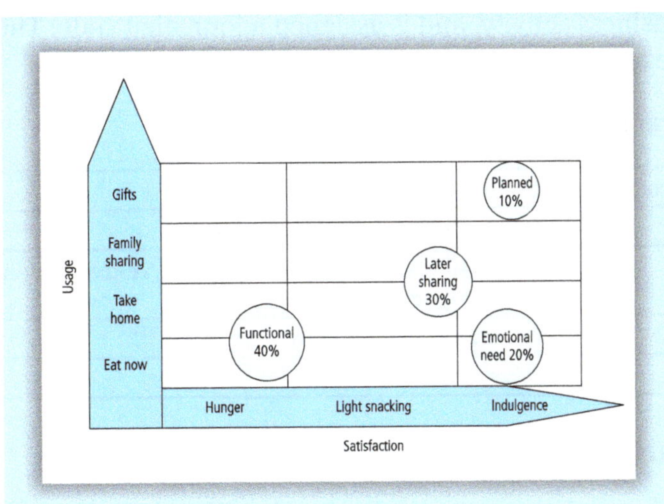

Bivariate segmentation of the chocolate market

Business Markets

Business markets can also be segmented in a number of ways, as shown in table.

The basic starting point for most B2B segmentation is the International Standard Industrial Classification (ISIC), which is a property of the United Nations Statistics Division. While this is a standard that is in widespread use, some countries have developed their own schemes. In the USA, Canada and Mexico, there is the North American Industry Classification System (NAICS). A 1400 page NAICS manual was published in 2007. In New Zealand and Australia there is the Australia and New Zealand Standard Industrial Classification (ANZSIC).

Business market segmentation criteria	Illustration
International Standard Industrial Classification	An internationally agreed standard for classifying goods and service producers.
Dispersion	Geographically concentrated or dispersed.
Size	Large, medium, small businesses: classified by number of employees, number of customers, profit or turnover.
Account status	Global account, National account, Regional account, A or B or C class accounts.
Account value	<$50 000 <$100 000 < $200 000, < $500 000.
Buying processes	Open tender, sealed bid, internet auction, centralized, de-centralized.
Buying criteria	Continuity of supply (reliability), product quality, price, customization, just-in-time, service support before or after sale.
Propensity to switch	Satisfied with current suppliers, dissatisfied.
Share of customer spend in the category	Sole supplier, majority supplier, minority supplier, non-supplier.
Geography	City, region, country, trading bloc (ASEAN, EU).
Buying style	Risk averse, innovator.

The ISIC classifies all forms of economic activity. Each business entity is classified according to its principal product or business activity, and is assigned a four-digit code. These are then amalgamated into 99 major categories.

Table: Illustrates several four-digit codes.

ISIC 4-digit code	Activity
1200	Mining of uranium and thorium ores
2511	Manufacture of rubber tyres and tubes; re-treading and rebuilding of rubber tyres
5520	Restaurants, bars and canteens
8030	Higher education

Customer Relationship Management

Governments and trade associations often collect and publish information that indicates the size of each ISIC code. This can be a useful to guide when answering the question, 'Which customers should we acquire?' However, targeting in the B2B context is often conducted not at the aggregated level of the ISIC, but at an individual account level. The question is not so much, 'Do we want to serve this segment?' as much as 'Do we want to serve this customer?'

Several of these account-level segmentation variables are specifically important for CRM purposes: account value, share of category (share of wallet) spend and propensity-to-switch.

Account Value

Most businesses have a scheme for classifying their customers according to their value. The majority of these schemes associate value with some measure of sales revenue or volume. This is not an adequate measure of value, because it takes no account of the costs to win and keep the customer.

Share of Wallet

Share of category spend gives an indication of the future potential that exists within the account. A supplier with only a 15 percent share of a customer company's spending on some raw material has, on the face of it, considerable potential.

Propensity-to-Switch

Propensity-to-switch may be high or low. It is possible to measure propensity-to-switch by assessing satisfaction with the current supplier, and by computing switching costs. Dissatisfaction alone does not indicate a high propensity to switch. Switching costs may be so high that even in the face of high levels of dissatisfaction, the customer does not switch. For example, customers may be unhappy with the performance of their telecommunications supplier, but may not switch because of the disruption that such a change would bring about.

Assess the Value in a Market Segment and Select which Markets to Serve

A number of target market alternatives should emerge from the market segmentation process. The potential of these to generate value for the company will need to be assessed.

The potential value of the segmentation opportunities depends upon answers to two questions:

- How attractive is the opportunity?
- How well placed is the company and its network to exploit the opportunity?

In figure identifies a number of the attributes that can be taken into account during this appraisal. The attractiveness of a market segment is related to a number of issues, including its size and growth potential, the number of competitors and the intensity of competition between them, the barriers to entry, and the propensity of customers to switch from their existing suppliers. The question of company fit revolves around the issue of the relative competitive competency of the company and its network members to satisfy the requirements of the segment.

- Segment attractiveness
    - Size of segment, segment growth rate, price sensitivity of customers, bargaining power of customers, customers' current relationships with suppliers, barriers to segment entry, barriers to segment exit, number and power of competitors, prospect of new entrants, potential for differentiation, propensity for customer switching.

- Company and network fit
    - Does the opportunity fit the company's objectives, mission, vision and values? Does the company and its network possess the operational, marketing, technological, people and other competencies, and liquidity to exploit the opportunity.

In principle, if the segment is attractive and the company and network competencies indicate a good fit, the opportunity may be worth pursuing. However, because many companies find that they have several opportunities, some kind of scoring process must be developed and applied to identify the more valuable opportunities. The matrix in figure can be used for this purpose. To begin with, companies need to identify attributes that indicate the attractiveness of a market segment (some are listed in figure), and the competencies of the company and its network. An importance weight is agreed for each attribute. The segment opportunity is rated against each attribute and a score is computed. The opportunities can then be mapped into figure.

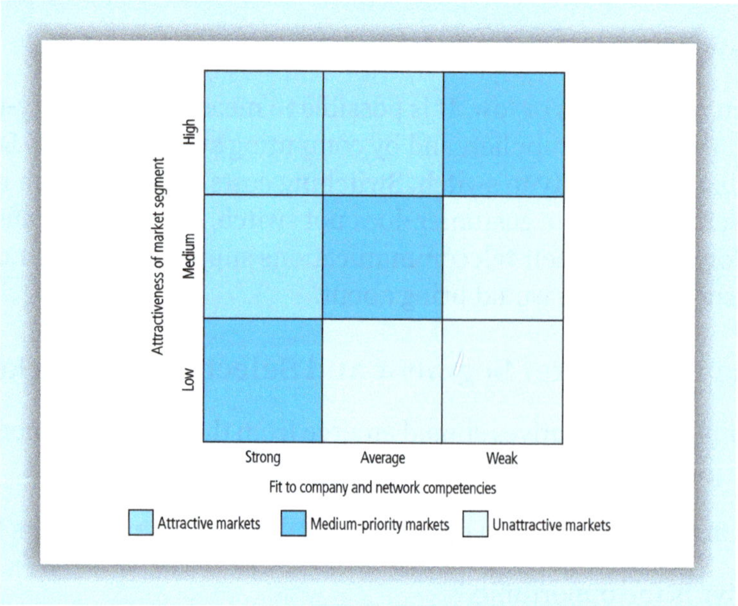

McKinsey/General Electric customer portfolio matrix

Sales Forecasting

The second discipline that can be used for CPM is sales forecasting. One major issue commonly facing companies that conduct CPM is that the data available for clustering customers takes a historical or, at best, present day view. The data identifies those customers who have been, or presently are, important for sales, profit or other strategic reasons. If management believes the future will be the same as the past, this presents no problem. However, if the business environment is changeable, this does present a problem. Because CPMs goal is to identify those customers that will be strategically important in the future, sales forecasting can be a useful discipline.

Sales forecasting, some pessimists argue, is a waste of time, because the business environment is rapidly changing and unpredictable. Major world events such as terrorist attacks, war, drought and market-based changes, such as new products from competitors or high visibility promotional campaigns, can make any sales forecasts invalid.

There are a number of sales forecasting techniques that can be applied, providing useful information for CPM. These techniques, which fall into three major groups, are appropriate for different circumstances.

- Qualitative methods:
  - Customer surveys
  - Sales team estimates.
- Time-series methods:
  - Moving average
  - Exponential smoothing
  - Time-series decomposition.
- Causal methods:
  - Leading indicators
  - Regression models.

Qualitative methods are probably the most widely used forecasting methods. Customer surveys ask consumers or purchasing officers to give an opinion on what they are likely to buy in the forecasting period. This makes sense when customers forward-plan their purchasing. Data can be obtained by inserting a question into a customer satisfaction survey. For example, 'In the next six months are you likely to buy more, the same or less from us than in the current period?' And, 'If more, or less, what volume do you expect to buy from us?' Sometimes, third party organizations such as industry associations or trans-industry groups such as the Chamber of Commerce or the Institute of Directors collect data that indicate future buying intentions or proxies for intention, such as business confidence.

Sales team estimates can be useful when salespeople have built close relationships with their customers. A key account management team might be well placed to generate several individual forecasts from the team membership. These can be averaged or weighted in some way that reflects the estimator's closeness to the customer. Account managers for Dyno Nobel, a supplier of commercial explosives for the mining and quarrying industries, are so close to their customers that they are able to forecast sales two to three years ahead.

Operational CRM systems support the qualitative sales forecasting methods, in particular sales team estimates. The CRM system takes into account the value of the sale, the probability of closing the sale and the anticipated period to closure. Many CRM systems also allow management to adjust the estimates of their sales team members, to allow for overly optimistic or pessimistic salespeople.

Time-series approaches take historical data and extrapolate them forward in a linear or curvilinear trend. This approach makes sense when there are historical sales data, and the assumption can be safely made that the future will reflect the past. The moving average method is the simplest of these. This takes sales in a number of previous periods and averages them. The averaging process reduces or eliminates random variation. The moving average is computed on successive periods of data, moving on one period at a time, as in Figure. Moving averages based on different periods can be calculated on historic data to generate an accurate method. A variation is to weight the more recent periods more heavily.

Year	Sales volumes	2-year moving average	4-year moving average
2002	4830		
2003	4930		
2004	4870	4880	
2005	5210	4900	
2006	5330	5040	4960
2007	5660	5270	5085
2008	5440	5495	5267
2009		5550	5410

The rationale is that more recent periods are better predictors.

In producing an estimate for year 2009 in Figure, one could weight the previous four years' sales performance by 0.4, 0.3, 0.2, and 0.1, respectively, to reach an estimate. This would generate a forecast of 5461. This approach is called exponential smoothing.

The decomposition method is applied when there is evidence of cyclical or seasonal patterns in the historical data. The method attempts to separate out four components of the time series: trend factor, cyclical factor, seasonal factor and random factor. The trend factor is the long- term direction of the trend after the other three elements are removed. The cyclical factor represents regular long-term recurrent influences on sales; seasonal influences generally occur within annual cycles.

It is sometimes possible to predict sales using leading indicators. A leading indicator is some contemporary activity or event that indicates that another activity or event will happen in the future. At a macro level, for example, housing starts are good predictors of future sales of kitchen furniture. At a micro level, when a credit card customer calls into a contact centre to ask about the current rate of interest, this is a strong indicator that the customer will switch to another supplier in the future.

Regression models work by employing data on a number of predictor variables to estimate future demand. The variable being predicted is called the dependent variable; the variables being used as predictors are called independent variables. For example, if you wanted to predict demand for cars (the dependent variable) you might use data on population size, average disposable income, average car price for the category being predicted and average fuel price (the independent variables). The regression equation can be tested and validated on historical data before being adopted. New predictor variables can be substituted or added to see if they improve the accuracy of the forecast. This can be a useful approach for predicting demand from a segment.

Activity-Based Costing

The third discipline that is useful for CPM is activity-based costing. Many companies, particularly those in a B2B context, can trace revenues to customers. In a B2C environment, it is usually only possible to trace revenues to identifiable customers if the company operates a billing system requiring customer details, or a membership scheme such as a customer club, store-card or a loyalty programed.

In a B2B context, revenues can be tracked in the sales and accounts databases. Costs are an entirely different matter. Because the goal of CPM is to cluster customers according to their strategic value, it is desirable to be able to identify which customers are, or will be, profitable. Clearly, if a company is to understand customer profitability, it has to be able to trace costs, as well as revenues, to customers.

Costs do vary from customer to customer. Some customers are very costly to acquire and serve, others are not. There can be considerable variance across the customer base within several categories of cost:

- Customer acquisition costs: Some customers require considerable sales effort to move them from prospect to first-time customer status: more sales calls, visits to reference customer sites, free samples, engineering advice, guarantees that switching costs will be met by the vendor.
- Terms of trade: Price discounts, advertising and promotion support, slotting allowances (cash paid to retailers for shelf space), extended invoice due dates.
- Customer service costs: Handling queries, claims and complaints, demands on salespeople and contact centre, small order sizes, high order frequency, just-in-time delivery, part load shipments, breaking bulk for delivery to multiple sites.
- Working capital costs: Carrying inventory for the customer, cost of credit.

Traditional product based or general ledger costing systems do not provide this type of detail, and do not enable companies to estimate customer profitability. Product costing systems track material, labour and energy costs to products, often comparing actual to standard costs. They do not, however, cover the customer-facing activities of marketing, sales and service. General ledger costing systems do track costs across all parts of the business, but are normally too highly aggregated to establish which customers or segments are responsible for generating those costs.

Activity-based costing (ABC) is an approach to costing that splits costs into two groups: volume-based costs and order-related costs. Volume-based (product-related) costs are variable against the size of the order, but fixed per unit for any order and any customer. Material and direct labour costs are examples. Order-related (customer-related) costs vary according to the product and process requirements of each particular customer.

Imagine two retail customers, each purchasing the same volumes of product from a manufacturer. Customer 1 makes no product or process demands. The sales revenue is $5000; the gross margin for the vendor is $1000. Customer 2 is a different story: customized product, special overprinted outer packaging, just-in-time delivery to three sites, provision of point-of-sale material, sale or return conditions and discounted price. Not only that, but Customer 2 spends a lot of time agreeing these terms and conditions with a salesperson who has had to call three times before closing the sale. The sales revenue is $5000, but after accounting for product and process costs to meet the demands of this particular customer, the margin retained by the vendor is $250. Other things being equal, Customer 1 is four times as valuable as Customer 2.

Whereas conventional cost accounting practices report what was spent, ABC reports what the money was spent doing. Whereas the conventional general ledger approach to costing identifies resource costs such as payroll, equipment and materials, the ABC approach shows what was being done when these costs were incurred.

ABC gives the manager of the claims-processing department a much clearer idea of which activities create cost. The next question from a CPM perspective is 'which customers create the activity? ' Put another way, which customers are the cost drivers? If you were to examine the activity cost item ' Analyse claims: $121 000 ' and find that 80 percent of the claims were made by drivers under the age of 20, you'd have a clear understanding of the customer group that was creating that activity cost for the business.

CRM needs ABC because of its overriding goal of generating profitable relationships with customers. Unless there is a costing system in place to trace costs to customers, CRM will find it very difficult to deliver on a promise of improved customer profitability.

Overall, ABC serves customer portfolio management in a number of ways:

1. When combined with revenue figures, it tells you the absolute and relative levels of profit generated by each customer, segment or cohort.
2. It guides you towards actions that can be taken to return customers to profit.
3. It helps prioritize and direct customer acquisition, retention and development strategies.
4. It helps establish whether customization and other forms of value creation for customers pay off.

ABC sometimes justifies management's confidence in the Pareto principle, otherwise known as the 80:20 rule. This rule suggests that 80 percent of profits come from 20 percent of customers. ABC tells you which customers fall into the important 20 percent. Research generally supports the 80:20 rule. For example, one report from Coopers and Lybrand found that, in the retail industry, the top 4 percent of customers account for 29 percent of profits, the next 26 percent of customers account for 55 percent of profits and the remaining 70 percent account for only 16 percent of profits.

Lifetime Value Estimation

The fourth discipline that can be used for CPM is customer lifetime value (LTV) estimation. LTV is measured by computing the present day value of all net margins (gross margins less cost-to-serve) earned from a relationship with a customer, segment or cohort. LTV estimates provide important insights that guide companies in their customer management strategies. Clearly, companies want to protect and ring-fence their relationships with customers, segments or cohorts that will generate significant amounts of profit.

Sunil Gupta and Donald Lehmann suggest that customer lifetime value can be computed as follows:

$$LTV = m = \left(\frac{r}{1+i-r} \right)$$

LTV = lifetime value

m = margin or profit from a customer per period (e.g. per year)

r = retention rate (e.g. 0.8 or 80%)

i = discount rate (e.g. 0.12 or 12%)

This means that LTV is equal to the margin (m) multiplied by the factor $r/(1 + i - r)$. This factor is referred to as the margin multiple, and is determined by both the customer retention rate (r) and the discount rate (i). For most companies the retention rate is in the region of 60 to 90 percent. The weighted average cost of capital (WACC), is generally used to determine the discount rate. The discount rate is applied to bring future margins back to today's value. Table presents some sample margin multiples based on the two variables: customer retention rate and discount rate.

Retention rate	Discount rate			
	10%	12%	14%	16%
60%	1.20	1.15	1.11	1.07
70%	1.75	1.67	1.59	1.52
80%	2.67	2.50	2.35	2.22
90%	4.50	4.09	3.75	3.46

For example, at a 12 percent discount rate and 80 percent retention rate the margin multiple is 2.5. From this table, you can see that margin multiples for most companies, given a WACC of 10 to 16 percent, and retention rates between 60 and 90 percent, are between 1.07X and 4.5X. When the discount rate is high, the margin multiple is lower. When customer retention rates are higher, margin multiples are higher.

The table can be used to compute customer value in this way. If you have a customer retention rate of 90 percent and your WACC is 12 percent and your customer generates $100 margin in a year, the LTV of the customer is about $400 (or $409 to be precise; i.e. 4.09 times$100). The same mathematics can be applied to segments or cohorts of customers. Your company may serve two clusters of customers, A and B. Customers from cluster A each generate annual margin of $400; cluster B customers each generate $200 margin. Retention rates vary between clusters. Cluster A has a retention rate of 80 percent; cluster B customers have a retention rate of 90 percent. If the same WACC of 12 percent is applied to both clusters, then the LTV of a customer from cohort A is $1000 ($400 X 2.50), and the LTV of a cohort B customer is $818 ($200 X 4.09). If you have 500 customers in cluster A, and 1000 customers in cluster B, the LTV of your customer base is $1 318 000, computed thus: ((500 X $1000) + (1000 X $818)).

The table can be used to assess the impact of a number of customer management strategies: what would be the impact of reducing cost-to-serve by shifting customers to low-cost self-serve channels? What would be the result of cross-selling higher margin products? What would be the outcome of a loyalty programme designed to increase retention rate from 80 to 82 percent?

An important additional benefit of this LTV calculation is that it enables you to estimate a company's value. For example, it has been computed that the LTV of the average US-based American Airlines customer is $166.94. American Airlines has 43.7 million such customers, yielding an estimated company value of $7.3 billion. Roland Rust and his co-researchers noted that, given the absence of international passengers and freight considerations from this computation, it was remarkably close to the company's market capitalization at the time their research was undertaken.

Data Mining

The fifth discipline that can be used for CPM is data mining. It has particular value when you are trying to find patterns or relationships in large volumes of data, as found in B2C contexts such as retailing, banking and home shopping.

An international retailing operation like Tesco, for example, has over 14 million Clubcard members in its UK customer base. Not only does the company have the demographic data that the customer provided on becoming a club member, but also the customer's transactional data. If ten million club members use Tesco in a week and purchase an average basket of 30 items, Tesco's database grows by 300 million pieces of data per week. This is certainly a huge cost, but potentially a major benefit.

Data mining can be thought of as the creation of intelligence from large quantities of data.

Customer portfolio management needs intelligent answers to questions such as these:

1. How can we segment the market to identify potential customers?
2. How can we cluster our current customers?
3. Which customers offer the greatest potential for the future?
4. Which customers are most likely to switch?

Data mining can involve the use of statistically advanced techniques, but fortunately managers do not need to be technocrats. It is generally sufficient to understand what the tools can do, how to interpret the results, and how to perform data mining.

Two of the major vendors of data mining tools have developed models to guide users through the data mining process. SAS promotes a five-step data mining process called SEMMA (sample, explore, modify, model, assess) and SPSS opts for the 5As (assess, access, analyse, act and automate). These models, though different in detail, essentially promote a common step-wise approach. The first step involves defining the business problem. Then you have to create a data mining database. Best practice involves extracting historical data from the data warehouse, creating a special mining data mart, and exploring that dataset for the patterns and relationships that can solve your business problem. The problem-solving step involves an iterative process of model-building, testing and refinement. Data miners often divide their dataset into two subsets. One is used for model training, i.e. estimating the model parameters, and the other is used for model validation. Once a model is developed that appears to solve the business problem, it can be adopted by management. As new data is loaded into the data warehouse, further subsets can be extracted to the data mining data mart and the model can be subjected to further refinement.

A number of different data mining tools are applicable to CPM problems: clustering, decision trees and neural networks.

Clustering

Clustering techniques are used to find naturally occurring groupings within a dataset. As applied to customer data, these techniques generally function as follows:

1. Each customer is allocated to just one group. The customer possesses attributes that are more closely associated with that group than any other group.
2. Each group is relatively homogenous.
3. The groups collectively are very different from each other.

In other words, clustering techniques generally try to maximize both within-group homogeneity and between-group heterogeneity. There are a number of clustering techniques, including CART (classification and regression trees) and CHAID (chi-square automatic interaction detection). Once statistically homogenous clusters have been formed they need to be interpreted.

CRM strategists are often interested in the future behaviours of a customer: segment, cohort or individual. Customers' potential value is determined by their propensity to buy products in the future. Data miners can build predictive models by examining patterns and relationships within historic data.

Predictive models can be generated to identify:

1. Which customer, segment or cohort is most likely to buy a given product?
2. Which customers are likely to default on payment?
3. Which customers are most likely to defect (churn)?

Data analysts scour historic data looking for predictor and outcome variables. Then a model is built and validated on these historic data. When the model seems to work well on the historic data, it is run on contemporary data, where the predictor data are known but the outcome data are not. This is known as 'scoring'. Scores are answers to questions such as the propensity-to-buy, default and churn questions listed above.

Predictive modelling is based on three assumptions, each of which may be true to a greater or lesser extent:

1. The past is a good predictor of the future but this may not be true. Sales of many products are cyclical or seasonal. Others have fashion or fad lifecycles.
2. The data are available but this may not be true. Data used to train the model may no longer be collected. Data may be too costly to collect, or may be in the wrong format.

3. Customer-related databases contain what you want to predict but this may not be true. The data may not be available. If you want to predict which customers are most likely to buy mortgage protection insurance, and you only have data on life policies, you will not be able to answer the question.

Two tools that are used for predicting future behaviours are decision trees and neural networks.

Decision Trees

Decision trees are so called because the graphical model output has the appearance of a branch structure. Decision trees work by analysing a dataset to find the independent variable that, when used to split the population, results in nodes that are most different from each other with respect to the variable you are trying to predict. Figure contains a set of data about five customers and their credit risk profile.

Name	Debt	Income	Married	Risk
Joe	High	High	Yes	Good
Soe	Low	High	Yes	Good
John	Low	High	No	Poor
Mary	High	Low	Yes	Poor
Fred	Low	Low	Yes	Poor

We want to use the data in four of the five columns to predict the risk rating in the fifth column. A decision tree can be constructed for this purpose.

In decision tree analysis, Risk is in the 'dependent' column. This is also known as the target variable. The other four columns are independent columns. It is unlikely that the customer's name is a predictor of Risk, so we will use the three other pieces of data as independent variables: debt, income and marital status. In the example, each of these is a simple categorical item, each of which only has two possible values (high or low; yes or no). The data from Figure are represented in a different form in Figure, in a way which lets you see which independent variable is best at predicting risk. As you examine the data, you will see that the best split is income (four instances highlighted in bold on the diagonal: two high income/good risk plus two low income/poor risk). Debt and marital status each score three on their diagonals.

Once a node is split, the same process is performed on each successive node, either until no further splits are possible or until you have reached a managerially useful model.

Predicted risk	High debt	Low debt	**High income**	**Low income**	Married	Not married
Good	1	1	**2**	0	2	0
Poor	1	2	1	**2**	2	1

Cross-tabulation of dependent and independent variables

The graphical output of this decision tree analysis is shown in Figure . Each box is a node. Nodes are linked by branches. The top node is the root node. The data from the root node is split into two groups based on income. The right-hand, low income box does not split any further because both low income customers are classified as poor credit risks. The left-hand, high-income box does split further, into married and not married customers. Neither of these split further because the one unmarried customer is a poor credit risk and the two remaining married customers are good credit risks.

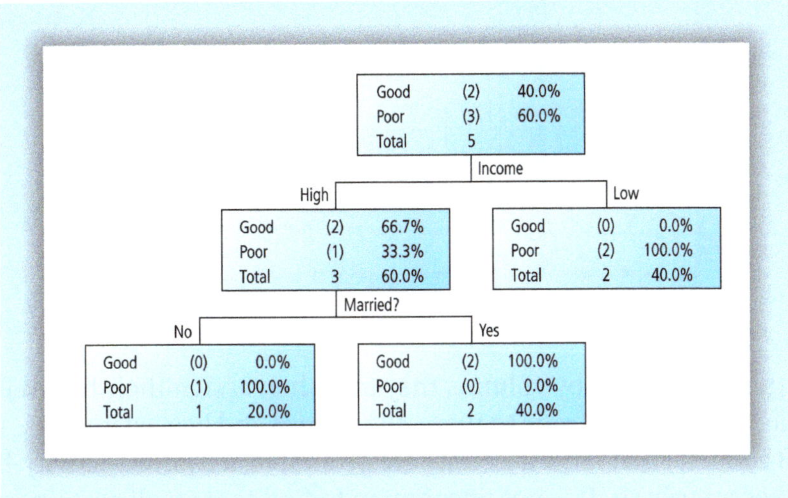

As a result of this process the company knows that customers who have the lowest credit risk will be high income and married. They will also note that debt, one of the variables inserted into the training model, did not perform well. It is not a predictor of creditworthiness. Decision trees that work with categorical data such as these are known as classification trees. When decision trees are applied to continuous data they are known as regression trees.

Neural Networks

Neural networks are another way of fitting a model to existing data for prediction purposes. The expression 'neural network' has its origins in the work of machine learning and artificial intelligence. Researchers in this field have tried to learn from the natural neural networks of living creatures.

Neural networks can produce excellent predictions from large and complex datasets containing hundreds of interactive predictor variables, but the neural networks are neither easy to understand nor straightforward to use. Neural networks represent complex mathematical equations, with many summations, exponential functions and parameters.

Like decision trees and clustering techniques, neural networks need to be trained to recognize patterns on sample datasets. Once trained, they can be used to predict customer behaviour from new data. They work well when there are many potential predictor variables, some of which are redundant.

CPM in the Business-to-Business Context

Many B2B companies classify their customers into groups based on sales revenue. They believe that their best customers are their biggest customers. Some of these companies consciously apply the Pareto principle, recognizing that 80 percent of sales are made to 20 percent of customers, as shown in figure below.

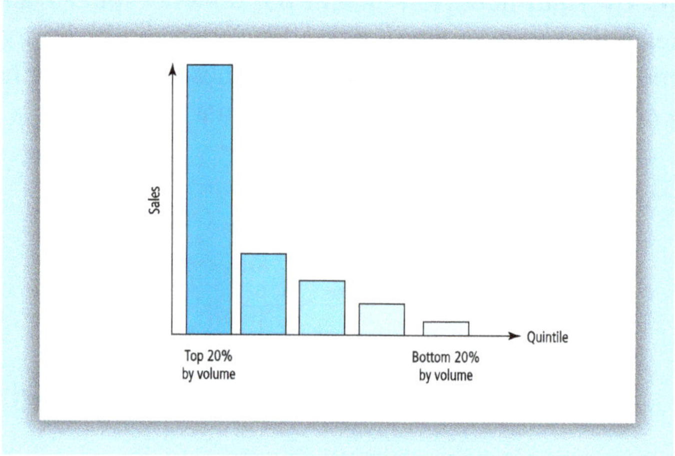

The Pareto principle, or 80:20 rule

Having clustered their customers by volume, they may then assign their best representatives, and offer the best service and terms of trade to these, the biggest and best customers. The assumption is often made in B2B contexts that large accounts are profitable accounts. Activity-based costing tells us that this is not necessarily so. It is not uncommon to find that small customers are unprofitable because their activity costs are greater than the margins they generate. Similarly, many companies fi nd that their largest accounts are also pareto table. Why? Large accounts create more work, more activity. The work of managing the account might require the services of a large number of people: a sales manager, a customer service executive and an applications engineer among others. The customer might demand customized product, delivery in less than container loads, just-in-time delivery, extended due dates for payment, and, ultimately, volume discounts on price. Very often it is the midrange sales volume customers that are the most profitable. Figure shows the profitability of customers who have been previously clustered according to volume. The chart shows that the top 20 percent of customers by volume, just as are the bottom 20 percent by volume.

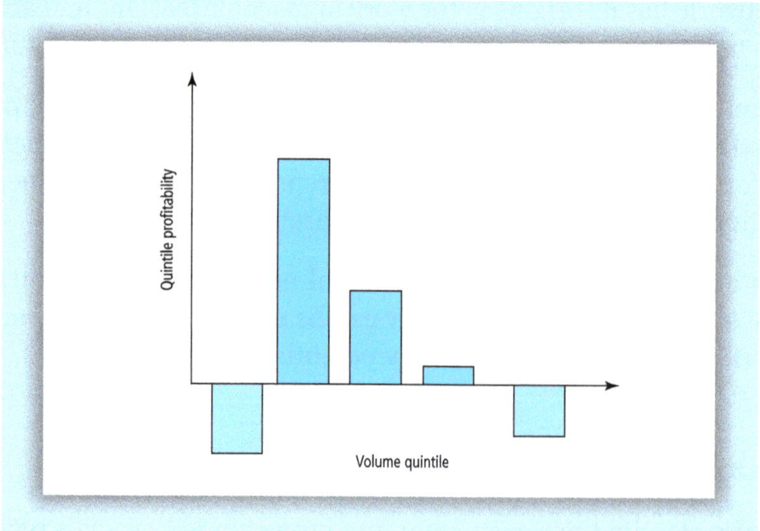

Customer profitability by sales volume quintile

When Kanthal, a Swedish manufacturer of electrical resistance heating elements, introduced ABC they found that only 40 percent of their customers were profitable. Two of their top three sales volume customers were among the most un-profit table. The most profitable 5 percent of customers generated 150 percent of profits. The least profitable 10 percent lost 120 percent of profit. The challenge for Kanthal was deciding what to do with the unprofitable customers.

Their options included implementation of open book accounting so their customers could see how much it cost to serve them, negotiation of service levels with customers, introducing transparent rules for migrating customers up and down the service level ladder, simplifying and standardizing the order process, introducing a self-service portal, negotiating price increases, sorting product lines into those that could be delivered restock and others for which advance orders were required, and rewarding account managers for customer profitability, both by percent margin and total Krona (Crown) value.

Customer Portfolio Models

Since the early 1980s there have been a number of tools specifically designed for assessing B2B companies 'customer portfolios. They generally classify existing customers using a matrix and measurement approach. CPM in B2B companies uses one or more variables to cluster customers; the most common single variable approach is to use sales revenue to cluster companies. You now know that this does not necessarily deliver a satisfactory profit outcome.

Bivariate models Benson Shapiro and his colleagues developed a customer portfolio model that importantly incorporated the idea of cost-to-serve into the evaluation of customer value. Figure presents the matrix they developed.

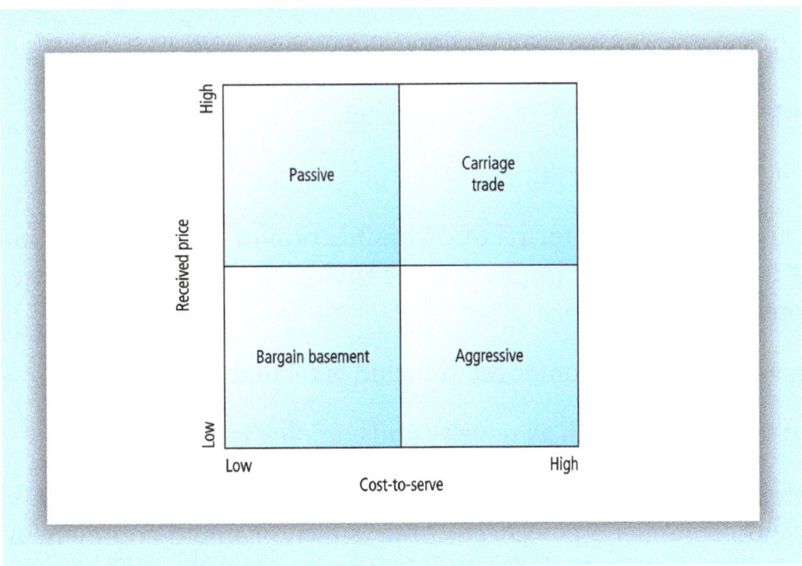

Shapiro et al. customer classification matrix

In this model customers are classified according to the price they pay and the costs incurred by the company to acquire and serve them. Four classes of customer are identified: carriage trade (often newly acquired customers who are costly to serve but pay a relatively high price), passive customers, aggressive customers and bargain basement customers. The important contribution of this model is that it recognizes that costs are not evenly distributed across the customer base. Some customers are more costly to win and serve and, if this is accompanied by a relatively low received price, the customer may be unprofitable. Table shows how costs can vary before the sale, in production, in distribution and after the sale.

Pre-sale costs	Production costs	Distribution costs	Post-sale costs
Geographic location: close versus distant	Order size	Shipment consolidation	Training
Prospecting	Set-up time	Preferred transportation mode	Installation
Sampling	Scrap rate	Back-haul opportunity	Technical support
Human resource: management versus representatives.	Customization	Location: close versus distant	Repairs and maintenance
Service: design support, applications engineering.	Order timing	Logistics support, e.g. field inventory	

Renato Fiocca created an advance in customer portfolio modelling when he introduced his two-step approach.

At the first step customers are classified according to:

1. The strategic importance of the customer.
2. The difficulty of managing the relationship with the customer. The strategic importance of a customer is determined by:
    - The value/volume of the customer's purchases.
    - The potential and prestige of the customer.
    - Customer market leadership.
    - General desirability in terms of diversification of the supplier's markets, providing access to new markets, improving technological expertise and the impact on other relationships.

The difficulty of managing the customer relationship is related to:

- Product characteristics, such as novelty and complexity.
- Account characteristics, such as the customer's needs and requirements, customer's buying behaviour, customer's power, customer's technical and commercial competence and the customer's preference to do business with a number of suppliers.
- Competition for the account, which is assessed by considering the number of competitors, the strength and weaknesses of competitors and the competitors' position the customer.

On the basis of this information it is possible to construct a two-dimensional matrix as in figure.

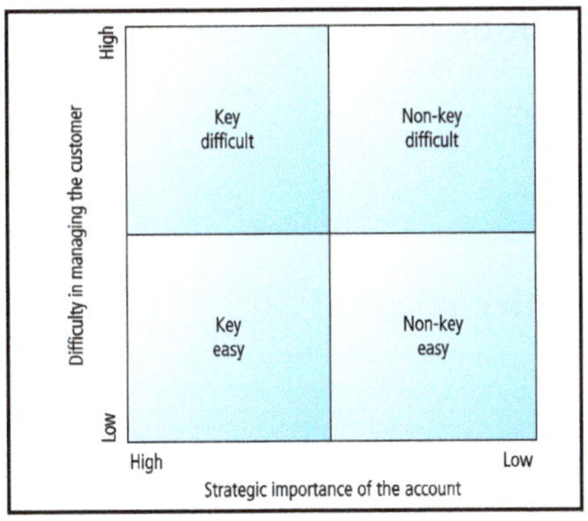

Fiocca's CPM model

The second step involves further analysis of the key accounts, shown in the left-hand cells of Figure. They are classified according to:

- The customer's business attractiveness.
- The relative strength of the buyer/seller relationship.

The attractiveness of the customer's business is strongly influenced by conditions in the customer's served market. Fiocca identifies these as market factors, competition, financial and economic factors, technological factors and socio-political factors, as detailed in table.

Market Factors

- Size of key segments served by customer.
- Customer's share of key segments.
- Customer's growth rate.
- Customer's influence on the market.

Competition in the Customer's Market

- Customer's position and strength.
- Customer's vulnerability to substitutes.
- Customer's level of integration.

Socio-Political Factors

- Customer's ability to adapt and fit.

Financial and Economic Factors

- Customer's margins.
- Customer's scale and experience.

- Barriers to customer's entry or exit.
- Customer's capacity utilization.

Technological Factors

- Customer's ability to cope with change.
- Depth of customer's skills.
- Types of technological know-how.
- Level of customer patent protection.

The strength of the customer relationship is determined by:

- The length of relationship.
- The volume or dollar value of purchases.
- The importance of the customer (percentage of supplier's sales accounted for by this customer).
- Personal friendships.
- Cooperation in product development.
- Management distance (language and culture).
- Geographical distance.

The data from this second step are then entered into a final nine-cell matrix, as shown in figure, which point to three core customer management strategies: hold, withdraw or improve.

There have been a couple of published validations of this model, but it has been criticized for its failure to consider customer profitability, and its rejection of non-key customers.

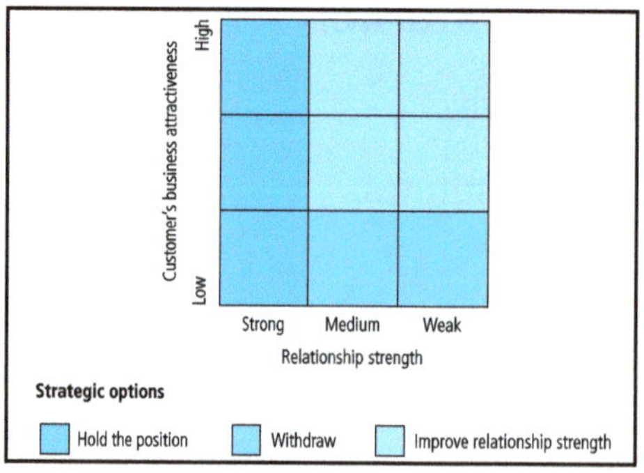

Fiocca's CPM model

Trivariate CPM Model

Peter Turnbull and Judy Zolkiewski have developed a three-dimensional CPM framework as shown in Figure The dimensions they propose are cost-to-serve, net price and relationship value. The first two variables are adopted from the Shapiro model. Relationship value, the third dimension, allows other strategic issues to be taken into account.

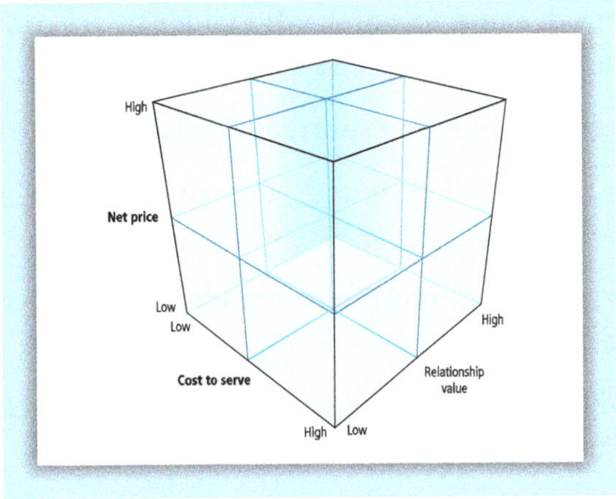

Turnbull and Zolkiewski's three-dimensional customer classification matrix

Relationship value is 'softer' or more judgmental than the other two dimensions. Among the questions considered when forming a judgment on relationship value are the following:

- Are the goods or services critical to the customer?
- Is the customer a major generator of volume for the supplier?
- Would the customer be hard to replace if he switched to another supplier?
- Does the customer generate cost savings for the supplier?

Additional Customer Portfolio Management Tools

In addition to specifically designed CPM tools there are a number of other tools in common use for strategic planning. These can also be very useful for CRM applications. These tools, however, operate at company- specific levels. This means that a CRM strategist would apply the tools to a specific customer to help in the assessment of that customer's future value. Among the tools are SWOT analysis, PESTE analysis, five-forces analysis and BCG matrix analysis.

Swot and Peste

SWOT is an acronym for strengths, weaknesses, opportunities and threats. SWOT analysis explores the internal environment (S and W) and the external environment (O and T) of a strategic business unit. The internal (SW) audit looks for strengths and weaknesses in the business functions of sales, marketing, manufacturing or operations, finance and people management. It then looks cross-functionally for strengths and weaknesses in, for example, cross-functional processes (such as new product development) and organizational culture.

The external (OT) audit analyses the macro- and micro-environments in which the customer operates. The macro-environment includes a number of broad conditions that might impact on a company. These conditions are identified by a PESTE analysis. PESTE is an acronym for political, economic, social, technological and environmental conditions.

An analysis would try to pick out major conditions that impact on a business, as illustrated below:

- Political environment: demand for international air travel contracted as worldwide political stability was reduced after September 11, 2001.
- Economic environment: demand for mortgages falls when the economy enters recession.
- Social environment: as a population ages, demand for healthcare and residential homes increase.
- Technological environment: as more households become owners of computers, demand for Internet banking increases.
- Environmental conditions: as customers become more concerned about environmental quality, demand for more energy efficient products increases.

The micro environmental part of the external (OT) audit examines relationships between a company and its immediate external stake- holders: customers, suppliers, business partners and investors.

A CRM-oriented SWOT analysis would be searching for customers or potential customers that emerge well from the analysis.

These would be customers that:

- Possess relevant strengths to exploit the opportunities open to them.
- Are overcoming weaknesses by partnering with other organizations to take advantage of opportunities.
- Are investing in turning around the company to exploit the opportunities.
- Are responding to external threats in their current markets by exploiting their strengths for diversification.

Five Forces

The five-forces analysis was developed by Michael Porter. He claimed that the profitability of an industry, as measured by its return on capital employed relative to its cost of capital, was determined by five sources of competitive pressure. These five sources include three horizontal and two vertical conditions.

The horizontal conditions are:

- Competition within the established businesses in the market.
- Competition from potential new entrants.
- Competition from potential substitutes.

The vertical conditions reflect supply and demand chain considerations:

- The bargaining power of buyers.
- The bargaining power of suppliers.

Porter's basic premise is that competitors in an industry will be more profitable if these five conditions are benign. For example, if buyers are very powerful, they can demand high levels of service and low prices, thus negatively influencing the profitability of the supplier. However, if barriers to entry are high, say because of large capital requirements or dominance of the market by very powerful brands, then current players will be relatively immune from new entrants and enjoy the possibility of better profits.

Why would a CRM-strategist be interested in a five-forces evaluation of customers? Fundamentally, a financially healthy customer offers better potential for a supplier than a customer in financial distress.

The analysis points to different CRM solutions:

- Customers in a profitable industry are more likely to be stable for the near-term, and are better placed to invest in opportunities for the future. They therefore have stronger value potential. These are customers with whom a supplier would want to build an exclusive and well-protected relationship.
- Customers in a stressed industry might be looking for reduced cost inputs from its suppliers, or for other ways that they can add value to their offer to their own customers. A CRM-oriented supplier would be trying to find ways to serve this customer more effectively, perhaps by stripping out elements of the value proposition that are not critical, or by adding elements that enable the customer to compete more strongly.

BCG Matrix

The Boston Consulting Group matrix was designed to analyse a company's product portfolio with a view to drawing strategy prescriptions. The analysis takes into account two criteria, relative market share and market growth rate, to identify where profits and cash flow are earned. Figure is a sample BCG matrix. The BCG claims that the best indicator of a market's attractiveness is its growth rate (hence the vertical axis of the matrix) and that the best indicator of competitive strength is relative market share (the horizontal axis). Relative market share, that is the market share of the business unit relative to its largest competitor, is claimed to improve the relative cost position due to the experience curve.

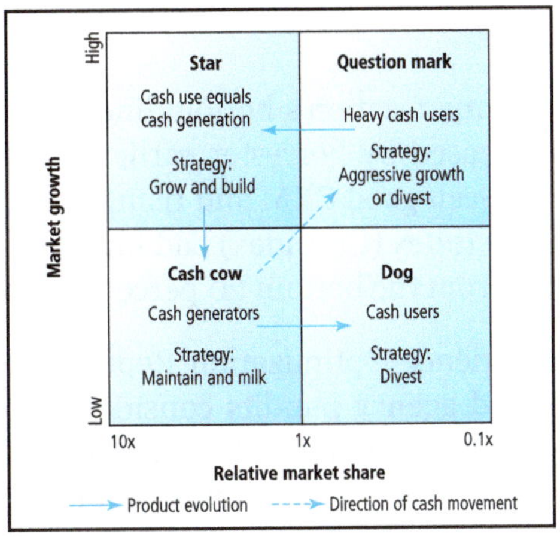

Boston Consulting Group matrix

The matrix categorizes products in a portfolio into one of four boxes and prescribes certain strategies: milk the cows, invest in the stars, ditch the dogs and then sort the question marks into those that you want to support as they become stars, and the remainder that you expect to convert into dogs.

A balanced portfolio of products contains question marks, stars and cash cows. Cash cows generate the cash flow that supports the question marks. As the question marks grow their relative market share, and become stars, they are establishing a position in the market that will eventually yield strong positive cash flows. This happens when a leading product maintains that position in a mature market.

From a CRM perspective, a customer with a balanced portfolio of products of its own has greater lifetime potential for a supplier than a customer with an unbalanced portfolio. A company with no new products in the pipeline will struggle to remain viable when the existing cash cows dry up. This happens as competitors fight to win market share and substitutes emerge.

Customer Experience Management

Customer experience management (CXM) is the management of customer interactions through each physical and digital touch point in order to deliver personalized experiences that drive brand loyalty and increase revenue, according to David Clarke, global chief experience officer at PwC. Brands accomplish CXM programs through a combination of software, analytics, research and data-management systems. In recent years, several brands have infused CXM with Artificial Intelligence (AI) and machine learning engines that help manage customer data and predict future interactions to allow brands to serve relevant content.

"Customer journeys are either historical or hypothetical," said Tim Linberg, chief experience officer at Verndale. "We can guide journeys, but we can't absolutely dictate them. And, moreover, a truly customer-centric organization wouldn't try to. What we can do, though, is use behavioral data, customer insights and marketing technologies to better understand and optimize every step of that journey. That's customer experience management."

Importance of CXM

Well, that's simple: it affects your organization's bottom line. No longer is making good products enough. According to a report released by Forrester earlier this year, the top-performing CXM brands see a direct correlation between good CXM and rising stocks. The top 20 percent of brands in Forrester's Customer Experience Index (CX Index) had higher stock price growth and higher total returns than companies drawn from the bottom 20 percent, according to Forrester researchers.

According to the "Customer Experience Optimization Report" Econsultancy and Ensighten, 96 percent of company marketers and agency pundits consider customer experience optimization somewhat important or critical. Also, 94 percent of marketers and 79 percent of agency respondents said that higher engagement and conversion rates are among the many benefits of CX optimization.

The future will still be about good CX. According to the 2017 Gartner Customer Experience in Marketing Survey released earlier this year, 81 percent say that in two years they expect to be competing mostly or completely on the basis of CX. And further, PwC's latest Digital IQ report found that 65 percent of respondents see CX as critical to advancing business performance, and 70 percent see it as crucial to achieving digital transformation.

How CXM Software helps?

A strong CXM program is only as good as the software behind it. Brands need to collect, track, manage, organize, analyze, personalize and execute relevant interactions with customers and prospects and can do this primarily through CXM software. Capterra, a product review site, provides reviews of nearly 300 CXM software platforms.

CXM software can also incorporate systems like CRM, web content management, personalization engines, web analytics and most platforms within the digital experience platform ecosystem. According to Tech Target, CXM software falls into a few buckets that include:

- Customer data analytics,
- Mobile marketing,
- Location-based services,
- Emotional analytics,
- Knowledge management systems.

Right CXM Tools for the Right Prospect and Customer

"Every customer, brand and campaign are unique," said Josh Martin, senior director of product marketing for Perfect Sense. "Therefore, delivering a good experience requires tools that allow companies to deliver the right content in the right context at the right time." Companies, he said, must first understand what customers they want to target. "This usually manifests itself as journey mapping," Martin added, "and allows content creators, marketing teams, product managers, etc. to create a personalized experience that delivers value to their users."

Having the right tools — instrumented correctly — is more important than having a lot of tools, Martin added. "A great customer experience," he said, "allows a brand to meet customer needs and be seen as helpful. To deliver this type of personalized experience across all channels, languages and content types, requires various marketing solutions. At the core is CRM, CMS and marketing automation. In the future, artificial intelligence will help drive content and experience optimization."

How do you bring good CX to life? By making connections, according to Clarke. Connect goals, POVs, responsibilities and ideas as they flow through the organization, according to Clarke. Connect cross-department teams and budgets to share in the commitment. Connect associate, customer and partner journeys. Connect systems and technologies to provide a platform for iteration, he added.

Technology does not Define CXM Strategy

To effectively manage CX, brands should not get distracted by newly available technology, according to PwC's Clarke. "Imagine your ideal CX: don't let technology define it," Clarke said. "Visualize all touch points across the digital and physical world. It is most important to ensure that you are providing customers with what they need, when they need it the most." This may mean deploying chatbot-based customer service, and other times it may mean reducing the number of clicks to get to purchase.

Brands should be thinking about democratizing CX. "CXM," Clarke added, "isn't an out-of-the-box solution. Great customer experiences are owned by the C-Suite and only happen through a matrix of co-dependent connections." It's not just on the marketing department to execute CXM. And it's not just about using a CRM. "It should be on the agenda across functions," Clarke said. "Having the customer in mind even when thinking of back-office system functionality has an effect on the customer. Don't silo the responsibility. Everyone affects CX."

Putting the Customer First

In conclusion, a good CXM program leads to a CX that is consistent across channels, frictionless and valuable to the consumer, according to Verndale's Linberg. "The promise of CXM for marketers is the ability to purposely move from 'ready fire aim' acquisition and retention tactics to a 'ready aim fire' approach that puts the customer first. This move towards true one-to-one marketing is enabled through technologies that unify customer data, and leverage artificial intelligence and machine learning to drive personalization at scale."

CRM and Customer Experience

Customer experience is forming during the interaction with your brand. It represents how clients percept your company during all stages of communication. People can be satisfied with the quality of your products but a complicated sales process or poor service will worsen overall impression.

This is the reason why your brand should find a way to effectively monitor and improve customer relations experience. A CRM (customer relation management) system can help you with it. In short, CRM is a strategy focused on managing relations with customers. This concept was applied to practice in CRM systems, software solutions which are used to manage contacts, sales, and complete histories of interacting with specific buyers and suppliers. Delivering a white glove customer experience can make the difference between your sales teams missing or exceeding their sales goals. It helps to determine whether a one-time customer becomes a repeat customer that actively promotes your company to their friends.

Why you should Care about Customer Experience?

If you have doubts about the importance of customer experience improvement, here are some facts. According to research by PWC, one-third of all surveyed customers abandon the company after a single bad experience. If there are more accidents, half of the customers will stop interacting with even their favorite brands.

A good customer experience can lead to greater trust and increase the likelihood the customer will recommend you to a friend or family member.

> "Customers are not just looking for good products and top-notch customer service. Those just meet expectations and are table stakes for any business," says Lemin. "Customers don't talk about average. They talk about different. Companies that can deliver at least one element of their customer experience in a different, unexpected way stand a better chance at success."

Nowadays people are not shopping just to get a product. They are looking for a great service which will grant them an excellent experience, and a story that they can tell. You may be surprised but 86 percent of people are even ready to pay more for it.

> "Consistency in delivering unique experiences leads to persistent brand storytelling," says Lemin.

Therefore, the importance of great customer experience should never be underestimated. Building an excellent experience will help you to attract new buyers and increase the loyalty of existing. Remember that in a broader sense businesses are built to meet customer demands. If on some point of interaction you fail to satisfy customers, they will leave you decreasing your income and lowering your reputation.

Customer Experience Measurement

Customer Experience Measurement is the practice of measuring customer experience at all touch points along the customer journey. It includes all customer actions. Before we start with the nits and grits of measuring CX, it is important to understand the importance of measuring customer experience.

Importance of Measuring Customer Experience (CX)

The most difficult task for any company is to make the organization more customer-centric, and measuring customer experience allows them to understand the needs of their customers and build a organization that is focused solely on the customer.

Measuring customer experience is not just an additional benefit, it is a necessity in today's age. It provides organizations with the necessary means to collect and analyze information to get a better perspective of the customer and their needs.

Measuring customer experience also allows organizations to find out what satisfies and dissatisfies their customers, and how to use that information to improve customer experience. Using this information, companies can better cater to their customer's expectations and continuously improve service quality. Not just understanding the customer, measuring customer experience also allows companies to measure how well their customer experience strategy is performing in terms of meeting business KPIs.

How to Start Measuring Customer Experience (CX)

Many organizations believe that measuring customer satisfaction is a good measure of customer experience. But, that isn't quite the case anymore.

Let's get into the details of how to measure customer experience along the entire customer journey.

Know your Customer

Most companies perform some kind of customer research to gather insights about their target audience. This information can be used in email marketing, SMS marketing, and other forms of targeted promotions. Understanding the customer allows business to think like them, and offer the right products & services to better engage them and provide superior experiences.

To start understanding your customers, it is crucial to know their most important needs and expectations in terms of what makes them satisfied and what it takes to retain them. Find out the key value factors in the minds of your customers. Make a map by creating a timeline of their journey and outlining what is important at each touch point along the journey.

Identify all Touchpoints

Analyze the customer journey from start to finish, and map the entire customer experience according to the customer's point-of-view. Pick the touchpoints that are moments of truth for the customer – ones that will etch your brand's experience into their memory forever. Develop touchpoint metrics for each touchpoint, or metrics that specifically measure the performance of each touchpoint.

Think of each touch point as an opportunity to improve customer experience. No touch point will ever be perfect – this is a continuous improvement process. It is your job to identify which area to focus on first along the customer journey. You can also use a customer experience mapping tool to map your customer journeys.

Work upon Key Problem Areas

Once all the touch points have been identified, identify the key problem areas and start working on them systematically. Identify and single out each problem, and devise innovative CX solutions to address these specific problems.

Choose the Right CX Metrics and Measure them

Now that you've taken the time to know your customer, identified all the touchpoints that matter, and worked on key problem areas – it's time to start measuring the results of your efforts by choosing the right business metrics to analyze.

Your primary objective should be to check whether the solutions you have proposed to your addressed problems are working or not, and how they can be improved further. If a solution isn't working, think of something else that might do the trick.

Use an appropriate data collection methodology to collect data about the various metrics defined above and find a way to collect insights on a regular basis. Set targets for each CX metric and continuously keep improving your organization's CX quality.

If you're using a customer experience tool with an inbuilt score for satisfaction or loyalty, use this as a starting point to help point you in the right direction. Track multiple metrics over multiple timeframes to guarantee success for your business.

Here are some customer experience metrics you can focus on-

- Net Promoter Score: NPS is an index that ranges from -100 to 100 that shows how willing a customer is in recommending a brand's products / services to other people. NPS divides customers into three categories – Promoters (loyal + satisfied), Passives (satisfied + unenthusiastic), and Detractors (unsatisfied + unenthusiastic). Generally, companies collect NPS data using surveys, and calculate the score by subtracting the percentage of detractors from the percentage of promoters.

- Average Handling Time (ART) / First Response Time (FRT): FRT shows how quickly agents are able to provide customer support to customer queries. AHT is the average amount of time taken to solve a customer's query. Quick response and handling times are usually linked to high customer satisfaction levels – research has proved this to be true. According to Forrester, 45% of US consumers will abandon an online transaction if their questions or concerns are not addressed quickly. According to Mckinsey, 75% of online customers expect help within 5 minutes.

- First Contact Resolution (FCR): FCR gives a measure of how well agents can solve customer queries the first time using surveys or statistical evaluations. If customers aren't able to get their queries resolved the very first time they contact you, they probably won't be satisfied or loyal for long.

- Customer Satisfaction Score (CSAT): Customer satisfaction score is the average score given to your brand according to customer answers based on a survey. Companies use CSAT scores to find out how satisfied customers were with specific products/services.

- Customer Effort Score (CES): Customer Effort Score is the score given to companies that shows the amount of effort customers have to put to execute a particular task. It has specific ranges, from Strongly Disagree to Strongly Agree with strengths ranging from 1 to 5. Companies should strive to make it as easy as possible to complete a particular task to maintain high levels of loyalty and satisfaction. They're giving you their time – the least you can do is make it easy for them to engage with you, right?

- Emotional Assessment using Plutchik's Wheel of Emotions: Robert Plutchik created a wheel of emotions in 1980 which depicted all the primary and secondary emotions in different colors. Use this combined with sentiment analysis capabilities through AI/Big Data to integrate emotions into your customer experience measurement strategy.

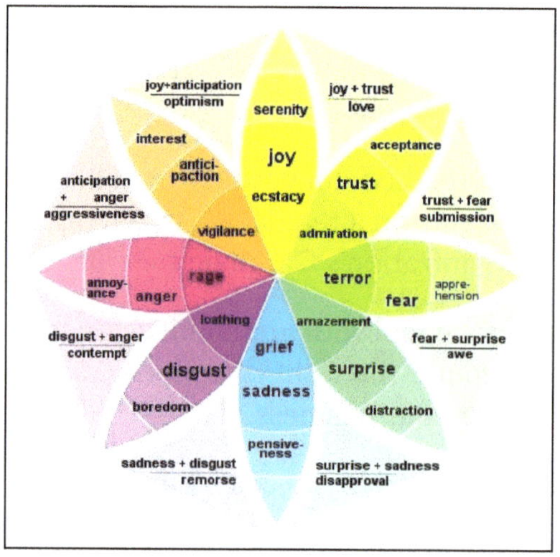

First Response Time

First response time is the most critical metric of great customer service. It is the time in which the customers receive the first response from the customer service agent after they submit a query.

While the other skills hold equal importance in place, providing response to customers in the shortest span of time is considered as one of the most essential skills. It especially works out for businesses where the long waiting time is resulting into higher customer frustration and increased churn rate.

How to Calculate Average First Response Time:

$$\frac{\text{Average 1st}}{\text{response time}} = \frac{\text{Total time taken to send the first response during the selected time period}}{\text{The number of tickets of tickets whose first responses were sent in the selected time period}}$$

Importance of First Response Time

Customers don't like to wait in queue for getting their issues resolved. Long wait times are destroying the essence of super customer service due to which the rate of customer defection is increasing. Thus, organizations need to closely study their first response time by doing a 360 degree monitoring of each department related in solving a case registered.

First response time plays a crucial role in determining the levels of customer satisfaction. Lower the time taken to provide response to a query, higher the level of customer satisfaction. It is not important to walk aloof in the crowd, but what matters is the kind of bond that an individual builds with the crowd. Same stands true for organizations as well where budding bonds with customers can help in future revenue generation.

Organizations can create SLAs or time frames for different cases. This will hold reps accountable for getting back to customers within a reasonable amount of time. Managers with the help of SLAs can also monitor the performance of individual agents to ensure higher levels of efficiency.

Also, the organizations should start analyzing the trend of average first response time to check whether it is increasing or decreasing over a period. Organization can be in trouble if the first response time consistently keeps on increasing.

In the below graph, you can see that the average response time is more than the SLA target. This means that the organization is lagging behind solving cases on the first go, i.e., the time being taken by the agents to contact customers after the case is placed is much more than the decided time frame. On the other hand the median line is fairly below the SLA target. Any signs of median line moving above SLA would be an indicator of inefficiency to close queries.

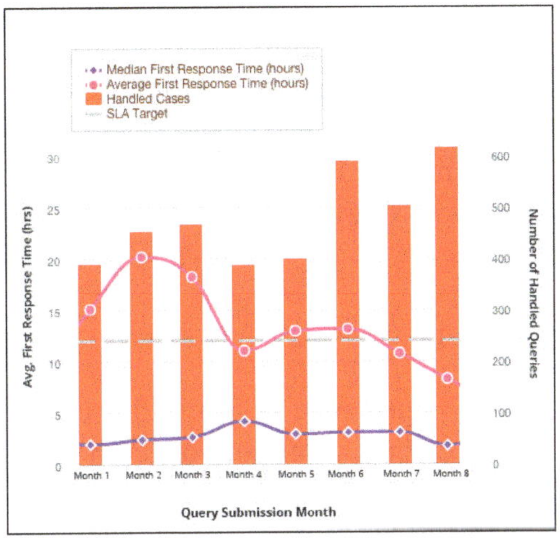

How to Reduce First Response Time?

If your organization is customer centric and is still thinking of ways to reduce the increasing churn rate, here is how you can rescue your customers from acute level of frustration:

- Provide effective training: Contact center managers should make it a habit of regularly analyzing the time taken by agents to respond to a particular query. Working on the average first response time taken by each agent can be of great help as it provides a clear picture of the managerial skills being used by each individual. What managers can do as a measure to reduce the first response time is by creating a SLA and by closely investigating the SLA targets being met in the team.
- On the basis of derived results, managers can train the agents lagging behind the SLA targets. Flexible training classes, suggestions, live demos can be provided according to the skills required for optimization of their workflow.
- Become omnipresent: One of the most effective ways of becoming a super performer is by being present on all channels of communications. Organizations who are setting themselves apart from the crowd are the one working on their response time by effectively providing resolution on email, social media, chat, voice and SMS. Omnichannel communication has truly captured the heart of customer service as the organizations a real view of the entire customer journey, i.e, the point from they placed a query to the point when the query got resolved. Thus, providing agents the power to become omnipresent can surely help in decreasing the first response time within a flash of time.

- Proactivity is the need of hour: Customer service agents can reduce the first response time by being proactive. They can analyze the buying behaviour and latest trends being followed in the market on the basis of which agents can design their service strategies to predict the requirement of the customers. Also, proactively going through the past history of the customer recorded in the CRM can be an additional donut for the agent. Agents can upsell and cross-sell with on the basis of the detailed analysis done before the call.

Is there a Universal Metric for Customer Experience?

When choosing a universal metric for customer experience, what comes to mind? NPS (Net Promoter Score) Score, CSAT (Customer Satisfaction) score, or CES (Customer Effort Score). Truth is – every company has their own definition of the customer experience score because the industry they operate in varies from company to company. A B2C company might look at the scenario differently as compared to a B2B company. For a B2C company, CES might be given more importance, whereas in B2B, NPS might be preferred. It really depends on the company, and how their business works.

CX Measurement Cheat Sheet

The best way to measure customer experience is to build a customer experience measurement scorecard, which helps identify the critical moments of truth for a customer and improve them strategically. Link KPIs and metrics with one another to form a measurement system along the entire customer journey. Identify lead and lag indicators for each section of the customer experience scorecard, and set goals for each metric.

Your CX Measurement Scorecard should include:

- Objectives: This is what you want to achieve – your end goal. e.g. improve customer retention.
- Measure: This is how you will measure what you are trying to achieve in your objective. It is always something quantifiable, realistic, and in your control to influence. e.g. churn rate.
- Targets: Targets define your objectives in quantifiable terms, i.e. in the form of numbers. e.g. churn rate < 10%.
- Key Business KPIs: This is the business KPI that drives your objective. e.g. revenue or number of repeat customers.

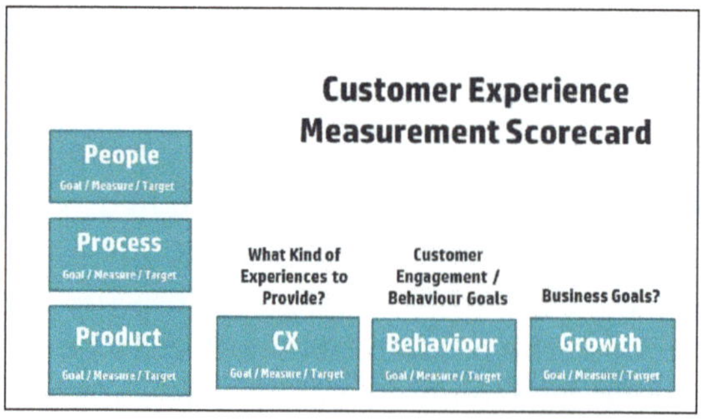

Here is a sample customer experience measurement scorecard you can apply to your business. This CX measurement framework should give you a clear idea about:

- Customer Satisfaction
- Visualizing the Entire Customer Journey
- Which Interactions Matter Most
- What Drives Your Customer Loyalty
- Where You Can Improve.

Strategies to Create a Great Customer Experience

In most cases, a customer's first point of contact with a company is usually through interacting with an employee (either by visiting a store or by speaking on the phone). This gives your business an opportunity to deliver excellent customer service.

However, customer service is only one aspect of the entire customer experience.

For example, if you book a vacation on the phone and the person you are speaking with is friendly and helpful, that's good customer service. Yet, if your tickets arrive early and the hotel upgrades your room, then that's a good customer experience.

That's how the two are different- Like most things in today's market place, customer experience has changed – it's more than person-to-person service and thanks to technology, companies can connect with their customers in new and exciting ways.

For example, using CRM software, you can view customer purchase history and to predict future needs even before the customer knows they need it. Having the ability to predict a future need will let you be proactive and attentive and, it means you can do things like:

- Provide related products based on purchase history.
- Create and deliver targeted email marketing campaigns.
- Understand the 360 degree view of the customer.

Customer service is still as important as ever, it's no longer the sole focus of customer experience. Now, the customer experience brings new ways to strengthen customer relationships through technological breakthroughs.

Ways to Improve the Customer Experience

Let's take a look at seven ways to create a great customer experience strategy to help you improve customer satisfaction, reduce churn and increase revenues.

Create a Clear Customer Experience Vision

The first step in your customer experience strategy is to have a clear customer-focused vision that you can communicate with your organization. The easiest way to define this vision is to create a set of statements that act as guiding principles.

For example, Zappos use their Zappos core family values and these values are embedded into their culture; which includes delivering wow through service, be humble and embracing change.

Once these principles are in place, they will drive the behavior of your organization. Every member of your team should know these principles by heart and they should be embedded into all areas of training and development.

Understanding Customers

The next step in building upon these customer experience principles is to bring to life the different type of customers who deal with your customer support teams. If your organization is going to really understand customer needs and wants, then they need to be able to connect and empathize with the situations that your customers face.

One way to do this is to create customer personas and give each persona a name and personality. For example, Anne is 35 years old; she likes new technology and is tech savvy enough to follow a video tutorial on her own, whereas John (42 years old) needs to be able to follow clear instructions on a web page.

By creating personas, your customer support team can recognize who they are and understand them better. It's also an important step in becoming truly customer centric.

Create an Emotional Connection with your Customers

You've heard the phrase "it's not what you say; it's how you say it"?

Well, the best customer experiences are achieved when a member of your team creates an emotional connection with a customer.

One of the best examples of creating an emotional connection comes from Zappos, when a customer was late on returning a pair of shoes due to her mother passing away. When Zappos found out what happened, they took care of the return shipping and had a courier pick up the shoes without cost. But, Zappos didn't stop there. The next day, the customer arrived home to a bouquet of flowers with a note from the Zappos customer service team who sent their condolences.

Research by the Journal of Consumer Research has found that more than 50% of an experience is based on an emotion as emotions shape the attitudes that drive decisions.

Customers become loyal because they are emotionally attached and they remember how they feel when they use a product or service. A business that optimizes for an emotional connection outperforms competitors by 85% in sales growth.

And, according to a recent Harvard Business Review study titled "The New Science of Customer Emotions", emotionally engaged customers are:

- At least three times more likely to recommend your product or service.

- Three times more likely to re-purchase.
- Less likely to shop around (44% said they rarely or never shop around).
- Much less price sensitive (33% said they would need a discount of over 20% before they would defect).

Capture Customer Feedback in Real Time

How can you tell if you are delivering a wow customer experience?

You need to ask – And ideally you do this by capturing feedback in real time.

Send a follow up email to every customer using post-interaction surveys and similar customer experience tools to automate the process. Of course, it's possible to make outbound calls to customers in order to gain more insightful feedback. It's also important to tie customer feedback to a specific customer support agent, which shows every team member the difference they are making to the business.

Use a Quality Framework for Development of your Team

By following the steps above, you now know what customers think about the quality of your service compared to the customer experience principles you have defined. The next step is to identify the training needs for each individual member of your customer support team.

Many organizations assess the quality of phone and email communication, however, a quality framework takes this assessment one step further by scheduling and tracking your teams development through coaching, eLearning and group training.

Act upon regular Employee Feedback

Most organizations have an annual survey process where they capture the overall feedback of your team; how engaged they are and the businesses ability to deliver an exceptional service.

But, what happens in the 11 months between these survey periods?

Usually, nothing happens. And this is where continuous employee feedback can play a role using tools that allow staff to share ideas on how to improve the customer experience and for managers to see how staff is feeling towards the business. For example, using project management software or social media tools, you can create a closed environment where your organization can leave continuous feedback.

Measure the ROI from Delivering Great Customer Experience

And finally, how do you know if all this investment in your teams, process and technology are working and paying off- Measuring customer experience is one of the biggest challenges faced by organizations, which is why many companies use the "Net Promoter Score" or NPS, which collects valuable information by asking a single straightforward question: "Would you recommend this company to a friend or relative?"

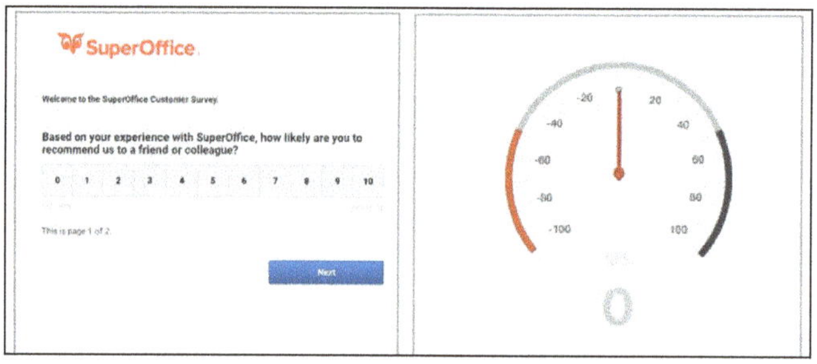

NPS, which was created by Rob Markey and Fred Reichheld at Bain and Company, is a highly suitable benchmark for a customer experience metric because a lot of companies use it as the standard customer experience measurement. And the fact that it's simple to implement and measure makes the NPS a favorite with company boards and executive committees.

Fundamentals to Deliver Value from Customer-Centricity

Organisations that embrace customer-centricity outperform their peers on revenue growth. However, if a customer-centric strategy is not approached in the right way, it can fail to deliver business value.

Successful customer-centric strategies and transformations require a holistic approach. While the strategy will likely differ for every organisation, there are 10 fundamentals we consider imperative to deriving business value from customer-centricity.

Assess and Understand your Level of Customer-Centricity

Assessing your organisation's level of customer-centricity against international best practice standards will not only help you pinpoint what good, bad and great look like, but also identify where you can deliver business improvements.

International best practice customer-centric standards often apply a Balanced Scorecard methodology to assess an organisation's strategic ability to deliver its value proposition to customers while also generating sustainable shareholder returns. This assessment should identify the level of continuous improvement of people, systems and business processes across the organisation.

However, simply conducting an assessment of customer-facing systems and practices is not enough. It needs to look holistically at how your entire organisational ecosystem contributes to the overall customer experience, including financial governance and HR processes, both front and back-end.

Assess Organisational Readiness

If your CEO's agenda doesn't include customer 'focus', 'obsession', 'intimacy' or similar, it's going to be tough to embark on a customer-centric journey.

Culture is key- Even if your CEO is already driving the customer-centric mandate, it won't be effective if it doesn't shift the entire culture towards customer-centricity. Think about employees in non-customer facing functions, like finance or production.

Assessing your organisation's readiness will help you understand the level of transformation required, whether an incremental or a complete transformation. A readiness assessment could be as simple as a traffic light assessment of 10 company attributes, or a more intensive and rigorous research project with scoring and benchmarking.

Assign Ownership and Accountability for Customer

Ownership and accountability of the customer is often left with the marketing department in many organisations. Yet having one department own the customer mandate can often result in a silo-ed effort and one that can be disconnected from other parts of the business. This scenario most often occurs when there is no mandate from the CEO or senior leadership team to support the delivery of the customer-centric vision.

Many global organisations are now addressing this issue by assigning Chief Customer Officer (CCO) roles to oversee the delivery of their customer-centric vision. The most successful CCOs go beyond paying lip service, by driving continued alignment across all departments to put the customer at the centre of everything they do. This often includes realigning operating models, distribution, value-chain, pricing, products and promotions to meet customer needs and deliver gross profits.

Understand your Customers and Conduct Diagnostics

Achieving customer intimacy is what successful customer-centric companies like Amazon and Walt Disney focus their strategic efforts on. This includes gaining an intimate understanding of the key customer groups that drive profits, their key behaviours, preferences, needs and wants. The current customer journey across your people, process and technology also needs to be thoroughly understood.

Customer research and analytics only forms part of this assessment. Practical diagnostic tools should also be used, such as Customer Journey Mapping, Service Blueprinting, Persona Development and Customer Discovery.

The Metrics that Matter

Developing and delivering a customer-centric strategy is irrelevant if it doesn't link to profits and growth. For example, if the key business metric that matters is Earnings before Interest and Tax (EBIT), you will need to demonstrate how your customer metrics drive EBIT.

Simplicity is king: Creating too many metrics makes it complicated to measure and act on the results, and challenging for your organisation to embrace. This is why some organisations choose one or two key metrics. For example, Customer Lifetime Value is often used as a key customer metric, as it can be directly linked back to profits.

Irrespective of the metrics that you choose, you must be able to assess whether your initiative is working and identify how you can make improvements. The most successful organisations often integrate these metrics into their official company financial reporting.

Develop and Assign Aligned Customer-Centric KPIs

Without assigning aligned KPIs across all teams, it can be challenging to deliver on integrated business objectives right across the organisation.

Take the simple scenario where Sales and Marketing have aligned KPIs around profitable customer acquisition and retention, but the Customer Service's departments KPIs are focused solely on productivity. Customer Service Reps try to reduce time spent on the phone to deliver cost savings, greater dissatisfaction results, as customers' problems are not resolved. This may trigger customers to leave the organisation.

Not only does this negatively impact Sales' and Marketing's KPIs, but also overall business results, as conflicting interests drive behaviour that goes against customer-centricity.

Understand, Review and Align your People Capability

Pivoting from a product-centric to a customer-centric operating model often requires an uplift in people capability via up-skilling, outsourcing or hiring-in new capabilities. For example, gaining an intimate understanding of your customers often involves the development of research and analytics capabilities. This may mean you need to hire new staff, up-skill existing staff or outsource to perform these activities.

Changing the mindset of staff to put the customer at the front and centre of their thinking can also require considerable training.

You may also want to review how different departments operate to ensure the customer is put at the forefront of their decision-making and processes. This could be as simple as refreshing collaboration processes between departments or conducting a complete structural realignment.

Optimise Organisational Processes and Technology

Customer diagnostics will enable you to pinpoint key customer friction points, such as back-office processes or customer-facing technology that negatively impact your current customer experience. The next step is to leverage these insights to develop or adapt processes and procedures across your organisation to deliver a seamless and improved customer experience.

This can be one of the most complex steps because it spans multiple business functions, and it may challenge the status quo in terms of who owns the process, customer, technology platforms and delivery. This is usually where organisations can benefit from an outside-in perspective to challenge in-built internal viewpoints and beliefs.

Create a Culture of Experimentation and Measurement

Embedding a rigorous continuous improvement culture is crucial to ensuring transformational initiatives are implemented effectively and are sustainable. Having a test and learn environment will help you transform new ideas and initiatives into winning business decisions.

Measuring the success of your key customer initiatives will help you understand the key performance drivers required to deliver continuous improvement. Visibility of customer metrics can also help drive increased cultural adoption of customer-centricity, especially financial customer metrics.

Implement a Change Management Program

A robust change management plan is crucial to delivering customer-centric success across your people, technology and processes. Employees need to buy-in to the concept, which can be challenging without a clear understanding of what is happening and why. Some simple impactful initiatives might be to get a cross-section of the business involved in developing a customer value proposition, or identifying an existing customer journey map for your organisation.

A customer-centric transformation is a cultural change as much as a change to actions, systems and processes. A holistic approach is required, often needing those responsible for change management to be dispersed across the organisation from the top-down, bottom-up and across.

Fundamentals of a Foolproof CRM Strategy

CRMs are proven to increase productivity, boost sales and improve customer communication. What was once strictly limited to larger organizations, is now being adopted by startups and SMBs.

If your goal is to deliver top notch customer service, it's certain that you must be planning to implement a CRM strategy, if you haven't already. Here are 5 fundamentals that would help you to build a foolproof CRM strategy.

Decide on your Goals

The aim of implementing a CRM is to help your business achieve its goals effectively. It's necessary to be clear on your objectives and to know how to achieve them. Break the objectives into small achievable chunks and connect that to how CRM fits to achieve the composite goal.

As you grow and evolve, your objectives will change along the way. Keep some space in your plan which will allow you to be flexible and revise your strategy on the fly.

Onboard your Employees

Your employees will be the ones executing the strategy, hence it is necessary to get them on board with your CRM strategy. Involve them early in the planning and implementation process. Explain to your employees how it will make their work easy and help them achieve the organization's objectives. Implement a change management plan that gives employees enough time to get used to the new system and ensures a smooth transition.

Empowering your employees with accountability and ownership will keep them motivated and move your CRM strategy in the right direction.

Understand your Buyer's Journey

Before analyzing your typical buyers' journey, re-visit your buyer persona. Start by answering the following questions:

- What are the traits of your ideal customer?
- Where do they live?
- What do they do?
- What are their pain areas?
- What do they appreciate in your product?

Knowing the answers to these questions will help you relate it with the buyer's journey (sales cycle). This will help you create and streamline content (emails, follow-ups, etc.) and workflows, and communicate according to the stage of sales funnel they are in.

Break Down Organizational Silos

Once you start collecting customer data, it is important to develop a culture of collaboration to improve the Customer Experience. Breaking down organizational silos is the key here. When your marketing, sales and customer service departments are not on the same page, the organization, as a whole, can be working at cross-purposes. When you promote cross-departmental collaboration, you'll be able to deliver better customer service. Also data collected by one department can be fed to another department to improve overall business operations.

Implement Data Management Best Practices

You will be collecting different data points like: name, address, company, email, designation, birthdate, nickname, qualifications, etc. While collecting this data, it is necessary to follow a set of standards to ensure these data points remain up-to-date. That means along with collecting new data, you should also delete junk records, update old records and sync data with any other systems you might be using along with CRM to collect and manage data. Also, there should be a universal format which everyone should follow while filling in information. Having this standard in place allows anyone with the rights to get access to information, thereby streamlining day to day operations.

References

- Strategic-crm: managementstudyguide.com, Retrieved 5 April, 2019
- How-to-create-a-crm-strategy: fitsmallbusiness.com, Retrieved 25 January, 2019
- Manage-your-customer-portfolio: thinkingportfolio.com, Retrieved 30 August, 2019
- Ways-crm-improves-the-customer-experience: nimble.com, Retrieved 12 April, 2019
- First-response-time-and-how-to-reduce-it: ameyo.com, Retrieved 7 May, 2019
- Customer-experience-strategy: superoffice.com, Retrieved 9 February, 2019
- Fundamentals-to-deliver-value-from-customer-centricity: customerthink.com, Retrieved 19 July, 2019
- Fundamentals-foolproof-crm-strategy: martechadvisor.com, Retrieved 13 March, 2019

4

Operational and Collaborative Customer Relationship Management

The entirety of services which allow a business organization to take care of customers' needs is known as operational customer relationship management. Collaborative CRM is an approach to customer relationship management where the different departments such as sales, technical support and marketing share the information gained from the customers. All the diverse principles of operational and collaborative CRM have been carefully analyzed in this chapter.

Operational CRM

Operational CRM can be defined as all the services that allow a business organization to take care of customers' needs. The system connects and supports an organization's sales, marketing, and customer service functions, thus building a framework that provides customer support.

In simple terms, your organization's CRM is the lifeline connecting your brand, team of employees, and the prospective customers. Its primary purpose is to streamline all business processes to offer the best customer experience. Some good examples of operational customer relationship management include contact and call centers, websites and data aggregation systems among others. To gain an edge against your competitors, getting access to information about your customers as well as getting a clear view of their needs is vital, and that is where high tech expertise in CRM becomes relevant.

Working of Operational CRM

Scheduling, automated communication, self-service management, performance tracking, lead sorting, cross-team collaboration and data analysis are a few of the day-to-day processes in a typical business across various departments. These are the processes that operational CRM will help with.

Considering that different departments are tasked with different roles in an organization (sales, marketing, and service), an operational CRM helps in aligning everyone's goals. This means that the CRM helps with linking of the marketing lead data with sales goals and that customer data, both prospective and current, is fed to the service team for them to provide the best customer support possible. This alignment of all departments within an organization is vital for it to automate various processes thus guaranteeing improved overall customer experience. Moreover, the alignment ensures businesses spend less on labor and strategically re-investing in other areas within the organization intended for growth.

Sales Automation

Several sales processes can be automated in a normal sales department including scheduling, automated communication, performance tracking, and leads sorting among others. A perfect operational CRM, therefore, should be able to track leads, prospects, and sales. However, a robust system can do much more including automating initial contacts all the way through setting up of the sales meeting and much more.

Business entrepreneurs no longer need to flip through their phone book or do random internet searches for potential customers. Instead, an operational CRM system is deployed to help the sales team make sales with targeted lead data.

Operational CRM and Sales Automation

Operational customer relationship management does more than just enhancing sales. It can also automate cross-sell communication, track sales performance, and maintain follow-up schedule.

Automated Reporting

There is a ridiculous competition in sales in the modern business world. Think of the sales team having to process a report every morning of goals and productivity.

Lead Distribution

An operational CRM helps your company to get the best leads to the best reps automatically. The system, in this case, sets your team up for success, unlike the old, manual way that lets leads languish on a list until you have the time to assign them.

Record Creation

A lot of time is wasted when the sales reps are manually entering customer details in your company's database or scheduling follow-ups. It is pretty evident that the majority of the leads have already left their information while visiting the website, signing up on a mail list, or responding to marketing campaign materials. With the help of an operational CRM, it becomes easier to create customer records for all leads from these sources. This way, the sales team will re-focus their energy into selling rather than doing data entry.

Meeting Scheduling

It is a daunting task to manage a busy sales rep's calendar. Operational customer relationship management has the potential of doing this work for the sales reps instead.

Marketing Automation

In any typical business organization, the marketing team is meant mainly to push marketing rather than sorting reports, classifying leads and manually analyzing data. These tasks should, instead, be handled by an operational CRM. Among the several marketing processes that can be automated in your organization include lead sorting, cross-team collaboration, performance tracking, and data analysis among others.

Operational CRM and Marketing Automation

Welcome Campaigns

An operational CRM ensures that you maximize every opportunity each time you are in contact with a potential customer. The system helps to put your company and brand in the best light rather than just waiting and hoping for the prospects to choose your company. The CRM system will help push the same in the right direction with automated welcome emails. Besides, doing this manually cannot be reliable in most cases.

Onboarding Campaigns

This is a process intended to ensure the customer that bought a product from your company can use it and love it. This way, they are likely to buy more or even tell their friends about your products. This is only achievable with proper communication with the customers. Onboarding campaigns are necessary in this case with the operational CRM deployed to automate contact with new customers to ask them how they are doing and invite you to call back in case they need any help. Most crucially, you need the customers to leave feedback. It has been established that when customers know you are still around and reachable after the sale, they are likely to use your products and talk about them.

Repeat Purchase Campaign

Having reached out to your customers after their first purchase, you should give them time before contacting them again. The second time you contact them, you will want to know about their first purchase and probably tell them about your new products. Statistics indicate that it is more difficult to get new customers than to get repeat sales to existing customers. Why not engage your operational CRM to help you with the repeat purchase campaign? Trust me; it will help you tap into the potential of an existing customer base.

Service Automation

Customer interactions give your company the opportunity to grow not only regarding making sales but also by providing the best customer support. This is where operational CRM comes in handy helping with various service processes including tracking problems, scheduling customer follow-ups, and supporting customers' self-service among others.

Operational CRM and Service Automation

Self-service – several service functions tie in directly to a company's CRM system. This may include paying of utility bills, purchasing movie tickets online, log in, returning of items purchased online and scheduling appointments among others. Upon customers accessing your system through a self-service channel or email, live chat or call, you get more information about the customers which is vital setting up targeted marketing campaigns that will boost repeat sales.

Benefits of Operational CRM

Having seen how an operational CRM can be used, it is clear that they are a great benefit to organizations focused on enhancing customer satisfaction and loyalty. Among the benefits of an operational CRM include:

- Enhancing marketing processes
- Improving internal communication
- Maximizing cross-selling and up-selling
- Increasing revenue and return on investment
- Enhancing customer satisfaction

Operational CRM using Short Message Service

The most ubiquitous and stable mobile technology namely Short Message Service (SMS) texting on cellular phones has great potential to support business toward customer relationship (create new and maintain). In 2001, 700 million mobile phone users worldwide sent an average of 20 billion SMS messages every month. Indeed, the volume of SMS messages sent in December 2001 was 30 billion worldwide and it was expected to grow to 100 billion by the end of 2002. In Europe, Norway leads the region with an average of 47 messages sent per month per user in 2001 while Philippines lead the Asia-Pacific region with 336 SMS messages. Given that the huge SMS messaging customer base could potentially serve as major component of the SMS commerce customer base, many commerce providers are becoming more interested in SMS commerce applications. Text Message Service (SMS) messages are handled by Short Message Service Centre (SMSC) that sending message in two-type of paradigm namely store-and-forward or forward-and-forget paradigm, these paradigm made SMS to be more effective communication compare to customer in some cases. In the store-and-forward paradigm, the system resends the message for some period of time until it is successfully received. In a forward-and-forget paradigm, the system sends the message to the end device without assurance of receipt or an attempt to redeliver in the case of failure. The most common application of the service is person-to-person messaging, however text messages are also often used to interact with automated systems, such as ordering products and services for mobile phones, or computer to mobile (or vice versa) messaging . SMS is becoming a widely used communication mechanism for mobile phone users, seeing that SMS facilitates person-to-person messaging, interactive information and entertainment services, and lately location based services.

Three consistent success indicators for SMS messaging are: (1) the cost-effectiveness and interoperability of the wireless infrastructure; (2) the high penetration of mobile phones (ubiquitous penetration levels of over 80% in some countries); and (3) the relatively low cost of the SMS messaging service. Also, some research believe meaningly interprets that cost of SMS does matter to consumptions. This functionality is increase of interest to service provider industry due to the service provider can interact with their customer anytime and effectively and more flexible compared to call customer one-by-one.

The system automates customer care using short message service. The message service comprises of reminders to maintain the customer's vehicle, administration (e.g., booking), home services, greeting/courteous message, and inform customers of new services.

Related Work and Motivation

As a business strategy "Customer Relationship Management (CRM) is a customer-focused business strategy that aims to increase customer satisfaction and customer loyalty by offering a more responsive and customized services to each customer was articulated that the objective customer relationship is to form customer's perception of an organization and its products through identifying customer, creating customer knowledge and building a relationship. Customer relationship management is extending into three levels; strategic, operational and analytical. To keep the customer service provider company have and add new one, the company need to make close relationship with customer, the relationship can be done by calling customers every day whether on the web, by phone, or via mail to give close attention personally. Operational CRM deals with automation and streamlining workflow at the front office which includes collecting data, processing transactions, and controlling workflow at the sales, marketing, and services. The analytical type deals with increasing customer and organization value using the customer data. Analytical CRM builds on operational CRM and analyze customer data to create information about the customer segmentation, customer behavior, and customer value to the organization using statistical analysis tools especially the data mining.

Initially, to make close relationship with its customers, service Provider Company made a mechanism to remind customer to maintain their vehicles. Service Provider Company notify and remind customer by phone, this mechanism was costly and took much time to remind customer one by one. Before remind notify and customer by phone, the front-office officer estimating the time when customer's vehicle should be maintain for the next period accordance to historical data retrieved from System and Application and Product in Data Processing (SAP). The estimation was done by using a tool, but the tool has a lack in estimation result, inaccurately. Base on result given by tool (i.e., list of estimated customer), then front-office officer notify and remind each customer to maintain their vehicle by phone (call customers one-by-one). Need much time to call all of customer and spend much money to remind customer by phone. Hence, front-office officer decided to choose and call potential customer. Accordance to this lack, we proposed new tool (more accurately result) and adopt Short Message Service (SMS) technology to notify, remind customer to maintain their vehicle and customer administration (e.g., booking service and booking home service). Utilizing Short Message Service to notify and remind customer can be the effective way, SMS guarantee delivery of notifications and alerts sent to single or multiple users and increased user productivity through instant delivery of notifications and alerts.

System Overview

To automate this proses (i.e., remind customer to maintain their vehicle, customer administration such as make an appointment and booking home service), first of all customer should fill in their phone number in application form. This phone number will be used to inform and notify the customer to maintain their vehicle when the time has come (the time will be estimate by system automatically). To forecast the time (customers will come to garage to maintain their vehicle for the next period); the service provider company should have two previous record of each car. System will use all previous kilometer records to forecast when customer will be come to garage and maintain their vehicles. After forecasting is complete, system will send text message to remind customer to maintain their vehicle for the next few day. The notification will be send to customer within two weeks before estimation day (if estimation day is 14th, then notification would be send on 1st). This mechanism chosen, we realize that customer will need time to decide when they will come to garage to maintain their vehicle.

In figure illustrates the whole proses of system development. Customer's historical data in database forecasted by system to gain the estimation date or day, and send reminder message accordance to estimation result. Database consist customer's historical service can be connected to SMS Server to supply data or can be uploading as external data (e.g., excel file or text file). Whereas figure illustrates the text message would receive by customer.

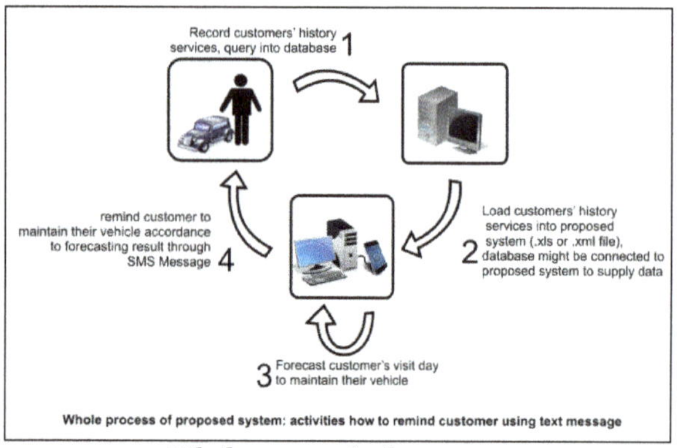

Whole process in the system

Message sent by System

The system development supporting two-way communication, it means customer can interact with service Provider Company through short message service. Customer can reply notification or reminder sent by system, and customer's reply might be considered as appointment or booking in case message format match in comparison to format defined by system. Message server will send a message alert if customer send wrong message format.

When customer replies the message sent by system, first of all system will check the SMS from the mobile phone and translate from Protocol Data Unit (PDU) format into plain text. In the PDU mode, a complete SMS Message including all header information is passed as a binary string (the opposite, text will be translate into PDU format before send to receiver). The translation message will be read and divide into three part (i.e., keyword, police number, address is optional for home service only) and compare keyword (in text message) to identified keyword (in message server). If the message format matched, system will store the message accordance to the format sent (there are two type of message format identified by system i.e., appointment and booking home service). The opposite, system will send a notification message inform that the message sent by customer was unidentified format or wrong format. Figure below shows how system read and respond the message sent by customer, then store the message in database when SMS server received right format. Figure illustrated alerting message due to invalid message format sent by customer. Throughout customers send a wrong format, system will send the alert message informed that the message sent by customer was unidentified by system. This repetition will always continue as long as system receives unidentified message format sent by customer.

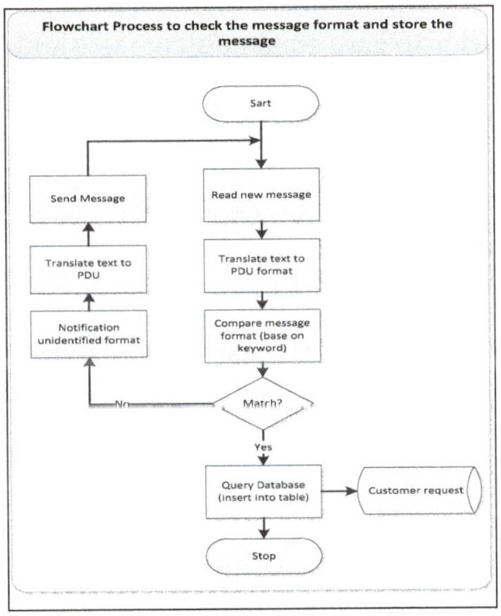

Reading and Responding Message

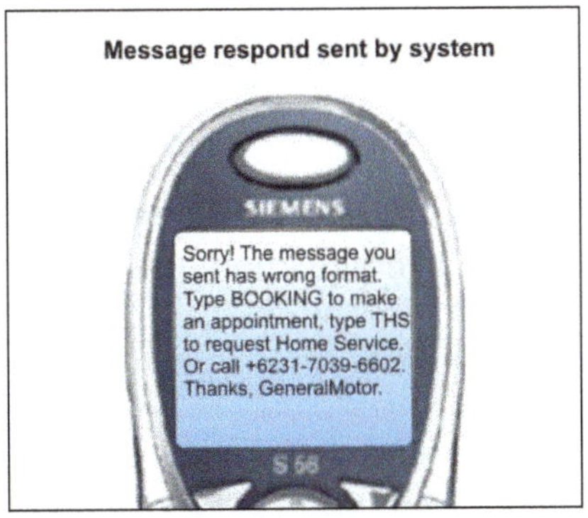

Message Alert Due To Invalid Message Format

To avoid this repetition happen steadily, alert message sent by SMS Server contains guidance how to reply message correctly corresponding message format identified by system. Customer might call the customer representative or customer service for further information or make appointment to maintain their vehicle.

Scenario Implementation and Analysis

To test and measure reliability of our model, we present three scenario; these scenarios are related to function that system should do.

The scenarios are:

- How to forecast when customer should to visit garage to maintain their vehicle.
- Reminder customer to maintain their vehicle trough Short Message Service (SMS).
- Alerting customer regards invalid message format.
- Submitting customer request into data.

These scenarios were representing whole proses of our system. We carried out all main proses of our system through these scenarios to gain good point of view how operational customer relationship management done using short message service through our proposed system.

Algorithm Scenario One

This scenario forecast shows how system forecast the time when customer due visit garage to maintain vehicle. Accordance the result of this scenario system will send short message to inform or remind customer to maintain the car. This scenario will forecast how long the car reaches next 10000 kilometers (generally, the car will be maintain when reach 10000 kilometers of usage).

Algorithm scenario one:

- Input: customers' service records
- Output: estimation day
- Begin

Step 1: Upload customers' service records contain (police number, address, kilometer stated, and execution date of maintenance) into system.

Step 2: Calculate average kilometer per day. Forecast how long the car will reach next 10000 kilometers (first of all system will count the average kilometer usage per day).

Step 3: Show estimation day of all customers.

Algorithm Scenario Two

Accordance to the result of scenario one, system will remind customers to maintain their vehicle using text message. System will send message to the nearest estimation result from day while estimating performed.

Algorithm scenario two:

- Input: police number, estimation day, phone number.
- Output: SMS Message, notification message that remind customer to maintain their vehicle.
- Begin.

Step 1: Make sure phone number was a valid input, and insert message to SMS_RECEIVER table (this table contains outgoing message).

Step 2: The SMS server will be always active. Translate the message into Protocol Data Unit (PDU) before ready to send.

Step 3: Check if the message has been Inserted into the SMS_RECEIVER table in the Local database as an outgoing Alerting massage, mark as sent. At the end, this message should be received by the DBA in his mobile phone. End;

As the result of our scenario, the outgoing message in the SMS_RECEIVER table should be same as the message that shall get to a customers' mobile phone.

Algorithm Scenario Three

As mention earlier, our proposed system supporting two-way communication. Customer can interact with system by reply the message. The third scenario will show how system read and process the message sent by customer and send alert message when customer sent invalid message format

Algorithm scenario three:

- Input: Text message (keyword).
- Output: Alerting text message due to invalid message format.
- Begin.

Step 1: Retrieve message from phone and translate message from Protocol Data Unit (PDU) format into text. Insert into INBOX table. Make sure the message in modem or phone deleted.

Step 2: Read new record in INBOX table and divide as parts and compare to format identified by system.

Step 3: if message format doesn't matched, then system will sent message alert due to invalid message received. Before send alert message, system will translate message into Protocol Data Unit format. End;

As a result the outgoing message should be same as the alert message that shall get to a customers' mobile phone.

Algorithm Scenario Four

This is the last scenario to test and measure our proposed model. This scenario will show how system responds the message sent by customers. Previous scenario show how system alert customer regards invalid format, this scenario system responds valid format.

Algorithm scenario four:

- Input: Text message (keyword)
- Output: Appointment or booking
- Begin

Step 1: Retrieve message from phone and translate message from Protocol Data Unit (PDU) format into text. Insert into INBOX table. Make sure the message in modem or phone deleted

Step 2: Read new record in INBOX table and divide as parts and compare to format identified by system.

Step 3: If message format matched compare to format message identified by system, system will submit a query corresponding keyword. In case keyword was an appointment system will query database as new appointment. Else, if keyword was a booking home service, system query database as booking service.

At the end of this scenario, system will creates new appointment or booking and save it in database corresponding the keywords. The keyword would be booking for appointment or THS to request home services.

The all of scenarios will always executes when send remind or alert message toward customers and read message sent by customers. Send message to ten correspondents or customers were conducted using three GSM operators they are Mentari, XL, and Simpati to test our systems. As the result of test we discovered average time of sending short message service less than 10 second. The performance is not affected by the connection between the computer and the mobile phone or GSM/GPRS modem (i.e. the SMS sending rate is about the same no matter the mobile phone or GSM/GPRS modem is connected to the computer through a serial cable, USB cable, Bluetooth link or infrared link) and does not depend on whether a mobile phone or GSM/GPRS modem is used.

Table: Delivery time to send message.

Delivery Time For Each Operators			
Number Message Sent	Mentari	Simpati	XL
1	15	10	9
2	10	25	9
3	40	20	8
4	20	10	30
5	15	9	15
6	10	20	10
7	10	30	15
8	9	53	9
9	9	9	8

10	8	9	6
Average time	14.6	19.5	11.9

Sending rate is or a GSM/GPRS modem is used). The determining factor for the SMS sending rate is the wireless network.

Marketing Automation

Marketing has evolved significantly over the years and has become more complex and perplexing than ever. Consumers are now using multiple media platforms to gather data and to stay up-to-date, making life difficult for marketers. However, with marketing automation features in its CRM, a business can streamline and optimize a variety of marketing tasks. This will increase the effectiveness and efficiency of the sales and marketing team by saving time on administrative tasks, delivering messages with the right content to the right audience, closing deals faster through increased automation, hence, increasing revenue and profits.

Marketing automation is an amazing technology but only if it is customized according to the needs and requirements of the business, otherwise it can prove to be counterproductive. For your convenience, here is a list of the key features that you need to look out for in a marketing automation platform.

Email Marketing

Emails are the principal communication channels with potential leads. With an automation tool, you can test your email content, create beautiful email templates that match your brand identity, preview your emails across platforms and devices and do advanced email reporting. Marketing automation in CRM incorporates Email marketing functionality and then expands on it by customizing content interactions through logic workflows e.g. you can send a 'Happy Birthday' message to a loyal customer and offer him a discount or send a 'Thank You' message when someone makes a purchase. This can make the difference between a happy customer and a lost prospect.

CRM Integration

Marketing automation platforms that integrate seamlessly with Customer Relationship Management platforms can be a very powerful weapon. Tight CRM Integrations will allow you to transfer lead information seamlessly between marketing and sales. Better alignment between marketing and sales will improve the effectiveness of campaigns. Your CRM system should talk to your marketing automation platform and your marketing automation platform should talk to your CRM system.

Lead Nurturing

Send the right information to the right prospects at the right time. Lead nurturing is the process of sending a series of automated emails that will trigger based on a person's behavior. Being able to nurture leads based on a variety of attributes (behavior, demographics, buying stage) is a highly sought after tool for marketers.

Campaign Management

Campaigns are the workflows you use to nurture leads along the sales cycle. Campaigns have both timed and triggered events. To run successful campaigns you need to send direct and personalized emails to a large number of people. Make sure the campaign management within your platform supports both inbound marketing and outbound campaigns as well.

Lead Management and Scoring

This is another fundamental feature of marketing automation software. Lead scoring enables marketers to concentrate on the most promising leads. Every customer receives a score, based on his activities. When a lead matures i.e. reaches a threshold value, it is assigned to a sales representative so that appropriate action can be taken. Being able to move leads through the entire marketing funnel is a challenging task and should be handled effectively by your Marketing Automation Platform.

Landing Pages

Also known as a Call to Action page, a landing page is any page in a website where traffic is sent specifically to prompt a certain action. Landing pages help increase conversion rates through targeted promotion. You can market multiple products to audiences using highly customized landing pages with very specific targeted content. Many marketing automation systems have excellent landing page builders. Make sure you select a landing page builder that is flexible and easy to use.

Social Marketing

Know what the customers and prospects have to say about your company's products and services, how they respond to email messages and website content, and then incorporate that data into your marketing automation platform. The marketing automation platform you select should have built-in social media marketing and management tools.

Visitor Tracking

Monitor every person who visits your website by tracking their behavior, including which pages they click, from where they access the website, what keywords they type on Google that direct them to your website, and so on. Many applications deliver real-time alerts to sales representatives when a lead, prospect or customer visits the website. Visitor tracking should also help you segment your database based on these tracked activities.

Benefits of Marketing Automation

Marketing Automation software can be useful if any business capitalizes on it effectively. SMBs especially can make use of this software to monitor and manage tasks while saving time using automation. The primary aim of this software is to provide a unified communication platform, where the marketing team can track and understand the marketing journey of a customer.

There are many benefits of using marketing automation software and you can read about the eight common benefits below:

Track Contacts

This software provides a unified platform using which businesses can track various customers on different channels easily. Understand and monitor your potential customers' web activities and buying behavior; record and respond to all communication channels; and deliver timely marketing messages to your customers. Using this software, you can gain insights about your customers and analyze their keenness to make the purchase.

Save Time

Using marketing automation software, businesses can automate their regular marketing tasks quickly while saving time to concentrate on other marketing strategies. Through this software, you can create multiple campaigns to send scheduled-customized emails to any number of customers; set-up auto-responders for daily follow-ups; or automate messages for various social media channels.

Build Relationships

Through this software, businesses can establish good relationships with their customers. The regular in-flow of data on daily customer activities helps personalize your interactions and improves them if need be. It helps you to deliver more valuable communication to your potential buyers and current customers, and build strong relationships.

Maintain Consistency

This software allows you to schedule your tasks in a timely manner to ensure that you are maintaining consistency in your process. Using this software, you can schedule timely follow-ups for all your customers' replies or achieve timely posting on all your social media channels without any delays.

Monitor Omni Channels

Using marketing automation software, you can monitor all the channels you use to interact with your potential buyers and current customers. From emails to social media, you can get detailed information on which customer did what and where, in minutes.

Create Reports

This software helps you track and monitor all the channels. Using this data you can create detailed reports and save them in the software itself. You can analyze the statistics and graphs on various campaigns and use these data to know which campaign did better. You can also organize and share these reports automatically with other teams or team members.

Lead Nurturing

Using marketing automation, you can simplify and automate the whole process of lead nurturing. You can easily clip prospects' and leads' information from various social media channels and add them directly. You can automate lead categorization using lead scoring and send personalized emails using email automation. You can also improve your follow-ups through auto-responders.

Detailed Profiles

This software helps you to create detailed customer profiles using email open rates, web behavior and responses. Various communication channels will help you gather new information about customers and after analyzing this data, you can add more points in your customer profiles.

Customer Service Automation

Customer service automation is more than just offering your customer convenience and faster processing. Customer service automation can cover a wide range of departments, including more personable automated messages, or auto-generated invoices. An enhanced customer experience includes meeting your consumers with professional and efficient service, but many employers fall into the trap of using technology as a substitute for a quality customer experience. Automation is a contentious issue around the world, because not only do people lose that face-to-face interaction with human beings, but what usually follows are massive job loses, as more employers seek to replace their workers with machines.

This method of automation usually does not last long, since many people still prefer old-fashioned human contact, and this is what truly delivers a superior customer experience. If you go to a grocery store, compare automated check-out centers to human cashiers physically scanning purchases. Despite room in the automated checkout lines, many customers prefer paying for their items with human cashiers. It might be more convenient to check out a few items with the automated system, but humans will inherently be more comfortable interacting with a human being rather than a computer.

The true essence of a good customer experience is balancing efficient technologies, while keeping your finger tapped on the pulse of consumer sentiment in order to deliver better service than your competition.

What does Ideal Customer Service Automation Looks Like?

CX automation not only benefits consumers, but your company as well. It does not mean you have to invest a vast amount of time and resources to keep up with the Digital Age. Benefits of automation translate into cost reduction, customer retention, better rate of return, and increased revenue. CX automation works because it all boils down to the customer. Before long, your consumer base will swell in numbers, and revenue will continue to flow.

The Specifics

The umbrella of customer service automation includes speedier processing of orders, quality calls, reduction of data entry errors and improved training. It also requires a level of creativity, such as using the best technologies to meet customer service demands, getting a sense of how your consumers perceive your company, and what they would like to see. Many companies already do this by having consumers fill out questionnaires, or drawing them in with prizes or contests in exchange for input.

Don't Forget your Employees

Customers are the most important, but employees define your company. Employees tend to be afraid of the word "automation," but our form of automation is a process that requires worker participation. Employees must be trained in the most cutting-edge technologies that will meet quotas, while still retaining that crucial human touch that so many customers prefer. What usually tends to happen is that technology will drive a wedge between the customer and worker, but our brand of automation should simplify things between both parties.

Speed is of the Essence

Worker and customer cohesion sounds good on print, but a lingering question is how long it takes to fully implement customer automation. Receiving top-notch service from your IT service is one thing, but you don't have years to wait for this function to come to fruition. Service automation is something that needs to happen in the short-term, as more of your competitors are upgrading their Salesforce capabilities. With our service, you'll get that unique touch, combined with the necessary haste in setting up a quality automation system.

Pros, Pitfalls and Best Practices

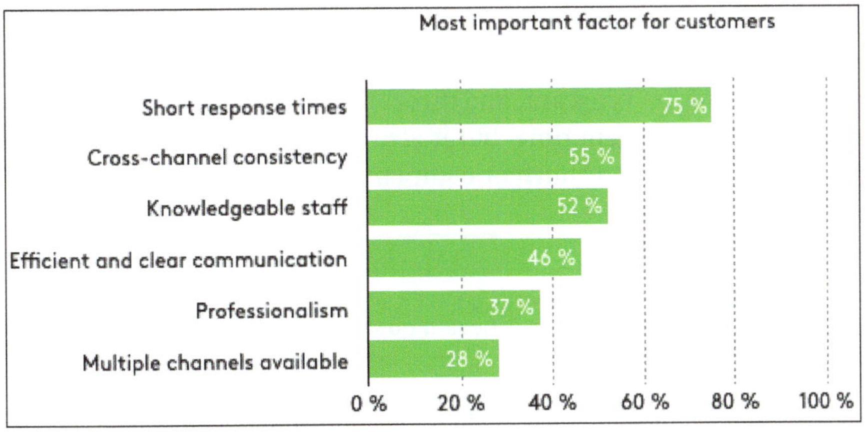

The automation of everyday life is not an unusual occurrence: from grocery shopping to the management of our very social life, we smoothly automate a great many tasks. Customer service automation is no exception.

As customers become both more tech-savvy and more demanding, their foremost expectation in terms of service is speed.

Customer service automation can help in that regard, and in others. However, the practice often gets a bad rap.

Benefits of Customer Service Automation

Implementing customer service automation processes can have several advantages. In short, automation removes or minimizes the human element in a given area of service. This removes the potential for redundancy, wasted effort, and human error.

Streamline your Process

Customer service automation can have a very beneficial effect on your team's workflow. For instance, your help desk system can be automated to provide scripted responses to the most recurring support scenario. This means that your human agents won't waste time typing out the same response several times a week.

The same program can also automate work flows by prioritizing and attributing tasks. These include responding to customers and following up on ongoing support situations. These small reductions in the effort expended daily by your team can add up to hours, even days, of time saved over the course of a year.

Introducing customer self-service resources, such as FAQs, and interactive knowledge bases, will allow customers to solve mundane problems and answer common questions without needing the help of a live agent. These automated solutions will leave the human support representatives more time to field the extra-difficult queries.

Reduce Friction for the Customer

When a customer gets in touch with customer service, long wait times is a giant pain point. To shorten them, you have several options: automating support channels, or hiring more agents.

The former can be achieved with the help of interactive voice recognition, or IVR. IVR lets callers interact with a voice recognition program, and direct them to the right interlocutor based on their needs. This not only saves your team time, but it also spares the customer a great deal of frustration, and gives them no incentive to churn or complain.

To take it one step further, customer service automation can allow you to preemptively do away with customer's friction points, thanks to predictive analytics. Call recording, voice recognition, and usage monitoring can help you keep tabs on how customers interact with your product, sales team, and support funnel. This lets you surveil product adoption and improve your customer retention, as well as zero in on frequent problem points in order to remedy them.

Lower your Costs

The other option to reduce wait times and expedite customer service is hiring more employees. This isn't necessarily feasible for your business. Perhaps you're starting out and funds are limited, perhaps recruitment is slow. Customer service automation lets you operate convincingly and efficiently with a more compact team.

While some automation services are costly to implement, many are available on a subscription basis. This means your support desk, your CRM software, your phone system, etc. You won't pay for more than you use, and you'll be able to easily scale your subscription to suit your needs.

Cater to an Emerging Demographic

Gen Y is in the process of overtaking Gen X and Baby Boomers in both numbers and purchasing power. Soon, the oft-reviled Millennial generation will compose the largest part of the customer pool. Having borne the brunt of countless jibes, it's obvious that this rising demographic is threatening those witnessing it.

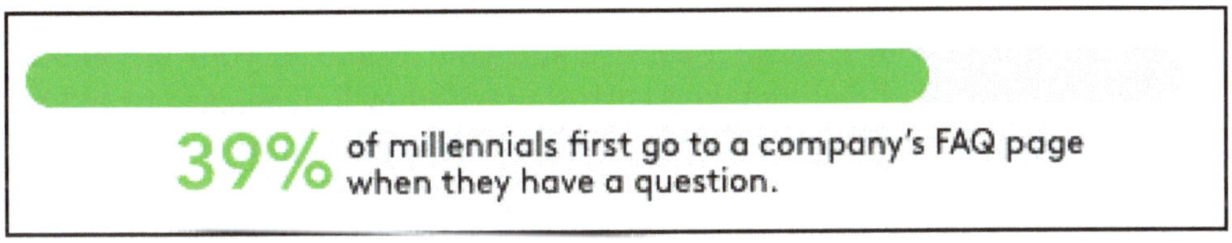

The entirety of Gen Y is often lumped together and characterized as lazy, entitled, and aloof. Another way to consider this is: as digital natives, Millennials are self-reliant, resourceful, and savvy problem-solvers. As such, they respond favorably to the possibility of automated service: 70% of Millennial women report being comfortable solving an easy issue without talking to a human, 60% of Millennials also feel good about themselves and the company when they are able to sort out a support issue on their own. Not only are Millennials comfortable with solving an issue with the assistance of automated customer service, they also welcome the opportunity to do so on their own, with an added benefit of bonding with the brand in question. Well trained and well informed customers are less likely to even require customer support, so Gen Y's resourcefulness is a quality businesses should embrace and enable, rather than resent.

The Pitfalls of Customer Service Automation

If the automation of customer service processes was both easy to implement and risk-free, then everyone would be set. That's just not the case. There are several potential bumps in the road to a successful automation strategy.

No Human Connection

The first is an obvious caveat: when you automate customer service, you necessarily tone down the human element of your support strategy. Customers can resent having to deal with a machine. Indeed, empathy, a quintessentially human ability, is an essential part of exemplary customer service. In one example, one brand found that emotionally engaging with customers reduced attrition and increased advocacy.

Let's return to the example of Millennials- While they welcome the opportunity to demonstrate self-sufficiency, they also strongly tend to patron brands with which they've formed an emotional bond. This search for reliability and identification can be severely hampered by customer service automation. It can be extremely off-putting to a customer looking for advice and support to be met with an automated service instead of a human agent.

Improper Configuration

Poor system design can really hurt your customer service automation system. If your IVR makes your customers go round in circles, if your chatbots can't understand a customer's issue, if call routing causes redundant conversations, then automation is more trouble than it's worth.

Likewise, if your various automated processes aren't available for analysis and cross-reference, then you won't benefit from the resulting insight and your customers won't get qualified informed service.

A Damaged Reputation

Customers will amalgamate your customer service and your brand. If your automated customer service leaves them frustrated of feeling taken advantage of, they'll disengage from your brand altogether. This can be the result of poor configuration, a lack of human presence, or both.

Dissatisfied customers are louder and more visible than contented ones, so the bad publicity resulting from inattention to detail can quickly sink your reputation.

Best Practices for Customer Service Automation

In order to avoid the pitfalls, here are some best practices to help your business pull off its customer service automation.

Pick your Battles

How to avoid alienating customers when it comes to customer service automation? The answer is to only select tasks and processes which invite automation in the first place. This includes repetitive support cases, self-service resources, knowledge bases, checkout pages, usage monitoring, etc. These are all rather thankless tasks; your customers and your team are both better off if they're automated. A good rule of thumb is: if a given automated process isn't collaborative and useful to your team, your customers or both, leave it out.

Nevertheless, a rule of thumb is just that; don't forget to cater to your precise audience. For instance, a repeat user might not need assistance with selecting a product or checking out, but a first-time user or one who returns after a long time away might need some guidance. An automated process which would save the former effort might cause the latter to feel frustrated or abandoned.

Likewise, customers expect consistency above all else across the different service channels you offer. That doesn't mean that all channels are equal when it comes to being automated. You wouldn't go to the trouble of introducing a supplementary channel if your customers won't use it; so don't automate a channel if it doesn't benefit your customers. A Chabot might be a solid idea, but it could also prove frustrating if the bot doesn't suit the needs of the customers.

Merge Service Channels

One way to make automated customer service more collaborative is to merge your service channels. Information silos are a major obstacle to a successful Omni channel strategy, and the same is true for automation.

If your automated channels and processes aren't mutually influenced and affected with your human representatives' tasks, then collaboration and efficiency will take a hit.

Your customers will have to repeat themselves if they have to escalate their issue to a human agent. Or they'll find themselves lost in an operational limbo. This lack of communication will greatly frustrate your team, not to mention your customers. Make sure that your automated processes can integrate with one another and with your other tools: such as by collecting chat logs, phone call recordings, support tickets, emails and more in a single interface for easy agent access and accountability.

Human Service Shouldn't Suffer

On that subject, customer service automation should benefit your team as well as your customers. The savings in time and funds shouldn't lead you to pocketing the difference and neglecting the humans in your team. The extra funds and available time can be reinvested in your human team to give them better training, better tools, and make them better equipped to work in tandem with the technology of automation.

Humans are the technology's backup, maintenance, and escape hatch. For the escalation of complex tasks and problems, humans are a necessity for your customers to receive efficient and empathetic service. Always give the customer the option to talk to a human if they'd rather take it slow. Customer service automation is a valuable tool, but it isn't a crutch for poor management or agent engagement.

Don't Forget to Test and ask for Feedback

Your customer service automation processes should be appreciated by your customers, useful to your team, and beneficial to your bottom line. To achieve this, they need to be up to date. Perfecting your strategy is a matter of continual testing and feedback collection.

First, testing will let you stay up to date with your software and keep it running smoothly. Your technical team is responsible for the upkeep of the automation software. Second, testing is necessary to refining your automation processes. Introduce change slowly, and in small segments at first. This will let your gauge the effectiveness and popularity of these changes.

It's necessary to ask your customers for feedback when you set out on your automation journey. Giving your customers a voice is an extremely important part of any customer service strategy, and automation is no exception. By monitoring how your customers interact with the changes you implement, you'll find out which are most welcome, and which do more harm than good. You'll need constant vigilance, as well as the willingness to impartially consider your own methods.

The learning curve is steep, but customer service automation will only ever be as successful as the planning behind it.

Collaborative CRM

Collaborative CRM is an approach to customer relationship management (CRM) in which the various departments of a company, such as sales, technical support, and marketing, share any information they collect from interactions with customers. For example, customer feedback gathered from a technical support session could inform marketing staff about products and services that might be of interest to the customer. The purpose of collaboration is to improve the quality of customer service, and, as a result, increase customer satisfaction and loyalty.

A Driver of Teamwork

Originally, CRM systems were designed to facilitate interactions with customers. However, in order to be efficient, these interactions need to be completed in a coordinated manner by all the different entities at play. Breaking down silos is the crux of collaborative CRM. Its features enable users to optimize teamwork, and in doing so, is a key element for the coherence of a Customer Relationship strategy.

A Vehicle of Customer Knowledge

Since data is centralized in one single tool, the different departments and divisions of a company can have a comprehensive view of their customers. This is referred to as the "360-degree view". For example, customer feedback collected by the customer service can be useful to the R&D department for future product developments. The results of a marketing campaign can become valuable arguments for the sales team. Collaborative CRM can also capitalize on in-house knowledge, even when employees decide to leave the company. In short, Collaborative CRM improves the performance of the company, in the short, medium and long term.

A Performance Lever

According to a study conducted by Software Advice, 74% of CRM users claim it has enhanced productivity and improved access to information. This is hardly surprising since, CRM software brings together a community of users, thereby promoting information sharing. With such a tool, you no longer have to go to five different people to get the latest version of a file. If you want to take this aspect even further, why not go for a mobile CRM solution? Mobile CRM is the best ally of your account managers, as it provides access to information in real time. What better way to facilitate communication between headquarters and the field.

Applications of Collaborative CRM

No matter how big or small your company may be, you need a CRM solution. It is the cornerstone of any Customer Relationship. This is what will enable you to manage all of your interactions effectively within your ecosystem.

Take the example of INRA, the first institute for agricultural research in Europe, and the second in the world: "INRA and its environment is a rich and complex ecosystem of partnerships between internal and external actors; we needed a collaborative, very customizable software, that would adapt to the needs of the different actors and secure the management of dematerialized data", explains Philippe Leroy, CRM project director.

Whether you are an SME or a large corporation, you certainly have customers, prospects and suppliers. Therefore, it is essential to choose a CRM solution which can meet your specific needs and which can integrate seamlessly with your existing IT system. Of course, to really make the most of the CRM solution you choose and foster cohesiveness among users, you will need to take time to check the features offered by your publisher.

Must-have Features

It is difficult to say what are the most useful features in a collaborative CRM because it depends on the challenges facing each company. However, here is a list of some general features which foster collaborative practices. It's up to you to define specifications which fully take account of your needs, and to choose a CRM solution which is open enough to meet them.

- Messaging (emails, tasks, calendar, etc.)
- Instant messaging
- News feed
- Document Management System (DMS)
- Knowledge base
- CTI (Computer Telephony Integration)
- Integration with office automation software

Access Rights management

With collaborative CRM, all the players of the company can access all relevant information about customers. The notion of "relevant information" is important here. A sales representative may not need to access the same data as a customer service representative, and vice versa. Therefore, it is essential to manage access rights to maintain data security, to simplify operations for users and, ultimately, to facilitate the adoption of the CRM tool.

What you need to Remember about Collaborative CRM

Collaborative CRM is designed to help users do their daily tasks in a more efficient way. This, in turn, will enhance satisfaction, not only on the part of your customers, but also of your staff. The company will therefore become more efficient, more effective and better structured. So, it's up to you now! Be sure to choose the publisher who can offer you the most appropriate collaborative CRM for your needs.

Ways Collaborative CRM Strengthens Engagement

Collaborative customer relationship management (CRM) synchronously shares customer data across various departments, including sales, marketing, service, and finances, to unify business processes with customer experience. Like all manifestations of CRM, collaborative CRM is designed to establish and grow customer relationships, but whereas traditional CRM focuses on automation, the cornerstone of collaborative CRM is customer engagement (CE).

Customer Engagement

The term has multiple interpretations and is therefore difficult to define. In certain cases, CE may refer to customer involvement. It's the outcome of customer experience and how that experience translates into action. That is to say, it's less about how customers feel and more about what they do. Loyalty and advocacy are closely tied to this type of CE.

But CE can also refer to the efforts a company makes to establish a connection with its customers. Collaborative CRM focuses on the latter to achieve the former: it enhances communication between an organization and its customers to obtain valuable information that leads to meaningful experiences.

How it Works?

Before addressing how collaborative CRM can boost engagement, it's important to understand the basics of how the system functions. The primary features of collaborative CRM include interaction management and channel management. Interaction management facilitates the development and implementation of contact channels; channel management relies on data synchronization and integration to streamline interaction media.

So how Exactly do these Features Lead to Better CE?

Paths of Communication

Collaborative CRM takes a multichannel approach to interaction and enables a customer to communicate with the company through a variety of touch points. Traditional means of communication, such as phone or face to face, are no longer enough to engage today's customers. Modern consumers are technologically savvy, and many therefore prefer interaction media that allow them to communicate with an organization through the Web or mobile apps. Collaborative CRM makes a company more available to its customers- it increases the opportunities customers have to interact with the organization at their convenience.

Self-Service Features

Customers don't always want to talk to a service agent to get things done—and with collaborative CRM, they don't have to. Web self-service, which includes searchable knowledge bases and troubleshooting tools, puts control back into customer hands and empowers them by allowing them to resolve issues on their own. Online channels don't have to be limited to support, either; customers can also, for example, add or request new services or products or change their address or billing information.

Companies can then mine these interactions for valuable insights into customer needs and make changes to products, services, or processes accordingly. Technical support can, for example, inspect article views or look up commonly searched terms through Web self-service to find out which problems affect customers the most.

Sharing Data

With collaborative CRM, no longer is information separated into departmental silos. Collaborative CRM synchronizes data among departments so that no one is left out of the proverbial loop. Information gained from sales can be shared with marketing; information gained from marketing can be shared with finances, and so on. For example, by analyzing data from sales, marketing can find out what types of products or services most interest customers. Departments can then use this information to alter their business strategies.

References

- Operational-crm: bpmonline.com, Retrieved 14 May, 2019
- Marketing-automation-crm: rolustech.com, Retrieved 4 January, 2019
- Benefits-of-marketing-automation-software, marketing-automation: agilecrm.com, Retrieved 11 March, 2019
- Customer-service-automation: sysgroup.net, Retrieved 10 June, 2019
- Customer-service-automation, customer-happiness: aircall.io, Retrieved 3 April, 2019
- Collaborative-crm: efficy.com, Retrieved 13 August, 2019
- Ways-collaborative-crm-strengthens-engagement: toolbox.com, Retrieved 20 February, 2019

5

Analytical Customer Relationship Management

Analytical customer relationship management deals with the analysis of customer data which has been collected from various sources, and then presents it in a coherent manner to enable business managers to make informed decisions. The chapter closely examines the key concepts of analytical CRM such as data analysis and customer-related database to provide an extensive understanding of the subject.

It is a systematic approach to analyze customer data and interactions to improve various business processes in Sales, Marketing and Service. The main purpose of Analytical CRM is to gather customer information from various channels and gain knowledge about customers' behaviors and buying pattern as much as possible. It helps an organization to develop new marketing strategy, campaign management, customer acquisition and retention.

Difference between Operational CRM and Analytical CRM

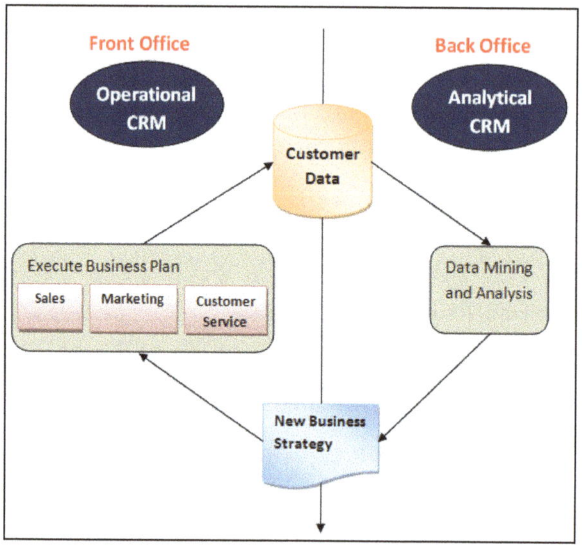

Operational CRM deals with automation of Sales, Marketing and Service processes that involve direct interaction of customers' requirements. Whereas Analytical CRM handles those operations that do not have direct dealing with customers. It analyzes customer data to enhance decision making capability of an organization.

Features of Analytical CRM

1. Gathers all relevant information about customers from various channels/sources and builds a knowledge base for an organization.

2. Analyzes customer data based on rules and methods set by business and prepares report to improve customer relationship and interaction.
3. Helps business to segment customers and run more customer centric marketing campaign to increase sales.
4. Decides what if scenarios – probability of a customer that purchases one product could buy another product.
5. Monitors events like customer may purchase gifts on his marriage anniversary.
6. Helps business to predict the probability of customer defection and take necessary steps.
7. Assists top management to do better financial forecasting and planning.

Benefits of using Analytical CRM:

1. Higher lead conversation rate.
2. Better customer experience by addressing their needs more effectively and efficiently.
3. Better market analysis before running a campaign.
4. Increase customer loyalty and satisfaction.
5. More accurate financial forecasting and planning.

Analytical CRM analyzes data coming from every aspect of business and generates reports:

1. Customer Analysis Report: This is the basic report based on analysis of customer knowledge base. This gives 360 degree view of a customer that helps a company to gain further insights about customer's needs and preferences.
2. Sales Analysis Report: This type of reports shows the organization's sales trend for a specified period – monthly, quarterly, yearly or any time frame that is significant for business. It provides support to streamline all sales opportunities by improving sales cycle. This helps managers to identify market opportunity, predict sales volumes and profit by analyzing historical sales data.
3. Marketing Analysis Report: This kind of reports helps to discover new marketing opportunities and improve marketing performance by maximizing Return on Investment (ROI). It decides marketing performance based on various parameters like region, channels, political influence. It also focuses on campaign planning and execution, product analysis.
4. Service Analysis Report: Service Analytics is a major area in Analytical CRM. It provides the insight about customer satisfaction, quality of service and areas of improvement in service. It finds out opportunities to cross sell or up sell products. It helps to track employee performance and productivity, tells management to conduct required training for employees.
5. Channel Analysis Report: Channel Analysis report helps business to understand customers' behavior across channels like email, phone call, social media or face to face interaction. This kind of knowledge can be used to interact with customers more effectively and efficiently.

For an organization, collection of customer data and its analysis is a continuous and iterative process. Decisions based on customer data and feedback become better and more accurate over the time.

Analytical CRM uses various data mining techniques like predictive modelling, supervised modelling.

Data Analytics in CRM Processes

Data analytics needs to be used to form responses to real time shifts in customer actions and behavior.

Effective CRM using data analytics has many stakeholders, including data mining practitioners and consultants, data analysts, statisticians, and CRM officers. Historically, business intelligence and data warehouses have been associated with back office employees. Over time, knowledge workers got directly involved in data analysis and developed abilities to perform rich and diverse analytical activities. Pervasive BI is the ability to deliver integrated right-time DW information to all users, including front-line employees, suppliers, customers, and business partners. As usage matured, requirements to include predictive analytics, event-driven alerts, and operational decision support have become the norm.

Data Analytics in the Customer Life Cycle

Customers'data may be found in enterprise-wide repositories, sales data (purchasing history), financial data (payment history and credit score), marketing data (campaign response, loyalty scheme data) and service data. All of these data create new opportunities to extract more value. As shown in figure, enterprise CRM supports all aspects of the customer life cycle. Ideally, CRM is "a cross- functional process for achieving a continuing dialogue with customers, across all of their contact and access points, with personalised treatment of the most valuable customers, to increase customer retention and the effectiveness of marketing initiatives".

From the business planning perspective, the CRM framework can be classified into operational and analytical. Operational CRM refers to the automation of business processes, whereas analytical CRM refers to the analysis of customer descriptive, attitudinal, interactive and behavioural information so as to support the organisation's customer management strategies.

Analytical CRM builds on the foundation of customer information. The role of analytical CRM continuously increases in enterprises. Analytical CRM is the use of data to develop relationship strategies.

The ability to access, analyse and manage vast volumes of data while rapidly evolving the information architecture has long been a goal at many enterprise institutions. An integrated approach to data analytics management requires a broad business perspective not just slamming in another software package. Typically, data analytics involves integration with the following infrastructure and tools:

- Analytical CRM (customer information storage.

- Business rules and decision automation engine. Predictive models can be integrated with a business rule engine, which drives the workflow).
- Predictive analysis, data mining, and statistical.
- Modelling tools.
- Visualization tool (business intelligence).

Typically, there are four phases of the customer lifecycle: Customer Identification, Customer Attraction, Customer Retention, and Customer Development. These four dimensions can be seen as a closed cycle of a customer management system. In order to gain a deep understanding of Data analytics in CRM processes, this section will introduce CRM functional technologies that are closely related to data analytics. Table outlines some of the most widely used CRM functional solutions, their definitions and their implementation benefits.

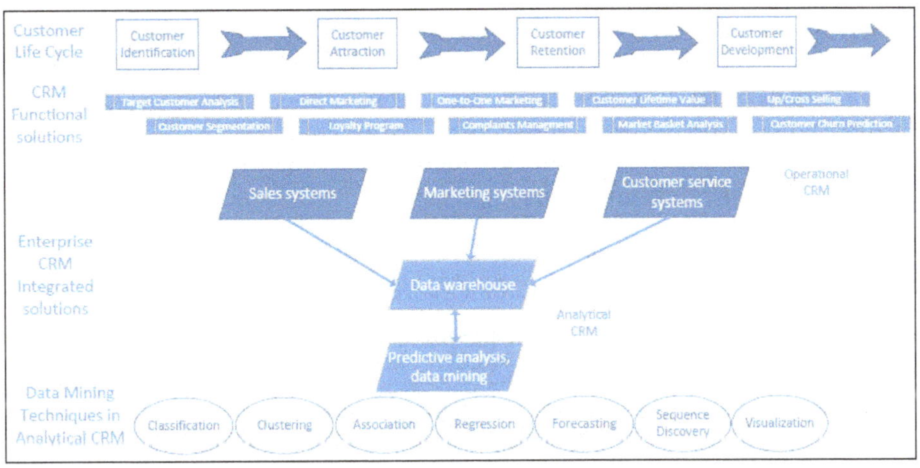

CRM supports the customer life cycle

There are nine existing examples of data analytics applications in industries which enhance operation processes to some extent.

CRM Functional Solutions

Target Customer Analysis

A target market analysis is a systematic and comprehensive assessment that allows identifying important characteristics about target markets and grouping them into categories based on those characteristics.

Customer Segmentation

Customer segmentation divides a customer base into groups of individuals that are similar in specific ways relevant to marketing, such as age, gender, interests and spending habits.

Direct Marketing

Direct marketing is a form of advertising which enterprises and organisations use to communicate directly to customers through a variety of media, including cell phone text messaging, e-mail, websites, etc.

Loyalty Program

Loyalty programmes are structured marketing strategies designed by merchants to encourage customers to continue to shop or use the services of businesses associated with each.

programme. These programmes exist covering most types of business, each one having varying features and reward schemes.

One-to-one Marketing

Personalised marketing is a marketing strategy by which companies leverage data analysis and digital technology to deliver individualised messages and product offerings to current or prospective customers.

Complaint Management

Complaint management re-establishes the satisfaction of the person who has lodged a complaint and reinforces the customer relationship.

Customer Lifetime Value

In marketing, a customer lifetime value is a prediction of the net profit attributed to the entire future relationship with a customer.

Market Basket Analysis

Market basket analysis (also called an association analysis) analyses purchases that commonly happen together.

Up/Cross-selling

Cross-selling is a practice of selling an additional product or service to the existing customer. In practice, businesses define cross-selling in many ways. It is often combined with crossselling and up-selling techniques to increase revenue.

Data Analytics Techniques

Methods for querying and mining big data are fundamentally different from traditional statistical analysis on small samples. Firstly, data mining requires integrated, cleaned, trustworthy, and efficiently accessible data, declarative query and mining interfaces, scalable mining algorithms, and big-data computing environments. At the same time, data mining itself can also be used to help improve the quality and trustworthiness of the data, understand its semantics, and provide intelligent querying functions.

Each data mining technique can perform one of the following types of data modelling or even more- Association, Classification, Clustering, Forecasting, Regression, Sequence Discovery and Visualisation.

Association

Association or association rule learning is method that is used to discover unknown relationships hidden in big data. Rules refer to a set of identified frequent itemsets that represent the uncovered relationships in the dataset. The underlying idea is to identify rules that will predict the occurrence of one or more items based on the occurrence of other items in the dataset. There are different algorithms used to identify frequent itemsets in order to perform association rule mining. The most known algorithm is the Apriori algorithm, but the Eclat and the FP- growth algorithm are also often used.

Classification

In data mining, classification is considered an instance of supervised learning, i.e., learning where a training set of correctly identified observations is available. Classification is the problem of identifying to which of a set of categories a new observation belongs, on the basis of a training set of data containing observations whose category membership is known. An example would be assigning a customer into "high risk" or "low risk" classes or assigning a diagnosis to a given patient.

Clustering

In data mining, clustering is the task of grouping a set of objects in such a way that objects in the same group (called a cluster) are more similar (in some sense or another) to each other than to those in other groups (clusters). Big data clustering techniques are classified into two categories: single machine clustering techniques and multiple machine clustering techniques, the latter have been drawing more attention recently because they are faster and more adapt to the new challenges of big data.

Forecasting

Forecasting is the process of making predictions of the future based on past and present data and most commonly by analysis of trends. A commonplace example might be estimation of some variables of interest at some specified future date.

Regression

Regression analysis is widely used for prediction and forecasting. In data mining, the regression analysis is a statistical process for estimating the relationships among variables. Most commonly, the regression analysis estimates the conditional expectation of the dependent variable given the independent variables, i.e., the average value of the dependent variable when the independent variables are fixed.

Sequence Discovery

Sequential pattern mining is a topic of data mining concerned with finding statistically relevant patterns between data examples where the values are delivered in a sequence. It is usually presumed that the values are discrete, and thus time series mining is closely related. Sequential pattern mining is a special case of structured data mining.

Visualisation

The purpose of data visualisation is to communicate information clearly and efficiently via statistical graphics, plots and information graphics. Effective visualisation helps users analyse and reason about data and evidence. It makes complex data more accessible, understandable and usable. Data visualisation combines technical and artistic aspects of data analysis. It is viewed as a branch of descriptive statistics by some researchers and as a grounded theory development tool by others.

The prediction model can have varying levels of sophistication and accuracy, ranging from a crude heuristic to the use of complex predictive analytics techniques.

Predictive Analytics for CRM

Predictive Analytics are all about finding the insights that will help you understand what might happen in the future. They help you recognize patterns in historical data, repeated transactions, and relationship cues. If you use predictive analytics effectively, you can facilitate a more proactive business approach.

There is a gigantic and horrifying sea of predictive analytic research & theory out there – so much so that it could make your head spin. So, for the sake of sanity, let's hone-in on three of the major predictive analytics types and how they can make you a smarter, savvier, sales or marketing professional.

The three predictive analytics we're going to discuss are:

1. Sequencing
2. Cross-Selling
3. Lack of Action

Sequencing

Simply put, sequencing has to do with analyzing probability. If a target performs action A (downloads a whitepaper), followed by action B (clicks on a pricing page), what is the probability they'll perform action C (buy the product)? This concept stems from the work of a Russian mathematician named Markov. Markov researched probability theory and determined that action C is equally as likely to occur if actions A and B occur first.

Seems easy enough- all you do is look at the historical patterns of behavior for A and B to determine your C outcome. But, what if you don't have a lot of historical data?

If you don't have enough historical data to analyze how two or more events affect the desired outcome, there's another way. Part of Markov's model includes an assumption about the data. Not surprisingly, it's called the Markov Assumption. If you consider only the last successful event to predict future behavior, you can assume the probability between that single event and the desired outcome is about the same as it would be otherwise. For example, ideally, we'd like to see Jane download a whitepaper, click a pricing page, and then buy a product. But Markov's Assumption says if someone who visited the site before Jane downloaded the whitepaper and then bought the product, it's likely that Jane will do the same. She doesn't have to download the whitepaper AND click the pricing page for us to assume she will buy the product.

What does that tell us? We don't need gobs and gobs of historical data to start a decent sequencing pattern. We can begin to discover sequences based on one action that leads to a purchase. That means you can initiate data sequencing today based on your most recent successful conversion, and then continue to tweak as you gather more and more historical data to cross-reference.

Ways to use Sequencing Analytics for Better Sales and Marketing

1. Marketing: One way marketing can use sequencing is with behavior-triggered email campaigns. If a person takes actions one or two, they are put into a specific track of the campaign. As you monitor the actions taken throughout each campaign, you'll begin to recognize the patterns to customize your messages going forward.

Two tips to keep in mind for your behavior-triggered campaign:

- Knowledge first, branding later- Create a campaign filled with rich, engaging content that will help the recipient. As they move through the cycle, sprinkle in your branding. The point is to establish trust and position your company as an insightful resource. Once the trust is earned, everything else will follow.
- Use mobile to help you sequence- More people than ever are reading emails on their mobile devices. Optimize your campaign for both desktop and mobile to help get a better grasp on your audience. Are you seeing more conversions from mobile? Weave that into your sequencing analysis to refine the approach. For example, make it easier for them to take action via mobile by replacing hyperlinks with buttons. Buttons are bigger and easier to touch on smaller screens.

2. Sales: Sequencing fosters proactive approaches to the buying cycle. For example, if someone visits your website, downloads a whitepaper, and requests a free trial of your product, you can assume they're pretty interested. Using the sequencing patterns, you can then predict that the next time someone downloads that whitepaper, it's probable that they're interested in the same thing. So, the proactive approach would be to reach out to that prospect. By reaching out you open dialogue that may be able to speak to any hesitations or concerns they have. Important note: There's a right way and a wrong way to reach out.

- Wrong way – "We noticed you downloaded our whitepaper on CRM integration this afternoon. Let's talk about it."
- Right Way – "Hi, you reaching out to local IT professionals about CRM integration. Is that something you're pursuing at this time?"

Don't act like a stalker (even if your sales process inadvertently makes you one). The right approach can make the sale without seeming creepy or overwhelming to the prospect.

Cross-Selling

What do you see when you make a purchase on a website like XYZ? As you go to check out, it shows you suggestions such as: People who bought this TV also bought this HD cable and these DVDs. They're using analytic data to figure out which companion products you're most likely to need/want based on your purchase — it's cross-selling. You can use predictive analytics in the same way.

Just as people who buy a TV often end up needing cables, people who buy one of your products or services may end up needing a companion product. Look back through transactional data from the last two years to see which products were most often purchased together. Then, use your predictive analytics strategy to plan the cross-sell strategy.

Focus on your current customers first when implementing a cross-sell strategy. First of all, you have more data available to you about their buying habits. Second, research has shown that cross-sells to existing customers are 60-70% more likely to be successful than those aimed at new customers.

Your CRM system contains much of your key customer data – so use it. If your social media feeds are integrated into your CRM data, that's even better. Use pattern analysis of Tweets, Shares, Likes, etc. for deeper insights.

Multichannel Analysis

You can start implementing your cross-selling data by:

- Showcasing companion products together on your website.
- Creating a bundled offer for two of your most popular products or services.
- Automating cross-selling in a confirmation email (Think XYZ website "Frequently bought together" tactic).

Lack of Action

The first two predictive analytics we covered have to do with interpreting the data around customers' actions. But, have you thought about the uses of predictive analytics for the opposite? If a customer you have frequent interactions with suddenly wanes in their communication, there may be a problem. Perhaps they're unsatisfied with something, or worse, they are thinking of severing business ties. Best case scenario, you realize their lack of action early enough to reach out to them and save the relationship, but you can't know to do that without first realizing there's a problem.

How do you use Lack of Action to your Advantage?

Look back on the customers who have left you. Can you pull out any patterns or trends? Use those patterns to create a fall-off model. For example, if you notice customers tend to respond slower (or not at all) to your emails prior to dropping your business, you can factor that in to your fall-off model. Think of your fall-off model as the ying to your analytics yang. When you combine the patterns from fall-off with your sequencing data, you can start to predict whether someone is likely or unlikely to buy. If they're more likely to buy, the marketing and sales departments can reach out to encourage the final push.

As the trend towards predictive analytics continue the activity management and sales forecasting of organizations will evolve to match. As humans, we are creatures of habit. Our behavior patterns tend to remain steady, and if you learn to read those patterns, you can vastly improve the effects of your sales and marketing efforts. Many CRM systems are starting to offer predictive analytics capabilities to keep up with this trend. Infor CRM, Salesforce, and Microsoft have all introduced predictive analytics in their latest releases, and another major CRM player, SugarCRM has one in the works. When it comes to predictive analytics, there's no time like the present! Use the power of your information for smarter sales and marketing, starting now.

Customer-related Database

Companies typically do not have a single customer database; instead, they have a number of customer-related databases. Large organizations, such as financial services companies, can have 20 or more customer systems, each with a separate database.

These databases capture customer-relate data from a number of different perspectives. Customer-related data bases might be maintained in a number of functional areas – sales, marketing, service, logistics and accounts – each serving different operational purposes. Respectively, these databases might record quite different customer-related data – opportunities, campaigns, enquiries, deliveries and billing.

Customer-related data might also be maintained by different channel managers – company- owned retail stores, third-party retail outlets and online retail, for example. Similarly, different product managers might maintain their own customer-related data.

Customer-related data can have a current, past or future perspective, focusing upon current opportunities, historic sales or potential opportunities. Customer-related data might be about individual customers, customer cohorts, customer segments, market segments or entire markets. They might also contain product information, competitor information, regulatory data or anything else pertinent to the development and maintenance of customer relationships.

Basic Principles for Maintaining the Customer Database

Maintaining the database means that users will be more likely to have their need for accurate and relevant data met. Accuracy and relevance are two of six desirable data attributes that have been identified data should be shareable, transportable, accurate, relevant, timely and secure. You can remember these desirable data attributes through the mnemonic STARTS.

S- Shareable
T- Transportable
A- Accurate
R- Relevant
T- Timely
S- Secure

S- Shareable

i. Data need to be shareable because several users may require access to the same data at the same time. For example, profile information about customers who have bought annual travel insurance might need to be made available to customer service agents in several geographic locations simultaneously as they deal with customer enquiries in response to an advertising campaign.

ii. Data need to be transportable from storage location to user. Data need to be made available wherever and whenever users require. The user might be a hot-desking customer service representative, a delivery driver en route to a pick-up, an independent mortgage consultant or a sales person in front of a prospect.

Today's international corporations with globally distributed customers, product portfolios across several categories and multiple routes to market face particularly challenging data transportation problems. Electronic customer databases are essential for today's businesses, together with enabling technologies, such as data synchronization, wireless communications and web browsers to make the data fully transportable.

iii. Data accuracy is a troublesome issue. In an ideal world it would be wonderful to have 100 percent accurate data. But data accuracy carries a high costs. Data are captured, entered, integrated and analysed at various moments. Any or all of these processes may be the source of inaccuracy Keystroke mistakes can cause errors at the point of data entry. Inappropriate analytical processes can lead to ill-founded conclusions.

In CRM, data inaccuracy can lead to undue waste in marketing campaigns, inappropriate prospecting by salespeople and general suboptimal customer experience. It also erodes trust in the CRM system, thus reducing usage. This leads to further degrading of data quality.

To counter this, usage volumes and data quality should be monitored. Data need to be entered at source rather than secondhand; user buy-in needs to be managed; data quality processes such as de-duplication need to be introduced. News agency and book retailer WHSmith attribute high response rates of CRM-enabled direct marketing to the accuracy of their database.

For example, an offer of Delia Smith's How to Cook book achieved an 8 percent response rate, significantly more than was the norm before their data quality project was implemented.

iv. Relevant data is pertinent for a given purpose. To check a customer's credit worthiness you need their transaction and payment histories, and their current employment and income status. To flag customers who are hot prospects for a cross-sell campaign, you need their propensity-to buy scores. In designing a data management system to support a CRM strategy, relevance is a major issue. You need to know what decisions will be made and what information is needed to enable them to be made well.

v. Timely data is data that is available as and when needed. Data that is retrieved after a decision is made is not helpful. Equally, decision-makers do not want to be burdened with data before the need is felt. Bank tellers need to have propensity-to-buy information available to them at the time a customer is being served.

vi. Data security is a hugely important issue for most companies. Data, particularly data about customers, is a major resource and a source of competitive advantage. It provides the foundation for delivery of better solutions to customers. Companies do need to protect their data against loss, sabotage and theft. Many companies regularly back-up their data. Security is enhanced through physical and electronic barriers such as fire walls.

Managing data security in a partner environment is particularly challenging, as it is essential that competing partners do not see each other's sales leads and opportunity information, despite being signed into the same CRM system through the same portal.

Ways to Develop a Customer-related Database

Database Functions

Databases support the four forms of CRM – strategic, operational, analytical and collaborative. Strategic CRM needs data about markets, market offerings, customers, channels, competitors, performance and potential to be able to identify which customers to target for customer acquisition, retention and development, and what to offer them.

Collaborative CRM implementations generally use the operational and analytical data as described below, so that partners in distribution channels can align their efforts to serve end-customers. Customer-related database is necessary for both operational and analytical CRM purposes. Operational CRM uses customer-related database to help in the everyday running of the business.

For example:

i. A telecoms customer service representative (CSR) needs to access a customer record when she receives a telephone query.

i. A hotel receptionist needs access to a guest's history so that she can reserve the preferred type of room – smoking or non-smoking, standard or deluxe.

ii. A salesperson needs to check a customer's payment history to find out whether the account has reached the maximum credit limit.

iii. Analytical CRM uses customer-related database to support the marketing, sales and service decisions that aim to enhance the value created for and from customers.

iv. The telecoms company might want to target a retention offer to customers who are signalling an intention to switch to a different supplier.

v. The hotel company might want to promote a weekend break to customers who have indicated their complete delight in previous customer satisfaction surveys.

vi. A sales manager might want to compute his sales representatives 'customer profitability, given the level of service that is being provided. Customer-related database are typically organized into two subsets, reflecting these operational and analytical purposes.

Operational data resides in an OLTP (online transaction processing) database, and analytical data resides in an OLAP (online analytical processing) database. The information in the OLAP database is normally a summarized, restructured, extract of the OLTP database, sufficient toper form the analytical tasks. The analytical database might also draw in data from a number of internal and external sources.

OLTP data needs to be very accurate and up to date. When a customer calls a contact center o enquire about an invoice, it is no use the CSR telling the customer what the average invoice is for a customer in her postcode. The customer wants personal, accurate, contemporary, information. OLAP data bases can perform well with less current data.

Information Requirements

The people best placed to answer the question' what information is needed?' are those who interact or communicate with customers for sales, marketing and service purposes, and those who have to make strategic CRM decisions.

A direct marketer who is planning an e-mail campaign might want to know open and click-through rates, and click-to-open rates (CTOR) for previous e-campaigns, broken down by target market, offer and execution. She would also want to know e-mail addresses, e-mail preferences (html or plain text), and preferred salutation (first name ?Mr? Ms?).

Operational and analytical needs like these help define the contents of customer-related databases. Senior managers reviewing your company's strategic CRM decisions will require a completely different set of information.

They may want to know the following:

Market segmented- Who are our current customers? What do they buy? Who else do they buy from? What are our customers 'requirements, expectations and preferences across all components of the value proposition, including product, service, channel and communication? With the advent of packaged CRM applications, much of the database design work has been done by the software vendors.

The availability of industry-specific CRM applications, with their corresponding industry specific data models, allows for a much closer fit with a company's data needs. Where there is a good fit out of the box, the data base design process for both operational and analytical CRM applications becomes one of implementing exceptions that have been overlooked by the generic industry model.

Some CRM vendors have also built in the extract, transform and load processes to move information from OLTP to OLAP databases although it is highly likely that a client will need to modify and customize the standard processes.

Customer Information Fields

Most CRM software has predefined fields in different modules, whether for sales, marketing or service applications. For example, in a sales application, a number of fields (columns) of information about customers are common: contact data, contact history, transactional history, current pipeline, future opportunities, products and communication preferences.

Contact Data

Who is the main contact (name) and who else (other names) is involved in buying decisions? What are their roles? Who are the decision-makers, buyers, influencers, initiators and gatekeepers? What are the customer's invoice addresses, delivery addresses, phone numbers, fax numbers, e- mail addresses, street addresses and postal address.

Contact History

Who has communicated with the customer, when, about what, in which medium and with what outcome?

Transactional History

What has the customer bought and when? What has been offered to the customer, but not been purchased?

Current Pipeline

What opportunities are currently in the sales pipeline? What is the value of each opportunity? What is the probability of closing? Is there a10 percent, 20 percent, 90 percent chance of making a sale? Some CRM applications enable sales people to allocate red, amber or green signals to opportunities according to the probability of success.

Opportunities

Whereas 'transactional history 'looks backwards, 'opportunity 'looks forward's. This is where opportunities that have not yet been opened or discussed are recorded.

Products

What products does the customer have? When were these products purchased, and when are they due for renewal? Have there been any service issues related to these products in the past?

Communication Preferences

What is the preferred medium of communication – mail, telephone, email, face-to-face, etc.? If it is e-mail, is plain text or html preferred? What is the preferred salutation? And the preferred contact time and location? Customers may prefer you to contact them by phone for some communications (e.g. an urgent product recall), by mail for others (e.g. invoicing), by e-mail (e.g. for advice about special offers) and face-to face for other reasons (e.g. news about new products).

These preferences can change over time. When a customer's preferences are used during customer communications, it is evidence that the company is responsive to customer expectations. Many companies allow customers to opt in to, or out of, different forms of communication. Customers may prefer to adjust their own preferences. Allows customers to opt to receive e-mail about six different types of content: terms and conditions of shopping at Amazon; new products; research surveys; magazine subscription renewal notices; information about and from Amazon's partners and special offers.

Identify the Information Sources

Information for customer-related databases can be sourced internally or externally. Prior to building the database it is necessary to the company to find out what data are available. Internal data are the foundation of most CRM programmes, though the amount of information available about customers depends on the degree of contact that the company has with the customer. Some companies sell through partners, agents and distributors and have little knowledge about the demand chain beyond their immediate contact. Internal data can be found in various functional areas.

i. Marketing might have data on market size, market segmentation, customer profiles, customer acquisition channels, marketing campaign records, product registrations and requests for product information.

ii. Sales might have records on customer purchasing history including regency, frequency and monetary value, buyers ' names and contact details, account number, SIC code, important buying criteria, terms of trade such as discounts and payment period, potential customers(prospects), responses to proposals, competitor products and pricing, and customer requirements and preferences.

iii. Customer service might have records of service histories, service requirements, customer satisfaction levels, customer complaints, resolved and unresolved issues, enquiries, and loyalty programme membership and status:

- Finance may have data on credit ratings, accounts receivable and payment histories.
- Your webmaster may have click-stream data.

Enhancing the Data

External data can be used to enhance the internal data and can be imported from a number of sources including market research companies and marketing database companies. The business intelligence company claritas, for example, offers clients access to their behaviour bank.

Lifestyle Selector Databases

These databases are populated with data obtained from many millions of returned questionnaires.

Experian, another intelligence company, provides geo-demographic data to its clients.

External data can be classified into three groups:

- Compiled list data.
- Census data.
- Modelled data.

1. Compiled list data: Compiled list data are individual level data assembled by list bureaux or list vendors. They build their lists from a variety of personal, household and business sources. They might use local or council tax records, questionnaire response data, warranty card registrations or businesses' published annual reports. Lists can be purchased outright or rented for a period of time and a defined number of uses. Once the list or its permitted use has expired, it must be removed from the database.

If you were a retailer thinking of diversifying from leisurewear into dancewear and had little relevant customer data of your own, you might be interested in buying or renting data from an external source.

Data could have been compiled by the bureau or vendor from a variety of sources, such as:

- Memberships of dance schools.
- Student enrolments on dance courses at school and college.
- Recent purchasers of dance equipment lifestyle questionnaire respondents who cite dance as an interest.
- Subscribers to dance magazines.
- Purchasers of tickets for dance and musical theatre.

2. Census data: Census data are obtained from government census records. In different parts of the world, different information is available. Some censuses are unreliable; others do not make much data available for nongovernmental use. In the USA, where the census is conducted every ten years, you cannot obtain census data at the household level, but you can at a more aggregated geo demographic level, such as zip code, census tract and block group.

Census tracts are subdivisions of counties. Block groups are subdivisions of census tracts, the boundaries of which are generally streets. In the USA there are about 225 000 block groups, with an average of over 1000 persons per group.

Census data available at geo demographic level includes:

- Median income.
- Average household size.
- Average home value.

- Average monthly mortgage.
- Percentage ethnic breakdown.
- Marital status.
- Percentage college educated.

For the UK census there are 155 000 enumeration districts, each comprising about 150 households and ten postcodes. The enumeration district is the basis for much geo demographic data. Individual-level data are better predictors of behaviour than aggregated geo demographic data. However, in the absence of individual-level data, census data may be the only option for enhancing your internal data. For example, a car reseller could use census data about median income and average household size to predict who might be prospects for a purchase promotion.

3. Modelled data: Modelled data are generated by third parties from data that they assemble from a variety of sources. You buy processed, rather than raw, data from these sources. Often they have performed clustering routines on the data. For example, Claritas has developed a customer classification scheme called PRIZM.

In Great Britain, PRIZM describes the lifestyles of people living in a particular postcode. Every postcode is assigned to one of 72 different clusters on the basis of their responses to a variety of lifestyle and demographic questions. Eighty percent of the data used in the clustering process is less than three years old.

Select the Database Technology and Hardware Platform

Customer-related database can be stored in a database in a number of different ways:

- Hierarchical
- Network
- Relational

1. Hierarchical database:

Hierarchical and network databases were the most common form between the 1960s and 1980s. The hierarchical database is the oldest form and not well suited to most CRM applications. You can imagine the hierarchical model as an organization chart or family tree, in which a child can have only one parent, but a parent can have many children.

The only way to get access to the lower levels is to start at the top and work downwards. When data is stored in hierarchical format, you may end up working through several layers of higher-level data before getting to the data you need.

Product databases are generally hierarchical. A major product category will be subdivided repeatedly until all forms of the product have their own record. To extend the family tree metaphor, the network database allows children to have one, none or more than one parent. Before the network database had the chance to become popular, the relational database superseded it, eventually becoming an ANSI standard in 1971.

2. Relational databases:

Relational databases are now the standard architecture for CRM applications Relational databases store data in two dimensional tables comprised of rows and columns. Relational databases have one or more fields that provide a unique form of identification for each record. This is called the primary key. For sales databases, each customer is generally assigned a unique number which appears in the first column.

Therefore, each row has a unique number. Companies also have other databases for marketing, service, inventory, payments and so on. The customer's unique identifying number enables linkages to be made between the various tabases. Let's imagine you are a customer of an online retailer. You buy a book and supply the retailer with your name, address, preferred delivery choice and credit-card details.

A record is created for you on the 'Customer 'database, with a unique identifying number. An 'Orders received 'database records your purchase and preferred delivery choice .An 'Inventory 'database records that there has been a reduction in the stock of the item you ordered. This may trigger a re-ordering process when inventory reaches a critical level.

A 'Payment 'database records your payment by credit-card. There will be one-to-many linkages between your customer record and these other databases. With the advent of enterprise suites from vendors such as Oracle and SAP, all of these databases may reside in the one system and be pre-integrated.

The choice of hardware platform is influenced by several conditions:

- The size of the databases- Even standard desktop PCs are capable of storing huge amounts of customer data. However, they are not designed for this data to be shared easily between several users.
- Existing technology- Most companies will already have technology that lends itself to database applications.
- The number and location of users- Many CRM applications are quite simple, but in an increasingly global marketplace the hardware may need very careful specification and periodic review. For example, the hardware might need to enable a geographically dispersed, multilingual, user group to access data for both analytical and operational purposes.

3. Relational database management system (RDBMS):

A relational database management system can be defined as follows: An RDBMS is a software programme that allows users to create, update and administer a relational database. There are a number of relational database management systems available from technology firms that are well suited to CRM applications. Leading RDBMS products are Oracle, DB2 from IBM, and Microsoft's SQL Server. Most RDBMS products use SQL to access, update and query the database.

The selection of the CRM database can be done in parallel with the next step in this process, selection of CRM applications. Modern database applications come together with their own database schema, which predetermines the tables and columns in the database structure. Each CRM vendor then supports a specified list of database technologies, for example, Oracle or SQL server. Indeed, it is possible to buy an entire platform, consisting of integrated hardware, operating system (OS), database and CRM applications. Leading platforms include UNIX, Microsoft and IBM.

The UNIX platform offers a number of hardware/OS/database options, such as Hewlett-Packard hardware, Digital UNIX operating system and Oracle database. The IBM platform employs AS/400 hardware, OS/4000perating system and DB2/400 database. Microsoft NT servers are becoming more popular for CRM applications, due to the ease with which they can be scaled and expanded.

Populate the Database

Having decided what information is needed and the database and hardware requirements, the next task is to obtain the data and enter it onto the database. CRM applications need data that are appropriately accurate.

We use the 'appropriately 'because the level of accuracy depends upon the function of the database. Operational CRM applications generally need more accurate and contemporary data than analytical applications. You may have personally experienced the results of poor quality data. Perhaps you have received a mailed invitation to become a do nor to a charity, to which you already donate direct from your salary.

This could have happened when a prospecting list that has been bought by the charity was not been checked against current donor lists. Perhaps you have been addressed as Mrs. although you prefer Ms. this is caused because the company has either not obtained or not acted or checked your communication preferences. One of the biggest issues with customer data is not so much incorrect data as missing data. Many organizations find it difficult to obtain even basic customer data, such as e-mail addresses and preferences.

The main steps in ensuring that the database is populated with appropriately accurate data are as follows:

1. Source the data
2. Verify the data
3. Validate the data
4. De-duplicate the data
5. Merge and purge data from two or more sources

1. Sourcing: Organizations must develop explicit processes to obtain information from customers, such as on initial sign-up or when concluding a service call. Organizations cannot rely on customer goodwill; data must be collected whenever interaction occurs.

2. Verification: This task is conducted to ensure that the data has been entered exactly as found in the original source. This can be a very labour intensive process since it generally involves keying the data in twice with the computer programmed to flag mismatches. An alternative is to check visually that the data entered match the data at the primary source.

3. Validation: This is concerned with checking the accuracy of the data that are entered. There are a number of common inaccuracies, many associated with name and address fields: misspelt names, incorrect titles, inappropriate salutations. A number of processes can improve data accuracy.

- Range validation: Does an entry lie outside the possible range for a field?
- Missing values: The computer can check for values that are missing in any column.
- Check against external sources: You could check postcodes against an authoritative external listing from the mail authorities.

4. De-duplication: Also known as de-duping, customers become aware that their details appear more than once on a database when they receive identical communications from a company. This might occur when external data is not cross-checked against internal data, when two or more internal lists are used for the mailing or when customers have more than one address on a database. There may be sound cost reasons for this (de-duplication does cost money), but from the customer's perspective it can look wasteful and unprofessional. De-duplication software is available to help in the process.

The de-duplication process needs to be alert to the possibility of two types of error:

- Removing a record that should be retained. For example, if a property is divided into unnumbered apartments and you have transactions with more than one resident, then it would be a mistake to assume duplication and delete records. Similarly, you may have more than one customer in a household, bearing the same family name or initials.
- Retaining a record that should be removed. For example, you may have separate records for a customer under different titles such as Mr and Dr.

5. Merge and purge: Also known as merge-purge, this is a process that is performed when two or more databases are merged. This might happen when an external database is merged to an internal database, when two internal databases are merged (e.g. marketing and customer service databases), or when two external lists are bought and merged for a particular purpose such as a campaign. There can be significant costs savings for marketing campaigns when duplications are purged from the combined lists.

Maintain the Database

Customer databases need to be updated to keep them useful.

Consider the following statistics:

- 19% of managing directors change jobs in any year.
- 8% of businesses relocate in any year.

- In the UK, 5% of postcodes change in an average year.
- In western economies about 1.2% of the population dies each year.
- In the USA, over 40 million people change addresses each year.

It does not take long for databases to degrade. Companies can maintain data integrity in a number of ways.

Ensure that data from all new transactions, campaigns and communications is inserted into the database immediately. You will need to develop rules and ensure that they are applied.

Regularly De-duplicate Databases

- Audit a subset of the files every year- Measure the amount of degradation. Identify the source of degradation: is it a particular data source or field?
- Purge customers who have been inactive for a certain period of time- For frequently bought products, the dormant time period might be six months or less. For products with a longer repeat purchase cycle, the period will be longer. It is not always clear what a suitable dormancy period is. Some credit-card users, for example, may have different cards in different currencies. Inactivity for a year only indicates that the owner has not travelled to a country in the previous year. The owner may make several trips in the coming year.
- Drip-feed the database- Every time there is a customer contact there is an opportunity to add new or verify existing data.
- Get customers to update their own records- When Amazon customers buy online, they need to confirm or update invoice and delivery details. Remove customers 'records when they request this.
- Insert decoy records- If the database is managed by an external agency, you might want to check the effectiveness of the agency's performance by inserting a few dummy records into the database. If the agency fails to spot the dummies, you may have a problem with their service standards users with administrative rights can update records. Database updating and maintenance is also enabled by database query language.

Common languages are SQL (Structured Query Language) and QBE (Query by Example). Maintenance queries available in SQL include update, insert and delete commands. You can use the commands to update your customer- related database. Insert, for example, adds a new record to the database.

Customer Data Management

Customer data management (CDM) is the process of collecting, analyzing, and managing your business' customer data while solving your customers' specific problems and provide valuable solutions to their issues while maintaining a superior level of customer satisfaction.

By delivering products, services, solutions, and content that offer real value to your audience, you stand to increase customer retention levels, improve brand awareness, and boost your bottom line.

Centered on leveraging consumer insights to improve your strategies and communications by using a highly data-driven process can also be referred to as Customer Intelligence (CI). If you wish to attract and retain your customers, it's critical to gain a clear understanding of your customer. Adopting a CI-driven mindset is essential.

Customer intelligence is not only methodical but will also provide the following benefits to your business:

- Creating customer loyalty.
- The ability to visualize real-time market changes.
- Enhancing your sales efficiency.
- Improving the ROI of your promotional and marketing activities.
- Developing more relatable, sustainable customer-driven business strategies.

Consumer-driven Insights you should know

To highlight the importance of effective customer database management, here is a hand-picked selection of facts, figures, and stats that you need to know:

- 95% of senior executives feel that data is a pivotal part of their business strategy development process. A testament to the potential of client data management.
- A moderate increase in Customer Experience (CX) driven by improved client data management generates an average revenue boost of $823 million over three years for a business with $1 billion in annual revenues.
- 53% of millennial consumers feel that store associates don't have the tools they need to deliver excellent customer service initiatives like mobile devices for looking up shopper profiles and providing product recommendations. By managing customer data more efficiently, you will be able to improve your business's customer-driven activities, both online and offline.
- A recent study discovered that 49% of marketers utilize data to enhance the customer experience.

Best Practices for Customer Data Management

It's clear that effective customer data management has the potential to maximize your business's potential in a number of ways. To help steer your ongoing success, here are 7 customer data management best practices for your reading pleasure.

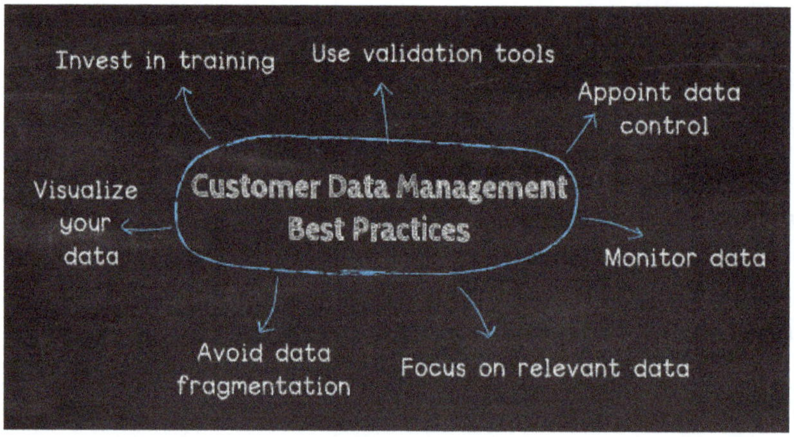

Invest in Training for your Employees

An employee that actively applies data analysis practices to their work can be as much as ten times more productive than someone with little or no practical experience in data analysis. The pivotal element that sets an experienced data analyst apart from a novice is the ability to understand the concept data on a comprehensive level, including the creation of a complete analytical report. This understanding yields a wealth of new resources and insights that can be used to enrich the business's overall data-centric strategies. Invest in training for your business and IT staff – with their buy-in (and newfound skills), you'll be able to conduct truly effective data management.

Smaller businesses should also consider the wealth of economical training options available today. The Internet makes it entirely possible to learn analysis through data analysis books and online courses, many of which are accessible at a low cost or free.

Use Validation Tools

Customer databases consist of millions of records, and each customer is equipped with their own address details, such as the zip code and other invaluable information. Records that fail to include this level of data can cause real problems in the communication process. When this situation occurs, address verification or validation tools can become incredibly useful – and it's possible to integrate them with almost any leading verification software with popular CRM or ERM systems.

Appoint Data Control

Concerning client database management, your analysis should be divided into departments where only a handful of people have full administrative privileges. Unless you take the necessary precautions, you run the risk of having to deal with multiple non-common data entries that may make your stats, facts, figures, and metrics inconsistent.

A good example would be acronyms for countries – you may input 'US' into your system, but someone else might have inserted 'United States'. Such inconsistencies can have a huge effect on the way data is organized through a host of different management systems within a company.

The best way to tackle this problem is to assign a special customer management group that knows all the necessary rules that govern your internal customer data creation. With the help of a decision support software, you may also expand this further into departments so that everyone is up-to-date on the right approach to customer data management.

Monitor your Data

Customer data is a state of constant flux, which is the number one reason to employ solid data monitoring principles. You may want to use specific notification techniques to maintain overall data quality and establish specific security policies that keep data organized and on point.

A bi-weekly scan of incomplete or erroneous records is essential to keep your database fully optimized and updated. Moreover, twice a week, you should also check your data for any unnecessary records and entries that should be cleaned – an essential component of client database management success. An online report generator can decrease the amount of time needed for these kinds of tasks and increase the quality of the data monitoring processes.

With concrete data monitoring principles, you are well prepared to get all your key metrics out of your data with a smart KPI software like datapine.

Focus on Relevant Data for Relevant Results

It's easy to get sidetracked with customer data management and optimize the particular CRM system in such a way that every available source of data is being tracked constantly. But sometimes, you will only need the very surface of all our available consumer data to make the most sound decisions for your company.

It can be overwhelming for anyone in the sales department to come across a plethora of data choices when the only thing that's really necessary is the understanding of which particular data set is most important for the business at any given time. To avoid these 'data overload' roadblocks, focus on implementing your sales report methods in a way that strives for better informational quality over data quantity – a priceless customer data management strategy.

Avoid Data Fragmentation where Possible

When it comes to customer data management strategy, in addition to selecting your consumer data wisely (mining for quality over quantity), implementing a cohesive information collection process is essential.

While you might get the vast majority of your customer insights from a small handful of tools, platforms, or sources, without the ability to view, interact, and analyze with your data from one central location, your information could become fragmented, making it less effective.

It's worth investing in customer data management software that allows you to collect, curate, and drill down into your consumer insights from one central location or live dashboard. That way, you will ensure cohesion and fluidity as well as a full and reliable view of the information that is most valuable to your business.

Visualize your Data

90% of the information transmitted to our brains is visual. Moreover, those who follow directions with illustrations thrive 323% more than people who follow text-only directions. By visualizing your customer data with the help of an online data visualization tool, aiming of using it to drill home an important set of insights or tell a story, you will make this all-important information widely accessible across the business.

If people can understand the data before them because it's more visually digestible, they will be able to develop initiatives that will ultimately enhance the level of customer experience you offer your audience, resulting in increased commercial success.

To put the power of data visualization into a real-world perspective, here are some data visualization examples that you need to explore.

Customer Database Management Examples

By leveraging the right customer database management system for your organization, you will be able to improve your marketing communications, sales initiatives, and customer experience efforts.

While we're on the subject, here are two examples of customer data management software dashboards based on marketing and service.

1. Marketing Performance Dashboard:

A working example of customer data management software (or customer data management system) in action, our marketing dashboard template hones in on the key areas of your customer-driven strategies and promotions with a view of making them more valuable, effective, and economically efficient.

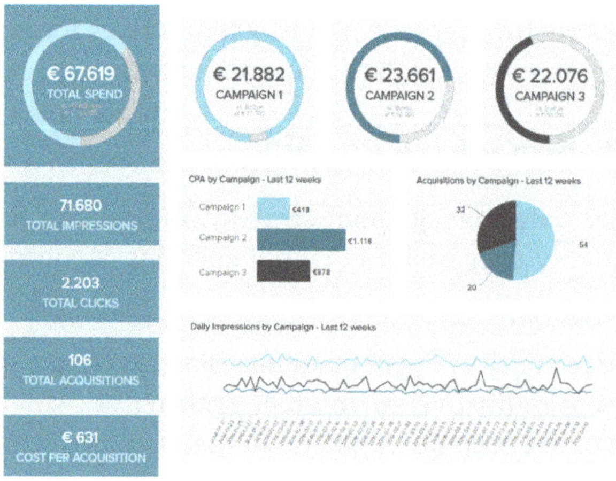

Primary KPIs

- Click-Through-Rate (CTR)
- Cost-per-Click (CPC)

- Cost-per-Acquisition (CPA).

By offering a digestible snapshot of marketing KPIs including CTR, CPC, and CPA, you will be able to sharpen your marketing initiatives to make them more economically viable as well as identify any weaknesses to touchpoints such as your website and landing pages to make your communications more engaging, inspiring, and results-driven.

2. Customer Satisfaction Dashboard:

There's no doubt about it: customer satisfaction is one of the most important elements of ongoing business success. Keeping your customers happy and engaged is the best way to foster brand loyalty and grow your audience over time. Our customer service dashboard will help you do just that.

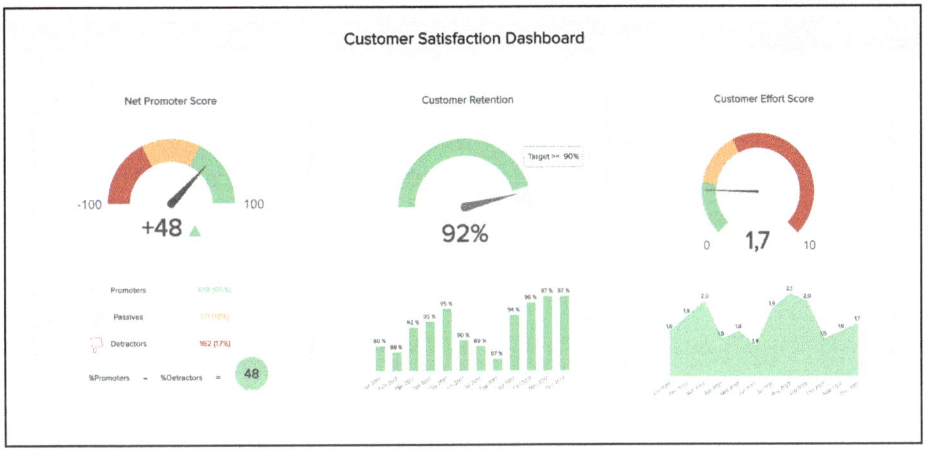

Primary KPIs

- Customer Satisfaction
- Net Promoter Score
- Customer Effort Score
- Customer Retention

With a mix of KPIs that help to monitor, measure, and analyze the success of your consumer-centric efforts in a host of areas, this client database management dashboard (or customer data management system) will help you boost your brand reputation, increase your customer retention rates, and grow your profitability indefinitely.

Although as a digitally transformed species, we've come an incredibly long way in recent years, we're still on a big learning curve concerning the analysis of key consumer metrics and the best customer data management strategy. Customer data management is continually evolving, so we have to work with our current capabilities to avoid the mistakes that could cost us our budget, and most importantly – our customers.

But by following the customer data management best practices, working with the right customer database management system for your organization, and using this wealth of invaluable insights to your advantage, you will be able to reach out and connect with your audience on a deeper, more meaningful level than you ever thought possible – and that, modern business warrior, is priceless.

Customer Data Integration

Customer data integration (CDI) is the process of collecting, organizing and distributing all available information about an organization's customers. CDI aims to maximize the use of this information throughout the entire organization to increase customer numbers, customer satisfaction and corporate profits. CDI uses data integration techniques and is a critical component of customer relations management (CRM).

Customer data integration may involve between six and 12 fields of data for every individual customer, such as name prefix, first name, last name, middle name or initial, name suffix, nickname, maiden name and professional or academic title. Complicating the data management further, much of this data changes frequently and becomes obsolete. For example, customers may change their names, move, get divorced or die. The value of the data is divided into five categories:

1. Completeness: Organizations may lack all the required data to make sound business decisions.
2. Latency: If data is not used quickly enough, it can become obsolete.
3. Accuracy.
4. Management: Data integration, governance, stewardship, operations and distribution all combine to make or break the value of the data.
5. Ownership: The more dissimilar customers are, the more difficult it will be to use the data to make decisions.

Accurate and comprehensive customer data retrieved through CDI has many uses and applications. These include:

1. Providing raw data for various service providers.
2. Optimizing product assortment, promotion, pricing and inventory rotation (merchandising).
3. Reducing waste.
4. Choosing the best locations for branch offices or outlets.
5. Supporting customer relationship management.
6. Supporting master data management.
7. Differentiating customers and their needs.

Data Warehouse for CRM

A CRM system is a package of applications that supports the above activities. Among various functionalities of a CRM system, below are functionalities that are ideally supported by a data warehouse or utilising the data from a data warehouse. Other functionalities may best be served by an Operational Data Store or front end applications.

- Single customer view
- Permission management
- Campaign segmentation
- Manage deliverability
- Customer services/support
- Customer analysis
- Personalisation
- Customer loyalty scheme

Let's discuss these functionalities one by one.

Single Customer View

One of the most important things in CRM data management is the concept of Single Customer View. This concept was raised because customers could be defined differently depending on the context and to which department we are talking to.

For example, a customer could be defined as follows:

- A customer is anybody who has purchased from us.
- A customer is anybody who has registered with us.
- A customer is anybody who has paid us.
- A customer is anybody who is currently subscribed to our newsletters.

And on top of that we have to deal with variations and complications such as:

- Order cancellations: What if the customer has ordered (purchased) from us but before we deliver the goods he cancelled his order? Do we count him as a customer? Hmm, maybe not.
- Contract termination: What if a customer signed a contract for a particular service from us for a year then the following year she did not renew the contract? Do we still count her as a customer? Perhaps not.

- Unsubscriptions: The customer has subscribed to our newsletter and then unsubscribed from that newsletter. Do we count him as a customer? May be not.
- Order life cycle: Order fulfillment process consists of many stages: quotation produced, contract signed, account opened, order placed, order dispatched (for physical goods), order fulfilled/delivered, consumed (for services), invoiced, paid, returned, credit note raised, refunded, account closed. So, at what stage do we recognized them as a customer? Different industries have different order stages.
- Even tough it is not technically a customer yet (technically it may be a prospect), some departments such as marketing need us to store the prospect data.
- When does a customer stop becoming a customer? When they no longer consume our products or services? In some industries such as waste management, the process of 'discharging' a customer is done in stages, for example: stopping the collections, removal of bins, settlement of accounts, deactivate customer status. In some industries there is not concept of stop becoming a customer. Once they purchase something they become customers forever.

So, practically speaking potentially we may need to store subscribers, registered users, purchaser and prospects as customers. What we do in the data warehouse is to build the customer dimension based on several different sources in the operational systems: order data, subscription and permission data, registration data and marketing data. Yes it's true that this will mean that we will have many attributes on the customer dimensions. And yes we do need to deduplicate the data, for example based on customer name, date of birth and address, or email address.

Single customer view simply means that we need to build a customer dimension that is solid, i.e. no duplication of data, complete (no missing customers) and correct. Deduplicate is not always easy, for example name can change when women get married, address changes when they move houses and email address changes over time too (a hard bounce could be an indication). Hence we need to use other measures such as time frame or data age (e.g. we can use the data if it is no more than 1 year old) or using other criteria such as Social Security Number, date of birth, etc. MDM and CDI vendors have a lot experience in this area, as well as data quality and data profiling software such as Trillium.

Permission Management

Regulations differ from country to country, but the basic principle is we can only send campaign to customers who have already given us their permissions to send it to them. Based on the scope, there are 2 kinds of permissions: subscription-based and general permission.

In a subscription-based scenario, we receive requests from customers for sending them a particular communication. For example, say we have 3 communications: weekly newsletter, low price alert and special offers. Customers can subscribe to these communications, either only to 1 communication, 2 communications or all 3 communications. In this case, if the customer subscribes to the low price alert, we can only send them low price alert, we cannot send them other communications. If we have a new communication, we cannot send it to subscribers of other communication. Instead, we need to build a new subscriber base for the new communication. Subscriber base is created by getting end users to subscribe to particular communication through website or promotions.

In the general permission type, customers do not subscribe to a particular communication. Instead, they give permission for us to send them a particular type of communication. For example, say we have 2 communication types: promotional items and subscription items. In this case the subscription items cover everything that is regular and promotional covers everything that is ad hoc. Another example: we can have 3 communication types: transactional (such as order confirmation emails and e-tickets), marketing (such as promotional campaign) and third party (such as campaign from our sister companies).

Permission is also categorized based on the communication channel or media, for example: by email, by SMS/text, by post, by telephone and by RSS feed. There is also a permission for sending (or not sending) *any kinds* of communication to customers. For example, a customer could call or email us asking to be excluded from any forms of communications.

For a multinational company, the permission is could be per locale. It is not necessarily country based, for example: Benelux, Nordic and Scandinavia are often mentioned as one locale, even though they consist of several countries. In those cases 1 office serving more than 1 country. It is possible that each locale has more than 1 language. We could also have several brands or names. For example, we could be operating in a certain country using 3 different company names, each having their own monthly newsletter or promotional campaign. Permissions can also have a validity period, e.g. only for 1 year. We need to take locale, language, brand and validity period into account when constructing the permission fact table and communication dimension.

Let us discuss the design. Permission data is ideally stored in a fact table, with all the above items as the dimension, plus the customer key, date the permission was given, source key and the permission ID as degenerate dimension if applicable. The measures or facts are number of subscribers, subscription price, there are 2 possible fact tables: subscription fact table if you use a subscription based permission, or general permission fact table if you use the general permission approach described above.

For an example let us discuss the design for subscription based type:

```
Fact table name: fact_subscription

Grain: each time a customer subscribes or unsubscribes to a communication.

Type: snapshot accumulative

Table creation script (ignoring partition for the time being):

create table fact_subscription

(customer_key int not null, — who the customer is

communication_key int not null, — what communication the customer is (un) subscribing to

channel_key int not null, — what media will be used (email, post, text, RSS)

promotion_source_key int not null, — which promotion is the source or cause of this
subscription
```

```
brand_key int not null, – which brand managing this (un) subscription

locale_key int not null, – which locale managing this (un) subscription

language_key int not null, – which language this (un) subscription event originated from

expiry_date_key int not null, – the date when this subscription is valid until

subscription_period_key int not null,- how long the subscription is valid for e.g. 3
months, 1 year

permission_id varchar(20) not null, – degenerate dimension from front end CRM system if
applicable

subscription_price money null, – how much this subscription costs

number_of_subscriptions int null, – 1 for a normal subscription, 0 for dummy

subscribed_dt datetime null, – date and time the customer subscribed

unsubscribed_dt datetime null, – date and time the customer unsubscribed, NULL if still
subscribed

is_active_flag tinyint not null, – 1 if the subscription is active, 0 if it is expired
or unsubscribed

created_dt datetime not null, – system date & time when this fact table record was created

last_updated_dt datetime not null – system date & time when this record was last updated

constraint pk_fact_subscription primary key clustered (customer_key, communication_key,
channel_key, subscribed_dt))
```

To get the subscribers' email address and customer name of Ivory weekly email campaign:

```
select email_address, customer_name from fact_subscription sub

join dim_customer cus on cus.customer_key = sub.customer_key

join dim_communication com on com.communication_key = sub.communication_key

join dim_channel ch on ch.channel_key = sub.channel_key

where com.communication_name = "Ivory Weekly"

and ch.channel_name = "Email"

and sub.active_flag = 1.
```

We could store the date the permission is given as a dimension, but we would recommend storing the timestamp on the fact table for 2 reasons: a) we don't loose the time of day element and b) it is easier to retrieve the timestamp data for campaign segmentation. It is not advisable to store the permission in the customer dimension because it would limit the grain to be per customer basis, rather than per customer, communication and date.

So permission management is the capability of a CRM data warehouse to store the permission, based on all of the items described above. And to always keep them up to date. The permission data needs to be made available to the campaign management system to support the campaign segmentation process. It is frequently used, i.e. every time the users create a campaign.

Campaign Segmentation

When creating a campaign, we need to have a list of customers to whom we are going to send it to. These end users are known as campaign target audience. Campaign segmentation process produces this list. Most CRM software has this capability. This is where the SCV play an important role. The richer the customer dimension, the more flexible we can create the segmentation. Segmentation criteria that are commonly used are:

- Permission
- Demographics
- Order data
- Campaign delivery
- Campaign response
- Customer loyalty score
- Customer profitability.

We will give an example on each of the above items so we are clear about what they are. Permission: all customers who subscribed to Norwegian weekly newsletter in the last 3 months. Demographics: all female customers age 20 to 40 who live in Milan. Order data: top 1000 customers (by order value, excluding VAT) who have purchased electronic products from us in the last 12 months. Campaign delivery: exclude customers who had more than 3 hard bounces more in the last 8 weeks. Campaign response: include all customers who have opened the last campaign. Customer loyalty score: include customers from the top tier with more than 500 loyalty points. Customer profitability: include all customers from band A with annual order value > $30,000.

Campaign Results

What we meant by campaign results are:

- Campaign delivery data, i.e. whether the campaign successfully reaches the target audience. For example, say we have an email campaign with 100,000 target recipients. Because of invalid email addresses, we only sent 99k and did not send 1k. Out of these 99k that went out, 96k were delivered to the target recipients' mail boxes and 5k were bounced. All this information is called campaign delivery data.

- Campaign response data, i.e. reactions from the customers receiving the campaign, perhaps by clicking on a link if it is an email campaign, or calling customer service center if it is a postal campaign.

- Orders resulting from the campaign, i.e. out of the customers who responded to the campaign, how many actually placed their orders, what did they purchase and what are their order values.

Once campaign segmentation is ready, CRM system executes a campaign and sends it to target audience. Data about to which customers the campaign were successfully delivered and to whom it was not delivered, along with the reason why it was not delivered, should be fed back by the CRM system to the data warehouse. We are not only talking about email campaign here, but also by post, by telephone, by text messages and by home page customisation. This campaign delivery data (i.e. sent, not sent, bounced and delivered) will be useful for future campaigns. One possible design for storing campaign delivery data in the data warehouse is a factless fact table, with customers, communication, date, channel, delivery status and reason as the dimensional keys.

Specific to email campaigns, when the campaign reaches the target audience email box, end user may open that campaign email and perhaps click on any particular offer in that campaign. These open and click through events are fed back to underlying data warehouse. No mechanism is 100% reliable, but one mechanism for logging open events is a transparent 1 pixel image inside the body of the email, with a query string containing a customer identifier on the image tag. The web log of this image is then processed daily and the hit of this image, along with the customer identifier and the timestamp, is stored in the campaign response database. A mechanism for logging click-through events is redirection, i.e. the link on the campaign email hits a landing page with the destination page URL and a customer identifier in the query string. A script behind the landing page then records the time of the event, the URL of requested page and the customer identifier into the campaign response database before redirect the user to the real page. The campaign response database is then fed back by the ETL to the data warehouse to be used for future campaign as additional criteria when doing segmentation.

Open event could be stored on the same fact table as the campaign delivery data.

An example of design for a campaign delivery data that contains the open data is below-

```
Fact table name: campaign delivery

Fact table type: snapshot accumulative

Grain: 1 row for each communication sent to each customer

Creation script:

create table fact_campaign_delivery (

customer_key int not null, – who the customer is

communication_key int not null, – what communication is delivered to the customer

channel_key int not null, – what media is used (email, post, text, RSS)

delivery_status_key tinyint not null, – 1 if successfully delivered, 0 if failed

reason_key int not null, – a positive integer containing failure reason, 0 if successful

open_status tinyint not null, – 1 if opened and 0 if not opened

number_of_opens int not null, – normally 1 if opened but can be more than 1

sent_dt datetime not null, – date and time the communication was sent to this customer

delivered_dt datetime null, – date and time the delivered was logged
```

```
bounced_dt datetime null, – date and time bounce event was logged

first_opened_dt datetime null, – date and time the message was first opened, NULL if not
opened

created_dt datetime not null, – system date & time when this fact table record was created

last_updated_dt datetime not null, – system date & time when this record was last updated

constraint pk_fact_campaign_delivery primary key clustered (customer_key, communication_
key, channel_key, sent_dt))
```

Because number of opens can be more than 1, if you want to record the date and time of the second and subsequent opens, you will need to put open in its own fact table, separate from campaign delivery. Normally it does not really matter that we don't get the timestamp of the 2nd and subsequent opens.

Click-through cannot be stored on the above fact table because the grain is different. The grain of click-through is 1 row for each link clicked on a communication.

An example of design is given below-

```
Fact table name: clickthrough

Fact table type: snapshot accumulative

Grain: 1 row for each link/URL on a communication, whether clicked or not clicked.

Creation script:

create table fact_clickthrough (

customer_key int not null, – who the customer is

communication_key int not null, – what communication is delivered to the customer

channel_key int not null, – what media is used (email, post, text, RSS)

URL_key int not null, – which URL on the communication

click_status tinyint not null, – 1 if it is clicked, 0 if not.

number_of_clicks – how many times the URL was clicked by the same customer

first_clicked_dt datetime null, – date and time the URL was first clicked, NULL if not
clicked

created_dt datetime not null, – system date & time when this fact table record was created

last_updated_dt datetime not null, – system date & time when this record was last updated

constraint pk_fact_campaign_delivery primary key clustered (customer_key, communication_
key, channel_key, URL_key)).
```

If you want to record the time the 2nd click happened, put each click on separate row and make the fact table type transactional. But normally it does not really matter, as long as we know the number of clicks. It is preferable to put each URL (whether it was clicked or not) in 1 row like above, with the number of clicks as a measure.

Some of the customers who responded to the campaign might place their orders. These orders are tracked using promotional code if it is a postal campaign, or using a identifier on the offer link if it is an email campaign, or using a standard software package such as Omniture SiteCatalyst if the order is placed online. Data that are normally fed back into the data warehouse to be used in future campaign are who the customer is, which campaign it is resulting from, and the usual order attributes such as product type, quantity and values. This way it would enable us to analyse campaign effectiveness, analyse customer behaviour and to monitor how much of the company revenue is generated from CRM activities, which could be used for ROI calculations or backing the proposal for future projects.

Customer Analysis

Various types of customer analysis could be performed in the data warehouse. To give you some ideas, below are some examples:

- Purchase pattern analysis, i.e. what kind of products or services does a particular group of customers purchase. The groupings could be based on demographics or campaign results. Based on the patterns we could try to forecast future purchases and relate it with inventory management, in particular the reorder level and purchasing lead time.
- Price sensitivity analysis, i.e. identifying changes in shopping and purchasing behaviour if the price changes. In this case we also group the customers for analysis, not individual customers. We try to identify if there are certain patterns which would be useful for setting future marketing strategies and operational directives.
- Shopping behaviour (especially for online businesses), i.e. identifying the factors associated with site traffic to measure the effectiveness of site design, checkout process design and help increase conversion rates. Shopping behaviour analysis is also conducted to gather the customer interests (which pages on the online store the individuals are more interested with), to be included as a factor when doing personalisation exercise such as site personalisation and personalised offers.
- Customer attrition analysis, or customer churn analysis, i.e. to answer the questions such as how many customers defected from us each week or month, how many new customers we are getting each week or month, what kind of customers we are loosing (in terms of profitability and demographics) and what kind of new customers we are gaining (in terms of product or service range and demographics). Also included in this kind of analysis is changes in the type of service or product that the customer is having (this does not apply for supermarket but it is applicable for health care and financial services, for example the type of account).
- Customer profitability analysis, i.e. revenue that we receive from the customer minus the costs associated to that customer, over a certain period (say weekly or annually). We want to know which customers we are loosing money from, and which customers are making money from. The formula to calculate the revenue side is normally not difficult but allocating the cost to each customer activity is technically and politically not easy.
- Fraud detection, i.e. large increase in credit card purchases which deviate significantly from the individual or group normal pattern (for financial service industry); unusual returns of

goods by the same customer (identified by name, post code and customer card number) within short period of time, compared with the daily and seasonal behaviour of the product line of suspected product code (this one is for retail industry); spiky account balances and unusual withdrawals/deposits (for banks), drops in recent invoice values not accompanied with lower usage activity (for telecom industry). Another method is to use 2 (or more) groups of samples, one containing the fraudulent transactions and the other representing good transactions. These groups are then fed into the mining model for training.

Each type of analysis requires different data model, and different industry requires different data model. For example, customer profitability fact table in utility sector (gas and electricity in particular) could be an incremental snapshot type, containing monthly snapshot of all accounts monthly revenues (calculated based on service types, rates and usage) and proportionate cost structure for the same period of time. The revenue may be per kwh but the base cost may be by weight (tons of coal) which makes the equation non-linear hence for some customers we could be making a loss and for others we are making handsome profit.

Although dimensional model can do a lot of analysis, in some cases we have to use multidimensional models, i.e. cubes. Many types of customer analysis especially those that involve predictive analytics, behaviour recognition, statistical analysis, non-linear estimation, cluster analysis and patterns finding, would require data mining running on multidimensional database, sometimes more than 1 MDB/cube. Some analysis would require building applications running multidimensional queries on cubes.

Personalisation

What we meant by personalization is tailoring our web site, products, services, campaigns and offers for a particular customer or a group of customers. There are large categories of personalisation: 1) we ask the customer what their preferences are, or 2) we guess their preferences based on their shopping behaviour, purchase history and demographic attributes. Once we know (or we think we know) the customer preferences, we offer them our products and services which we think would suit their preferences. Examples of personalisation are:

- Price and product alerts, i.e. we let the customer know if what they like appears in our data warehouse. Price alerts are notification to the customers when there are special offers (lower price) on certain products or services that satisfy their criteria, for example if they would like to fly to certain cities or purchase certain type of digital camera. Product alerts are notification to the customers when a certain product appears in our database. For example: they declare their favourite singer or musical preferences, then we notify the customers when a certain album or single that suit those preferences appear in our database. The basic working principle is matching: on the one hand we have many suppliers supplying us with thousands of products and services every day and on the other hand we have a lot of customers with certain preferences. All we have to do is to match them automatically.

- Personalised offers, i.e. we offer our customers certain products or services that we think match their needs or profile. There are 2 broad categories on how to choose the products or services: a) based on their past purchases (or shopping/browsing if it is an online store), and b) based on the customer attributes. Example of past purchases: because a customer purchased Canon

S300 ink jet printer 3 months ago, they may need BCI-24 colour ink cartridge today. Example of customer demographic attributes: the customer had a 3 months old baby so she may need baby products. For online stores and online services, customers could be identified by using cookie or asking them to login and once identified we could track their shopping behaviour, i.e. which product or service category they are spending a lot of time on, etc.

- Recommendations, which is basically the same as personalised offer. But this term is normally used when the customer is still shopping on the web site (for online businesses), unlike the term 'offers' that normally used when they are not shopping, i.e. via email or post. Recommendation tends to be targeted to *one* customer, where as personalised offers can be targeted to a *group* of customers that satisfies certain criteria, for example, those in certain age range or live in certain cities.

- Site personalisation (specific to online businesses), i.e. the web site contains different products and services (and prices) depending on who the customer is. There are 2 methods which are widely used to identify the customer: login and cookie. Login is the most (if not the only) certain way of identifying who the customer is, i.e. by supplying credentials, such as user ID and password. Serving the same purpose as login are: bio metric ID (such as finger print), challenge response device (such as a device that displays different response numbers every time it is activated, based on certain seed number which has been planted into the device) and security token (such as security card). Using cookie is probably 50-60% at best, never achieve 80% certainty. Some people disabled cookies on their browser, some installed certain plug-in on their browser which prevents cookies, some people regularly cleaned their temporary Internet files including cookies and of course some people don't use their own, permanent computer, i.e. Internet café, a friend's house, a shared home computer, an office or campus computer, library's PC, etc.

The content of site personalisation may be generated by a CRM system (as an XML), by setting up a campaign that is executed once a day. The logic behind this campaign does a data mining on a multidimensional data warehouse or, if we prefer a simpler way, by running a rule-based logic stored as metadata against the dimensional data warehouse. These rules are conditional rules, e.g. similar to if then statement but with a lot of IFs. Price and product alert do not need a dimensional data warehouse. They can run on a 3rd normal form ODS. Or even on the front end CRM system.

One of the logic behind personalised offer (and recommendation) is 'what similar people are interested in'. 'Similar people' can be quite a challenging term to implement. Some of the most popular classification techniques are nearest neighbour, neural networks and classification trees. Nearest neighbour is classification of customers based on their position in multidimensional space. Imagine that each dimensional attribute or each distinguishing factor that contributes to the grouping is a vector or arrow. The direction of the arrow is determined by the value of the attributes. A customer is defined by joining all the arrows by putting the beginning of the next arrow at the end of the previous arrow. This way a customer consists of all their dimensional attributes. Customers that are close to each other are classified as "similar". Close or far is defined as multidimensional distance, i.e. square root of sums of all components' squares. The difficult thing to do here is assigning numeric values to the dimensional attributes. As we all know dimensional attributes are mostly non-numeric. If the dimension has a hierarchy (such as city or location) then the numeric score depends on whether they have the same parent or grand-parent.

Classification trees method is using a diagram where a branch has 2 sub branches. At each branch whether we go to sub branch 1 or sub branch 2 depends on the value of the attributes which is compared to certain criteria (normally a constant). Starting at the trunk, after following all the branches and sub branches we will arrive at the leaves. Now if we bring say 1 million customers to through these paths, some of them will end up at leaf 1, some at leaf 2, some at leaf 3, etc. The leaves are what we call classes. A customer is said to be "similar" if they are in the same class, or a nearby class, which is defined by the number of levels.

Customer Insight

Customer information is not useful without its intelligent analysis. Analysis is always evolving and finding new ways to increase revenues through customer insight. Customer data plays vital role to build customer insight. Customer insight is a model to view available customer data and to analyze customer behaviour over period of time.

Using a data warehouse one can create rich customer dimension and use it to create customer insight. Business analyst can analyze complete customer data set in following ways:

Customer Shopping Analysis

Using historic order data, customer-shopping behaviour is analyzed. For example, business analyst can find answers to all the following questions by doing customer data analysis:

- How many times customer has purchased from us?
- What is time gap between two consecutive purchases?
- What is the purchase pattern?
- What product has he purchased most?

By answering above questions business user can understand customer-shopping behaviour and can design future marketing strategy to retain that customer.

Customer Permissions Analysis

Permissions play vital part in defining customer data. Every enterprise has different set of rules to define these permissions. These permissions are stored in data warehouse for future analysis of customer permissions. For example, as described above in permission management section customer/subscriber can subscribe to different communications types over time period and all these historical subscription events are stored in subscription fact table. Business user can use CRM tools to do subscription analysis for different subscribers over period of time.

Customer Loyalty Scheme

Customer loyalty scheme is the way to reward high valued customers and build loyalty among customer bases. Many enterprises use customer scoring/point based system to build loyalty-based program. Customers are scored based on their previous shopping behaviour and points are calculated accordingly. Customer scores can be stored in customer dimension. CRM system uses these customer scores to design campaigns and group customers as per their loyalty points. Different customers are offered different promotions as per their scores.

Below we illustrate which tool is best to serve various CRM functionalities: data warehouse (DW), online transaction processing system (OLTP, i.e. front office application) or Operational Data Store (back office integrated operational database in 3rd normal form). If the cell does not have a 'Yes' in it, it does not mean that the tool cannot do the functionality. It may be possible, but it's not the best tool to serve that purpose.

Customer Support

Customer support is one of the important aspects of CRM industry. Many companies use various CRM tools to build customer support systems. Support system helps to solve customer queries, provide them promotional updates etc. For e.g. Customer call center to update billing address or phone number etc.

Many companies use ODS to store latest customer's data to provide quick and efficient search capability to fetch up customer's information. The underlying ODS database can be populated from OLTP databases or from data warehouse (in rare cases) for latest customer information. Many CRM vendors provide tools and techniques to transfer data between ODS and data warehouse. ODS can be populated from data warehouse/Data Marts for customer specific data which is not persisted in OLTP databases.

Functionality	OLTP	DW	ODS
Single Customer View – Subscribers – Bookers – Registered users – Customer matching		Yes	Yes
Permission management – Subscription based – Tactical campaigns – ISP feedback loop – Communication preferences	Yes	Yes	Yes
Segmentations – Order data – Demographic data – Campaign delivery – Campaign response – Customer loyalty score – Customer profitability		Yes	Yes
Campaign Content – Promotional Offers – Routine Newsletter – Purchaser Lifecycle – Subscriber Lifecycle – Cross-selling	Yes		

Campaign Results – Delivery rates – Open rates – Click through rates – Conversion rates	Yes	Yes	
Customer Support – Complaint Handling – Cross selling – Pre-consumption support – Consumption support – Emergency support – Post consumption	Yes		Yes
Customer Analysis – Purchase pattern – Price sensitivity analysis – Shopping behaviour – Customer attrition analysis – Customer profitability analysis – Fraud detection		Yes	
Personalization – Alerts/Notification – Special Offers – Recommendations		Yes	Yes
Customer Loyalty Scheme – Scheme Administration – Customer scoring – Classification – Satisfaction survey		Yes	Yes
Order processing – Quotation – Registration – Custom pricing – Placing orders – Contract management – Order confirmation	Yes		
Finance – Invoicing – Payments – Refunds – Arrears – Account management	Yes		

CRM-Data Mart

A CRM system should offer the famous 360-degree view of the customer. Existing business systems have already collected a lot of customer-related information. For example, ERP, WWS or order systems contain customer and product master data as well as orders, sales and sales. The accounting system contributes open items and credit data.

In addition, growing CRM landscapes often produce other special systems with customer relationships in addition to the operative CRM system: mobile CRM, e-mail marketing or customer portals. All of these systems generate and consume customer data. This shows the heterogeneity, especially in the B2B area.

Against this background, the simple individual system-to-individual system integration falls short. Even when connecting a new CRM with several existing systems, it makes sense to choose a systematic integration approach using a CRM Data Marts. The CRM Data Mart is the binding central office for all customer-related data. Integration interfaces couple the data mart with any system that generates or requires customer data. It avoids multiple point-to-point links between individual systems that are difficult to coordinate and difficult to control during operation. In particular, the CRM Data Mart easily integrates additional systems, creating more agility.

Metadata as a Worthwhile Option

The center of the data mart is a relational database. Customer-related data is stored here in a clean, extensible data structure, the so-called normal form. Data from CRM, ERP etc. are transferred periodically and after appropriate transformation into these central structures. If the CRM data mart is to grow strategically, then a meta-level worth the data is systematically and machine-readable - also in terms of content, d. For example, in sales figures, it explains whether credits have already been offset or not.

Analytical CRM

Only a mature CRM data mart offers the often-evoked 360-degree view, because it includes both data from the CRM itself and data from other systems with customer reference. This allows analyzes of all aspects of numbers - even those that mix classic business data with sales data. Thus, contribution margins of individual customers can be determined with the inclusion of sales and marketing costs, and well-founded customer segmentation is possible. It is now also possible to tackle difficult questions: Which type of customer is worth a campaign for? Are there any business events that require special actions?

Particularly in the B2B area, hard, operational reports are required. So-called customer fact sheets make it easier for field staff to work. To do this, they summarize the most important information for a visit preparation in blocks, such as: contact persons, last contacts, open tasks, turnover overview, open items or current orders. Ideally, such a fact sheet can be accessed directly in operative CRM in the customer context - even if it includes data from the data mart. This is made possible by web-based and programmable reporting solutions.

Differentiation to the Data Warehouse

The example Customer Fact Sheet shows that detailed data plays a major role in the CRM environment. The large data warehouses, such as SAP BI, often groan under the weight of the usual business evaluations. In this scenario, the CRM data mart quickly provides operational scores that are below the "radar line" of the data warehouse. In the sense of a division of labor, the CRM Data Mart can pre-aggregate customer-related information and then pass it on to the strategic data warehouse. This is especially true when special data sources, such as Notes databases, are to be included, for which some ETL tools often do not provide interfaces. In the SME sector, the CRM Data Mart can be a pragmatic introduction to the overall topic of Data Warehouse and BI.

Types of Data Analysis in CRM

OLAP (Online Analytical Processing)

Despite its varied interpretations, 'data mining' has acquired an almost mystical allure over the past decade, although its widespread interpretation is as an activity associated with querying increasingly detail data -"drill down," as it's called – in-fact, data mining is a heavily specialized sub categories of analysis that has specific application from both with in outside CRM.

In-fact, the term drill down is more appropriately applied to the practice of online analytical processing, known as OLAR. OLAP has become the most popular type of decision support analysis, allowing the average business person to explorer data online with the aim of focusing on data at a lower and lower level of the data hierarchy. Most often, this mean generating an online report, analyzing the result, and submitting a more detailed query in order to understand the result data.

OLAP generally focus on proving a set data attribute from a data base organized around certain dimension, such as time and location, thus a user can request the companies regional sells revenue for all baby care products by region or by store. He can request the report detailing regional revenue for each month with in quarter.

Although OLAP is generally lumped into the data mining rubric-usually by software vendors eager to claim the data mining moniker-it normally relies on data that has been summarized according to particular dimension, data mining involves the identification of meaning full pattern an rules from detail data, usually from large amount of data, thus, instead of analysis customer segment to determine who is likely to churm as with OLAP, data mining would examine individual customers, touching each of the millions of records in a database.

OLAP analysis required the analysis to have a query or hypothesis in mind, but data mining can generate information to show pattern and relationship without the analysis knowing about them. Data mining can identified cluster of customers who buy similar products.

For instance, home office workers who buy PCs, power supplies, toner, printer cables, waste papers baskets, and coffee, with an OLAP tools, the anlaysist would have to guesses which product a home office workers would purchase and then identified customers making such a purchase. OLAP analysis typically examine category grouping such as PCs, printer cable, and toner [computer related products] but might not organized out of category purchase such as coffee and waste baskets.

Where Theory meets Practice-data Mining in CRM?

Data mining tool identified pattern in data and deliver valuable new information that can increase a company understanding of itself an its customers. Data mining is commonly used to help data analysts search for information they don't yet no to look for, often involving no hypothesis. It has helped companies uncover a diverse set of new knowledge, from a customer next purchase to optimal store layouts to the most favorable release data for a movie in preproduction.

There are many different types of data mining algorithms, some esoteric and not easily applicable to business problems.

Although the specific algorithms themselves might vary- decision trees and neural networks are fundamentally different but can both we used to predict behavior the following three types of data mining particularly germane to CRM:

Prediction

Prediction the use of historical data to determine future behaviors- Predictive modeling generates output that populates of "models" or structure to represent the results. For instance, a predictive model can indicate the next product a customer is most likely to purchase based on historical purchases buy that customer and other customer who have purchased the same product.

Sequence

Sequential analysis identifies combination of activities that occur in a particular order . business use sequential analysis to determine whether customers are doing thing in a particular order. It can help a business distill behavior from events captured from various operational systems around a company to determine patterns. For instance, a bank or telecom companies can learn more about a given customer or customer segment by examining patterns in the slowdown of purchases or in service cancellation.

Association

Association analysis detects groups of similar item and events. It can we used to detect items or events that occur together. The association algorithm is often applied to market – basket analysis to help business understand products being purchase together. By understanding customer and product affinities, a company can make important decisions about which products to advertise or discount and which customers should be targeted of certain product.

One central difference between data mining and other types of decision support analysis is that data mining usually involves statisticians or product specialists intimate with the use of the correct algorithm and their application to business problem, as well as with the specific data mining software.

Although the business persons rarely mines the data herself, she might use data mining results- either represented graphically in a visualization tool or deployed to a data base for general query access to help make important decision about managing customer relations.

There are myriad uses for the three types of data mining just describe, from targeting brand new customers by modeling existing customer's response pattern to avoiding high risk prospects through risk prediction or forecasting a customer's life time values. Many companies acquire dedicating data mining servers, on to which they load customer data record to build models and explore various customer behavior patterns such activities are usually processing- intensive so standalone data mining plate forms avoid impacting processing on other systems.

These servers are usually linked to a company's data warehouse, enabling data analysts to easily access customer data to experiment with various pricing plans, for example, or to create dynamic customer segments for testing new campaigns and performing what-if analysis.

Each type of data mining can DVD player commutes to work on the train, causing the retailer to reallocate much of its marketing budget from daytime television commercials to newspapers ads and billboards. The company saw sales of these players shoot up 43 present after changing its ad media.

Understanding the impending behaviors of customers and prospects is the key to data mining, and where CRM is concerned, two data mining applications in particular stand out: click stream analysis and personalization.

Click Stream Analysis

IT department have become giddy over capturing click stream-the data that illustrates a Web visitor's footprint around the site, how long he stayed, what he did during his visit, and when he returned. They're the equivalent of a camera in a department store recording a shopper's every move.

Click stream data-usually stored either as a part of a company's data warehouse or in a dedicated click stream data store sometimes called a "data warehouse"-is growing hand-in- hand with corporate e-commerce activities.

One client of mine, a general merchandise retailer who has joined the e-tailing ranks, want its Web site to be as "sticky "as possible and has begun analyzing click stream data to surmise why customers might leave the site prematurely. The company has sharpened its analysis to determine the value of abandoned shopping carts. When a customer leaves the site in the midst of a shopping trip, whatever the reason, the company looks to see what products were in the cart.

The data is then compared with similar data from other abandoned carts to examine:

1. How much revenue the abandoned cart represented. In other words, how much revenue was lost because of the customer's early departure.
2. Whether the products in the cart were high-profit items or loss leaders.
3. If the same product were found in other abandoned carts.
4. The volume of products and the number of different product categories in the cart.
5. Whether the total bill for the abandoned carts consistently fell within a certain dollar range.
6. At what point during the shopping trip the cart was actually abandoned when the customer saw the shopping charge. When the site required a personal survey before confirming the purchase.
7. How the average and total bills for abandoned carts compared with "un-abandoned" carts-those that made it through the checkout process.

The result of this analysis can trigger some interesting theories. For instance, perhaps none of the products in the cart was appealing enough to a particular customer to motivate her to continue shopping or the customer was put off by frequent inquiries asking her whether she was ready to check out or possibly, at a particular dollar total, the customer thought the better of the entire shopping trip and bailed.

Finally, perhaps the number or mix of products in the cart reminded the customer of another site that offered a steeper discount for similar purchases.

Admittedly, some of these theories are mere guesses. But when examined regularly and with consistent metrics, click stream can reveal some interesting patterns. The fact is, whatever the customer's reason for leaving the site and a cart full of merchandise, the e-tailor can take a verity of actions based on both hard findings and less-than-certain extrapolations the e-tailor can use these results to tweak the design and contents of its Web site and monitor resulting improvements.

Pattern might indicate product affinities, suggesting cross selling and up selling strategies. And when combined with customer's demographic, psychographics, and past behaviors, click stream data can bring the understanding of customer behavior to a whole new level.

The latter option is perhaps the most intriguing: rather than simply examining a customer's navigation patterns and guessing about which actions to take, the retailer can navigation patterns and guessing about which actions to take, the retailer can combine those patterns with more specific customer data-his previous purchases in that product category, key demographic and psychographic data, or his lifetime value score, for example-to provide a holistic view of that customer's value and interest.

It might have been a one-time-only shopper who was lost, but in other cases a high-value customer might have left the sit on multiple occasions. A tailored e-mail message electronic coupon perhaps target one of the products left behind on a prior trip-could make all the difference the next time that customer decides to log on.

The following scenario, based on a real-life case studies illustrates how click stream data, when integrated with other key data from around the enterprise, enhances opportunities to personalized customer communications. Most marketing managers won't be looking our analyst, shoulders individual click streams. But understanding our customer's navigation around the site can help a company decide how to lure him back.

You have several choices, your companies usually tactic for all registered visitors who visit the site but don't make a purchase it is to mail them to coupon for $5 off a new pair of fashion eye wear. However, this particular visitor was looking at contacts. He'd probably trash the glasses coupon as soon as it arrived in the mail.

A better choice might be to e-mail the visitor a discount code-a coupon is given a unique code so no one but the given customer can redeem it- for $10 off a new pair of hard contacts or three pairs of disposable lenses a predictive model could confirm this as the best course of action your profit on contact lenses is usually good, and the shopper seemed on the brink of making a purchase besides, e-mailing the offer is a lower cost option that the U.S. postal service and would probably result in quicker turnaround time.

Along with this more personalized tactics, you could also monitor the referring Web site for other referred shoppers who have researched or purchased connect lenses, if connect lens activity is particularly high, you might concerned placing a more customized banner ad on the partner's sit and even provide better financial incentives for the partner when new connect lens customers click through.

With the e-mail strategy, the customer more likely to return to sit and you're almost guaranteed purchases.

The problem with this scenario is that even through analysis is involved, it's still dangers. The fact that you're looking at only a single customer touch point can mean his problems and a bad decisions. If your click stream database contained behavior history on this shopper, things might turn out differently.

You would have more information about the customer, and you'd know the following:

1. This isn't the customer's first visit to your Web site.
2. He has made three other purchases on three separate occasions.
3. The products he has purchased have all been on sale.

In short, you would understand that you Web visitors are what's known as a "cherry picker" someone whose only purchase low-margin products when they're being promoted. No cross-selling, no up-selling, no true loyalty. He'll be back again, too, when he finds the next markdown.

If you had this information, you would understand the optimal marketing tactic for this customer: do nothing: do nothing, any further marketing to him would be a bad investment. Of course, you're perfectly happy to have this customer return to your site of his own free will.

But you've already invested too much money in an unprofitable. Each times retailer price-subsidizes product for cherry pickers, it is losing an opportunity to sell that product it a more valuable customer. The retailer is in fact investing in an undesirable customer relationship.

Personalization and Collaborative Filtering

The practice of tailoring communications directly to a customer segment or, increasingly, to an individual customer. The premise of personalization is that, by collecting sufficient customer data, a company can market to an individual's unique needs, both now and in the future.

Personalized communications is the principal techniques via which companies can convince customers they understand them and that their information-which the company often uses thanks to the customer's explicit permission-is mutually beneficial.

The goal is to deliver accurate product recommendations; content geared to individual preferences, and targeted promotions for individual Web visitors-and in real time. When done right, personalized means not only maintaining customer loyalty, but also driving purchases higher leverages detailed information about individual and can dictate some very tactical decisions.

The following analysis topics from a drugstore e-tailor suggest the level of individual detail and resulting tactics personalization can provide:

1. For people who have bought or expressed interest in vitamin supplements, which other products are likely to buy.
2. How likely is customer X to buy prescription drugs online?

3. What other items are likely to be in a shopper's market basket if he buys, say, decongestant?
4. Which products are most similar to brand eye drops the customer chose?

Personalization can take various forms. It can involve customizing actual Web pages, including a Web site's look and feel, according to the features favored by an individual visitor. Many Web sites allow the visitor to customize the site according to her preferences, eliminating format variations and allowing her a private window into the company. Use the search function often? Move the search window to the top of the page. Like customization, so called localization can focus site content to the visitor's particular geographic area.

Notice that the personalization leverage established rules that dictate, for instance, which products might be purchased might be purchased together or whether a certain Web pages should precede or follow another.

When a visitor to a software Web site buys Quicken, the site might suggest he buy Quicken: The Official Guide before going to the checkout screen. Rules- based personalization most often involves rules that have been hard-coded into the software. For this reason, it's often difficult to maintain and support.

The other type of personalization, adaptive personalization, learns as it goes. More commonly known as collaborative filtering, this type of personalization gats smarter as it observes customer behaviors and applies them to new circumstances. For instance, if a gardening e-tailor using collaborative filtering observes that shoppers tend to buy low-cost perennial flowers at the same time they order gardening tools, the Web site might begin suggesting a flat of pansies to all customers who buy bulb planters.

Collaborative filtering uses the behavior of other "like" visitors as the basis for its recommendations. Collaborative filtering tools are often more complex, and thus more expensive, than rules-based personalization. The most celebrated example of collaborative filtering is purchase circles, in which Amazon factors in the buyer's past purchase and geography to suggest what readers who live in her neighborhood and have similar interests might be reading.

The more similar shoppers buy, the smarter Amazon becomes about their preferences, and the more accurate are the site's recommendations. Several customers you know are cherry pickers on other booksellers' Web sites during special promotions, but they always return to Amazon because "they know me better."

Perhaps the most telling delineation in personalization is in whether or not the user knows its happening. In the permission marketing scenario Web visitor voluntarily provide personal information to Web sites where they believe there will be some sort of Quid pro quo: the company will use the information to provide a value added service such as periodic discounts or special- interest newsletters. Some sites can personalize content without making the shopper aware that the products he's seeing are different from those of fellow shoppers-who might have different profiles and web retailers who combine eCRM with detail customer data and advanced personalization can customize content and screen layouts for individual visitors to increase the site's stickiness and the shopper's propensity to buy.

On the other hand, companies such as Lands' End simply ask customers what they like, whether or not they make a purchase. The company's My Personal Shopper feature shows Web visitors various product combinations and solicits their feedback.

This practices is different from the "inferential" personalization in which a company applies complex logic to infer a customer's preferences "referential" personalization simply stores a customer's responses to questions or surveys, making those answer part of her profile so they can be used to cross-sell her additional products.

Although custom content seems innocuous enough-it tantamount to reorganizing a brick and mortar store's layout according to the way the shopper likes to move around the store-it can also have more controversial uses.

Revealed to be selling the same DVD movie for different prices to different shoppers/this practices, known as dynamic pricing, turned the concept of consumer choice on its head. The Web, famous for offering shoppers the opportunity to find the best deal with a simple mouse click, was now allowing sellers the opportunity to differentiate consumers and their price sensitivity.

Dynamic pricing actually leverage CRM technology and detailed customer data to let a company, say, compare a shopper's desire for the product with his perceived ability to pay for that product. For the first time, consumers are the ones competing for the best deal.

Arguments for and against dynamic pricing raise issues of consumer privacy as well as goodwill. After all the more a shopper buys on a company Web sites, the more information the site has on the buyer and the weaker the buyer's negotiating power.

In the past several years, Airlines were routinely accused of raising tree online fares for frequently fliers-there most loyal customers who are more likely to fly a particular carrier because of the mileage perks. And, in a now in famous public relations gaff, coco cola was alleged to have been considering a vending machine that raised the price of beverages when the temperature soared in.

In defending dynamic pricing, e-tailor point to their brick-and mortar counterparts who have been engaging in the practice for years. Drug stores have been known to price cold medicines higher in chillier climates, and the short age of Sony play station to units last Christmas trove price up sharply/Kmart used the short age as a way of rewarding loyal customers first, steering play station availability to loyal shoppers on the company's blue light(dot)com Web site, "in the Web world, where consumer data can include a shopper's home addresses, income level, number of children, and even his resolve to purchase a product, dynamic pricing-along with a number of other personalization techniques-can be implemented more quickly and to the wider number of the shoppers.

Good or bad, Amazon's dynamic pricing experiment might have gone unnoticed all together if it hadn't been for the Web. In an ironic twist participants in an internet chat room begins comparing their movie receipts and discover that price seemed higher for the regular customer.

Amazon claimed the dynamic pricing was simply are test and denied plans to for mailed the practice. But the example proofs the Web has affected both business and social communication to the point where even CRM can sometimes be are double-edged sword.

References

- What-is-analytical-crm: techonestop.com, Retrieved 2 June, 2019
- Data-Analytics-in-CRM-Processes: researchgate.net, Retrieved 12 March, 2019
- Predictive-analytics-crm: techadv.com, Retrieved 11 May, 2019
- Customer-related-database-meaning-and-principles, customer-database: businessmanagementideas.com, Retrieved 20 July, 2019
- How-to-develop-a-customer-related-database, crm: businessmanagementideas.com, Retrieved 3 February, 2019
- Customer-data-management-best-practices: datapine.com, Retrieved 14 June, 2019
- Customer-data-integration-cdi: techopedia.com, Retrieved 18 August, 2019
- Using-data-warehouse-for-crm: wordpress.com, Retrieved 8 May, 2019
- Crm-data-mart: midrange.de, Retrieved 6 April, 2019
- Main-types-of-data-analysis-used-in-crm: businessmanagementideas.com, Retrieved 30 January, 2019

Permissions

All chapters in this book are published with permission under the Creative Commons Attribution Share Alike License or equivalent. Every chapter published in this book has been scrutinized by our experts. Their significance has been extensively debated. The topics covered herein carry significant information for a comprehensive understanding. They may even be implemented as practical applications or may be referred to as a beginning point for further studies.

We would like to thank the editorial team for lending their expertise to make the book truly unique. They have played a crucial role in the development of this book. Without their invaluable contributions this book wouldn't have been possible. They have made vital efforts to compile up to date information on the varied aspects of this subject to make this book a valuable addition to the collection of many professionals and students.

This book was conceptualized with the vision of imparting up-to-date and integrated information in this field. To ensure the same, a matchless editorial board was set up. Every individual on the board went through rigorous rounds of assessment to prove their worth. After which they invested a large part of their time researching and compiling the most relevant data for our readers.

The editorial board has been involved in producing this book since its inception. They have spent rigorous hours researching and exploring the diverse topics which have resulted in the successful publishing of this book. They have passed on their knowledge of decades through this book. To expedite this challenging task, the publisher supported the team at every step. A small team of assistant editors was also appointed to further simplify the editing procedure and attain best results for the readers.

Apart from the editorial board, the designing team has also invested a significant amount of their time in understanding the subject and creating the most relevant covers. They scrutinized every image to scout for the most suitable representation of the subject and create an appropriate cover for the book.

The publishing team has been an ardent support to the editorial, designing and production team. Their endless efforts to recruit the best for this project, has resulted in the accomplishment of this book. They are a veteran in the field of academics and their pool of knowledge is as vast as their experience in printing. Their expertise and guidance has proved useful at every step. Their uncompromising quality standards have made this book an exceptional effort. Their encouragement from time to time has been an inspiration for everyone.

The publisher and the editorial board hope that this book will prove to be a valuable piece of knowledge for students, practitioners and scholars across the globe.

Index

CPSIA information can be obtained
at www.ICGtesting.com
Printed in the USA
LVHW060901030122
707669LV00002B/295

9 781682 859810